Whatever Happened
to the Egyptian Revolution?

Whatever Happened to the Egyptian Revolution?

Galal Amin

Translated by
Jonathan Wright

The American University in Cairo Press
Cairo   New York

First published in 2013 by
The American University in Cairo Press
113 Sharia Kasr el Aini, Cairo, Egypt
420 Fifth Avenue, New York, NY 10018
www.aucpress.com

Dar el Kutub No. 13680/12
ISBN 978 977 416 589 4

Dar el Kutub Cataloging-in-Publication Data

Amin, Galal
        Whatever Happened to the Egyptian Revolution? / Galal Amin; translated by Jonathan
    Wright.—Cairo: The American University in Cairo Press, 2013
        p.   cm.
        ISBN 978 977 416 589 4
        1. Egypt—History   I. Wright, Jonathan   II. Title
        962.055

1 2 3 4 5   17 16 15 14 13

Designed by Adam el Sehemy
Printed in Egypt

Contents

Introduction

It has been two years since the outbreak of the revolution of January 25, 2011, which within less than a month brought to an end one of the worst eras in Egyptian history, the era of Hosni Mubarak, who ruled Egypt for close to thirty years and presided over declines in the Egyptian economy, social conditions, and Egypt's status in the Arab world and internationally.

Egyptians were overjoyed that the revolution had succeeded in getting rid of the head of the regime and putting an end to the idea of dynastic succession by Mubarak's son, and hopes rose that in the wake of Mubarak's downfall the whole regime would be uprooted and Egypt would embark on a renaissance and a new era of progress. But the revolution soon ran into many obstacles, creating anxiety and fear that the high hopes might not be fulfilled.

This book includes chapters dealing, first, with many of the symptoms of corruption and decline that led to the January 25 revolution. It then explains the reasons why the revolution created such optimism for a bright future and lays out the causes for concern that have arisen now that the outlook is gloomier. The book also contains chapters on what could constitute components of a renaissance in Egypt, democratically, economically, in social justice, and through shaking off dependency, if we succeed in dispersing those clouds of gloom.

The story told in this book ends with the elections that brought in Dr. Muhammad Morsi as the new president. The conclusion describes the growing anxiety felt by many Egyptians, even after the fairly free elections of both parliament and president. It also tries to explain how a very promising revolution may very well have turned out to be abortive.

Part 1

Causes of the Revolution

Worse than Unemployment

1

Whenever I returned to Egypt after an absence of any length, as soon as I set foot in the airport, I would be struck by some manifestation of a class-based society: junior staff waiting for senior staff, someone carrying passports for an important group of people and completing the passport formalities on their behalf so that they could get out of the airport before anyone else, or the staff of tour companies, mostly university graduates, who could not find better employment than holding up a sign with their company's name for passengers to see, and so on.

As soon as I started putting my bags on the bus that takes you from the airport to the parking lot, two young men would appear from nowhere, then three of them and then four, all competing to help me and my wife carry our bags. Then, as soon as the bus stopped and I started taking the bags off, another four young men would appear from nowhere, competing to perform the same task.

I noticed that those competing to do this job didn't look the way porters used to look in Egypt. They were better dressed and younger, but the look of degradation on their faces was more distressing than the facial expressions of the old-time porters.

In such situations I would usually feel guilty in a way I had not felt all the time I was abroad, because travelers in Europe, the United States, or even in other Arab countries never come across such situations. Yes, of course, there are rich and poor, but not in this way. Yes, society there can be divided into classes, but they do not have the same privileges for the upper classes that you see in Egypt from the first moment you arrive, or the same servility among those beneath.

Social stratification is a very old phenomenon, of course, whether in Egypt or the rest of the world, but it has not always created this feeling of guilt on one side or bitterness on the other, because until recently the upper classes believed sincerely that they deserved their lives of luxury, as they were of a different breed because they were from distinguished families or simply because they owned vast tracts of farmland. In most cases they considered their wealth and their distinguished status to be a sign of God's favor, and until recently the lower classes took this explanation for granted. "Yes, we are of inferior stock, born to lowly families without status or land, which shows that we are out of favor with God for some reason or other," they would tell themselves.

Over the past hundred years things have happened to undermine these ideas or greatly weaken them on both sides of the divide. Race, color, pedigree, history, and religion cannot justify these class distinctions. It's all a matter of outright injustice, and what makes matters worse is that everything is now obvious: the poor all know exactly how the rich live, if not from the luxury cars they see in the street, then from television, and they know that the upper classes can obtain all this opulence only by cheating.

The sense of bitterness on one side and the sense of guilt on the other were bound to grow, even if everyone pretended otherwise.

"I know full well how you obtained your money or your job." That's what those stuck at the bottom of the ladder tell themselves, while the others, even if they never say so in public, know that they are basically impostors who got where they are by force or by fraud.

In such a climate it's hardly surprising that we find plenty of things to complain about loudly: new and unfamiliar types of crime, sexual harassment, bigotry, religious fanaticism, and so on.

2

There were two young men standing at the movie theater entrance, neither of them more than thirty years old, and their only job was to check tickets. One of them might escort you into the theater to show you your seat. There's nothing strange about that, but the surprise was the way they treated us, my wife and me, as soon as I gave them the tickets. I've come across such situations before, but every time the shock makes it seem like the first. From the first word they uttered it was clear they were thinking only of their tip. We had arrived half an hour before the film started, so they suggested we sit in the movie theater's snack bar and promised they would come and tell us as soon as it was time to go in. I disliked the degrading way they were speaking and I found the situation most unpleasant: two good-looking young men wearing smart suits (no doubt the management required it) yet prepared to beg for tips in this manner.

I took another two steps and another young man of similar appearance came up to me, with a young woman in hijab next to him, helping him with his work. What kind of work was it? He was inviting me to take part in a competition, the gist of which I did not quite understand, but I gathered from what he said that if I won I would get a prize.

After recovering my composure I went back to one of the men who had met us when we came in and asked him a few questions:

"What's he after, that man who offered me a prize?"

"He's the agent for a travel company that's trying to promote its business, and the competition and the prize are part of the promotion."

"What did you study at university?" I asked him (I was almost certain he had a university degree).

He said he had a degree in computer science.

"And your colleague?"

"He studied commerce, in English," he said.

"Are you married?"

"Yes, and I have two kids: a boy, two years old, and a girl of six months."

"Do you live with your family or your wife's family?" I asked.

"No, we live in a rented apartment."

"How much is the rent?"

"Four hundred and fifty pounds a month," he said.

"Don't get upset if I ask how much you earn."

"Two hundred pounds."

"Does your wife work?"

"How could she work when we have two kids that age? And suppose my wife did go out to work, when would we be together, when I work from four in the afternoon until midnight?"

"Do you have another job in the morning?"

"No, because they sometimes ask me to work in the morning instead of the evening."

Then I realized how important the tips were; not just important but a matter of life and death. Was it surprising then that this young man and his colleague should treat me in such a degrading manner? I left him and went to the restroom. I saw another man standing at the door waiting for me. This man differed from the others in age but not in the impression of degradation he conveyed. He was older and thinner and his face suggested he was malnourished. It was a familiar sight that nonetheless gave me an agonizing feeling with a touch of anger every time I saw it. Not anger with the man, but with what drove him to behave in this way.

The poor man didn't know what he could do or what service he could offer me in order to get a reward. But he knew how important it was to get the reward, which he had done nothing to deserve. Was that precisely what caused the feeling of humiliation so evident on his face? I guessed that this man did not receive any wage whatsoever. If the movie theater owner was only paying the young ticket taker two hundred pounds a month, he had probably offered this man a choice between a job without a salary or no job at all, and the man had taken the job in the hope that customers would take pity on him.

This phenomenon is much more widespread in Egypt than we imagine: jobs that must number in the millions in what is called the service sector. Someone selling goods or a service knows that the buyer expects him to provide some small additional service, like the car owner at the gas station who expects someone to fill his tank instead of doing it himself, or the customer at the supermarket who expects someone to help him bag his groceries or carry them to his car, or the hotel guest who expects someone to come and carry his bags, or the passenger getting on a train who wants someone to show him to his seat, and so on.

But employers don't want to cover the cost of providing these small services. Since they know that Egypt has millions of unemployed people looking for any work, they exploit their weakness by giving them a choice between remaining unemployed or doing these jobs for no pay (or for insignificant payment) and relying on their ingenuity in dealing with customers.

This phenomenon, which is now widespread in Egypt, is not an old one. It did not exist to any noticeable extent in the time of the monarchy, under President Gamal Abd al-Nasser, or under President Anwar al-Sadat.

The phenomenon prevalent when Egypt was a monarchy was what economists call disguised unemployment. Men would work at way below their full capacity, but not in this peculiar position of intermediary between customers and employers. That was the case with the surplus labor in the countryside, and with peddlers and shoe shiners in the cities.

In the time of Abd al-Nasser disguised unemployment sharply declined as a result of agricultural reform and industrialization, though it gradually reappeared in the civil service and the public sector when the drive for industrialization lost momentum after the 1967 war with Israel. But in the time of Abd al-Nasser we did not see the pernicious phenomenon I'm talking about. Nor did we see it to any noticeable extent under President Sadat because of the job opportunities available through migration to oil-producing countries.

All these outlets have been firmly shut for the past quarter-century. The number of jobs in agriculture and industry is growing too slowly, the emigration rate has fallen sharply because of the fall in demand for Egyptian workers in oil-producing states, and the Egyptian government has withdrawn from the business of giving jobs to all graduates and is cutting expenditures in the hope that the private sector will do what the government used to do. But the private sector is in the state I explained above: its motto is supply and demand, whether of commodities or labor. If someone is ready to work for no wage, why pay them a wage?

Whenever I open the window at home in the morning I see a young man of about twenty-five from Upper Egypt. I know his life history well because I have met him so often in my street. I know that his father did the impossible to make sure he completed his secondary education and then to get him into university to obtain a degree in business. Now, after he and his father did everything possible to get him a job that matches his qualifications, he has ended up with the job of wiping dust off the fancy cars parked in front of the building opposite mine. His hopes, just like the hopes of the men I have already described, depend on the generosity of the car owners, but this generosity is not assured and cannot be calculated precisely so he cannot rely on it when deciding whether or not to get married, for example. There are other needs that are more important and more pressing, including sending some of what he earns to his mother, who has stayed in Upper Egypt.

After seeing the 'workers' at the movie theater, I recalled some statistics presented by a prominent economist, a specialist in employment and unemployment, as evidence that the employment situation in Egypt has improved. The economist stated proudly that the unemployment rate in Egypt fell from 11.7 percent in 1998 to 8.3 percent in 2006. I said to myself, "There's something very strange about this, because the unemployed don't keep waiting for jobs until they die of hunger. They have to find jobs of some kind to feed themselves and their families. After getting computer science diplomas or degrees in business studies and then completely despairing of life, they must have agreed to take on the jobs I have described, and so the eminent economist can then deduct them from the rolls of the unemployed, and the ministers of investment and economic development can mention them in their statistics as evidence of achievements in reducing unemployment. But how should one really describe the work they are doing?"

3

There is a new way to die, known to Egyptians only for the last twenty years or so. What you do is pay several thousand pounds to someone whose specialty is smuggling people to Italy or Greece, then you get into a vehicle along with a group of other desperate people, cross the border into Libya, and get on a rubber boat with about fourteen other people. The boat takes you to somewhere off the coast of Italy or Greece, then you leave the boat and rely on yourself in swimming to shore, in a place where you hope the coastguards will be few. You slip past the guards and find yourself in a country where one can work illegally, unlike in Egypt, where there are no jobs, legal or illegal.

The problem is that the rubber boat is vulnerable to the rough seas of the Mediterranean and the traffickers usually overload it with people, so there is a serious risk of drowning before you reach the coast of Italy or Greece. Many such boats have sunk in the last few years. One of the most recent drowning incidents involved seven young men from the villages of Zanqar and Nousa in Daqahliya Province who were trying to slip into Greece. One of the survivors said that the boat capsized only thirty yards off the Greek coast.

I say this is a new way for Egyptians to die, and of course I mean poor Egyptians because rich and middle-class Egyptians do not die this way. If they want to go to Italy or Greece, they get on a plane or a ship. It's a new way for poor Egyptians to die because they used to die at home of hunger or of grief, or on the roads in bus accidents because the brakes were worn or the driver was exhausted from long hours at the wheel or from the stress of driving on Egyptian roads. When poor Egyptians did die of drowning, it would be on a ferry that was badly maintained or not seaworthy in the first place. For poor Egyptians to drown from a rubber boat that isn't designed to cross the Mediterranean is what's new, but it's not the only new aspect of this way of dying.

There's another important aspect: that the poor Egyptians who die this way are not usually illiterate. In fact, many of them have university degrees, and despite these degrees (or maybe because of them) they have not been able to find suitable work at a reasonable salary. When illiterate Egyptians leave their villages and decide to emigrate, they rarely go anywhere other than the Gulf countries or Libya, so they are rarely exposed to the danger of drowning off the coast of some European country. This way of dying is closely linked to the phenomenon of growing unemployment among graduates over the past twenty years, because they are the ones who feel the painful gap between their aspirations, reinforced by the education they have received, and the wretched reality of their lives and their inability to meet their most basic demands: a reasonable job and a home that enables them to get married.

4

In an old film by the famous Italian director Vittorio De Sica, made about half a century ago, there's a story that's as funny as it is moving. It's about the conditions that prevailed in some of the poorest regions of southern Italy, where unemployment was common and finding rewarding work was just about impossible, and so it was impossible to get suitable housing. In order to obtain somewhere to live, some of the poor young men would resort to the following ruse: they would find an empty piece of state-owned land, bring anything they could find that could be used as a substitute for bricks or stone, and build a small room under cover of darkness and as quickly as possible. By daybreak the building would be done and the police could not do anything against them because the law banned the demolition of any building with a roof, except through complicated judicial procedures that the police considered to be pointless. What mattered was that the building should have a roof. If the police happened to arrive before the roof was complete, it was all over; the building would be knocked down and all the efforts of the unemployed young men would go to waste.

The reader can imagine how a very amusing film could be made on this subject. The whole story becomes as funny as it is tragic, like a game of cat and mouse between the poor and the police over whether the poor will be able to put the roof on before the police arrive. During this tragic game the poor often found it useful to assign someone as lookout, to monitor the police from afar and warn the others if the police were coming, whereupon they would quickly do something to trick them, either by trying to divert them to somewhere else or by covering the missing part of the roof with anything, even with newspapers or old rags. The attitude of the police toward them varied according to the temperament or mood of the policeman. There was one hard-hearted policeman who would insist on arresting them and demolishing the room, and another decent one who voluntarily looked the other way while they finished building the roof or who pretended that the roof was real when it was not at all, and so on.

Something similar happens every day in Cairo and for similar reasons. As unemployment has increased in Egypt, the number of people seeking jobs of any kind to keep body and soul together for themselves and their children has grown year by year. I noticed that the number of people doing what economists call marginal work has increased rapidly in recent years: shoe shiners, peddlers, and street traders with minimal stock of cheap goods and a daily turnover of no more than five or ten pounds, whose profits might be no more than a third or half of that amount, selling meager quantities of limes or tomatoes, a few loaves of bread, or a few blocks of low-fat white cheese, and so on. The police constantly harass them on various pretexts: that they are blocking the streets and obstructing traffic, that they are getting in the way of pedestrians on the sidewalk, that they are giving foreign tourists a bad impression of Cairo, or that they are a security threat if a senior official is on his way to or from work, and so on. So the police confiscate their goods: they pick up their crates and baskets and throw them into police trucks, and the tomatoes or limes spill into the street as the traders scramble helplessly to pick them up. Then they run after the police vehicles, begging for mercy and shouting that the police have taken all their capital (which in fact amounts to just a crate or a basket), and the answer they hear is that if they want they can recover their goods from the police station after all the necessary procedures have been followed.

In these police vehicles I have seen many kinds of 'capital': baskets of pretzels, shoe shiners' boxes, various cheap children's toys mixed up with combs and plastic mirrors that the owners a few moments ago were offering for sale, shouting out, "Anything for a pound." Sometimes you find that the traders themselves have got into the police vehicles with their goods and their crates, since they see no sense in watching their only source of livelihood disappear out of sight without going and trying to recover it, as if it were a pound of their own flesh that was being confiscated.

These people often assign one of their number to stand watch at the corner of the street down which the police might come, to monitor their movements and give the others an early warning as soon as he sees a policeman coming. When the warning comes, the others hurriedly gather up their goods and disappear in the blink of an eye, or hide their goods in a nearby place where they have an agreement with the owner and pretend that they are doing something else.

When you have a close look at the policeman who comes to enforce the law and confiscate their goods, you find that he's no better off than they, for life has not been any kinder to him. The way he treats them, whether cruelly or with compassion, varies according to his temperament and his mood, or depending on whether his own superior treated him harshly or compassionately that morning. However the policeman or his superior behave, this game of hide and seek is bound to recur day after day in Cairo's streets and public squares, as if it were part of the nature of things and the way of the world. People have to eat to live.

5

I can understand that someone might love a particular woman or a particular man, but that someone would love 'humanity' as a whole strikes me as a dubious proposition.

That's because people, by nature I believe, find it easier to direct their emotions toward a particular person than toward abstractions such as "all humanity," "freedom for everyone," or "women as a whole," and so on. If someone were to claim that they did not love anyone in particular but that they did love people as a whole, we would be right to doubt their sincerity until they produced some evidence.

In my own life I have known socialists and communists of this kind, people who talk a lot about how they hate "the exploitation of man by his fellow man." But then I find they have been exploiting their wives or their friends in the most appalling fashion. Some of them also have not given back books they borrowed from me, despite firm promises that they would do so, because in their eyes I am an exploitative bourgeois unworthy of compassion while it is only the proletarians who deserve compassion, and not a particular proletarian but proletarians in general.

I remember reading an article in which the British philosopher Bertrand Russell described meeting the communist leader Vladimir Lenin after the revolution in Russia. Lenin was describing what the socialist revolution had done to the big landowners whose land the revolutionaries had confiscated. Russell said he was surprised and shocked to see on Lenin's face, as he talked, signs of extreme cruelty that Russell could not reconcile with the empathy implicit in what Lenin said about impoverished peasants.

I remembered these incidents when I read reports in 2009 of how a group of women who worked in a youth center in Sixth of October City had been tormented. The head of the Ministry of Youth Affairs in Giza had issued a decree terminating their secondment to the center to punish them for failing to obey strict orders to turn up at the Cairo stadium on a certain day. The women had good excuses, which the official ignored. Nahid Abd al-Hakim, for example, did not carry out the order because she was pregnant. Nahid Abd al-Khalik was nursing her infant son, who is a polio victim. Iman Abdallah, Seham Sabri, Rabia Yassin, Dalia Abd al-Qader, Ahlam Mahmoud, Fatma Sayyid, and others had similar excuses.

The occasion that prompted the Ministry to issue the strict orders that this group of wretched women was compelled to disobey was a women's marathon presided over by Suzanne Mubarak, the wife of President Hosni Mubarak. The government newspaper *al-Ahram* described the marathon as part of the objectives of Suzanne Mubarak's Women's International Peace Movement, which include "supporting the participation of women in the process of peacemaking" and "providing safe communities for women and children."

6

On the first day of the Eid al-Fitr holiday in 2006, dozens (some say hundreds) of young men attacked a number of women in the center of Cairo within sight of other people, including policemen, and everyone felt that something new and serious was happening or that something serious had started to come to light when we had not thought that things had gone so far.

The basic conclusion that emerged from that incident, especially as it took place a few days after we discovered that in some cities and villages the drinking water had been contaminated with sewage water (dozens of people were taken to the hospital and some died), was that the Egyptian government, after thirty years of highly reckless and selfish policies, had reduced a considerable proportion of the Egyptian population to a standard of living not fit for human beings.

It did this by starving a large number of Egyptians, neglecting to educate them, and failing to provide them with rewarding jobs, to build houses that were fit for human habitation and that would enable them to marry and settle down, to provide public transport that they could use with dignity, and so on. These Egyptians, who might account for 40 percent of the total population, most of them young, turned into creatures that wandered the streets aimlessly and without hope, thinking only about the basics of life, such as providing food for themselves and their families, seeking sexual satisfaction by pressing themselves up against women on public transportation (and now in the street) or through common-law marriages that the couple knew had no legal value, committing murders to steal paltry amounts of money, or becoming addicted to cheap drugs that relieved them of the burden of thinking about the cruel reality around them and at the same time reduced the pangs of hunger. Some sought a way to escape the country in the hope of finding a livelihood abroad, such as by going to Saudi Arabia on the pretext of performing the minor pilgrimage and then slipping off into the desert when it was time to go back to Egypt (as a large proportion of Egyptian pilgrims have done recently), or accepting offers from human traffickers to take them across the Mediterranean to Italy, where they could swim ashore and slip into the country in the hope that the Italian police would not see them, and then look for work there, even if the engineers among them have to work as porters, the accountants as hotel staff, and the lawyers as newspaper vendors, assuming they manage to avoid death by drowning on the way.

These are young men who have nothing to lose—no wives, no children, no decent jobs, and no money. Their fathers and mothers, trying to survive, are too busy to care. They have no hope for the foreseeable future of having a family, a job, or any money. They don't seem to worry about how the people around them see them or about the hatred and contempt that their deeds might provoke, because they are hated and despised in any case. There is nothing to distinguish them from the herds of thousands of young men lost in the streets and they have nothing to fear from the police because a high proportion of policemen are not much different from these lost young men. Just look at the wretched expression on the faces of the police, from complete despair, their bodies frail from starvation, their degradation, their inability to brush away a fly, let alone pursue young men trying to molest a woman in the street. Most policemen have the same problems of poverty, hunger, bad housing, and poor marriage prospects, besides the daily abuse they face from officers who have problems that may be somewhat different in quality but stem from the same source as the problems of the wretched policemen and the young unemployed—corruption and a state that is lax and negligent. What could possibly motivate a poor policeman or even a dynamic officer to protect a girl or a woman who is being harassed in the street in this pervasive climate of frustration?

A very small category of Egyptians does not feel this frustration: those for whom the streets are swept every morning, for whom the roads are closed for hours if the message comes that they want to go out driving, for whom luxury houses are built and luxury foodstuffs imported, who get engaged and married to young men and women of the same class that monopolizes the luxury food and drink and the beaches, and reserves for its children the jobs, the houses, and the fabulous weddings. This category of Egyptians has even monopolized the newspapers, for it is noticeable that the state-owned newspapers didn't publish anything about what happened on the first day of the Eid al-Fitr holiday until it was the talk of the whole world and had been reported on foreign radio stations. The state-owned newspapers, after waiting a week without writing a word about it, began to look rather suspect and in the end had to say something. Yet, when you read the coverage of the subject in the government's prime daily, it would have been better if they had not written anything at all. The coverage ranged from implicit defense of the young men, saying they went out to have a fun time on the occasion of the holiday, to criticism of the young women for going out when the streets were crowded, to denial that anything serious had happened at all and portrayals of the police as having done their duty in full.

Several weeks earlier we had been told that members of this lucky sector, which had ruled over the Egyptian people for ages, and their children, who intended to take their place as rulers, didn't read what was written in the independent and opposition newspapers because they did not have time to listen to complaints. They had more important preoccupations, basically connected to preparing Egyptians to accept the news that the son was going to take his father's place as ruler. In my opinion they were wasting their valuable time on something that was pointless, because amending Articles 76 and 77 of the constitution or re-amending them in order to enable the president's son to succeed him was no longer of interest to the vast swath of Egyptians whose circumstances I have just described. Perhaps the objective in amending this or that article was to convince certain foreign governments and organizations that the son's succession would take place "democratically." But maybe these governments and organizations were also uninterested in whether this or that article was amended or preserved as it is because these governments and international organizations are in reality only interested in ensuring that this lucky group of Egyptians soon sells off this bank or that company to foreigners and that they do not say a single word in opposition to what this country or that organization is doing in Iraq, Lebanon, or any other country. So, in order to ensure that this bank or that company is sold and that this small and lucky group continue to monopolize the luxury food and drink, the housing, the beaches, and the fabulous weddings, it is fine to starve a high proportion of the Egyptian people and make them homeless in this manner, so much so that one can sometimes see policemen looking for scraps of food in garbage bins, and hundreds of young Egyptians, in order to resolve their psychological and sexual problems, resort to remorseless assaults on any woman they find in the street.

In the newspapers after that Eid al-Fitr I read that the police had received hundreds of reports of sexual harassment over the holiday. The number of instances that did not come to the attention of the police must have been high.

Then I heard from an Egyptian academic who was teaching a group of young Americans who had come to spend a few months in Egypt to learn Arabic that they had had a very unpleasant experience over the Eid al-Fitr holiday, which they had spent in Alexandria. The women were harassed while walking along the seafront. The harassment mainly took the form of vulgar remarks, as the Egyptian young men mistakenly thought that the women didn't understand Arabic, but sometimes the harassment went beyond vulgar remarks. The women and the young American man who was with them were very upset and angry, but they did not know how to deal with the crowd of young Egyptians, who were egging each other on and did not seem to care about anything.

A few days after the holiday I saw an amazing photograph in an Egyptian newspaper, showing the minister of population and family affairs (a recently created ministry in Egypt) leading a small demonstration (judging from the picture, it seemed to be within the walls of Cairo University), flanked by two eminent women who hold important jobs related to education and population, surrounded by a small number of men and women. They were carrying banners, and under the picture I read that the demonstration was in protest against sexual harassment.

The demonstration struck me as surprising because I believe the problem is too complicated for a demonstration to contribute toward solving it. In fact, it is much too complicated to be solved by the three institutions that the three eminent women head or work for, unless they are assisted by policies to be adopted by many other ministries and institutions, and unless it is part of an effort that continues for a good length of time, about as long as the time that has elapsed since the start of this appalling deterioration in the state of young Egyptians and Egyptian society, which in the end has led to the phenomenon of sexual harassment on the scale we have seen in recent years and to other similar phenomena. What exactly happened to bring this about?

For more than forty years I have relied on the Helwan metro to get to work. At first I used to take the metro to Bab al-Louq station, but twenty years later (when it became part of the underground network) I would take it to Tahrir Square. I stopped doing this four or five years ago when it became hard for me to climb the seventy-six steps between the platform at Tahrir Square (or Sadat) station and street level.

Throughout this period the metro struck me as the best way to get to Tahrir Square. In the first twenty years (from the mid-1960s to the mid-1980s) the only disadvantage was that at certain times of the day it could be very crowded, when the workers came out of the factories in Helwan or from the barracks in Maadi. It would be difficult even to find a place to stand in the train and you could not be sure you would be able to get off when it stopped at your station. In fact, it could get so crowded that if the other passengers wanted to get off at some other station you would have to get off with them, against your will, pushed off by the mass of bodies. But this was a minor problem that could be avoided by avoiding the times when the workers came off work.

When the metro became the underground, with an increase in the number of carriages and the greater frequency of the trains, the crowding problem was greatly alleviated. But two or three years before I stopped using the metro almost completely I was surprised by the appearance of a problem that was new not only to me but also to Egypt. On the way back from Tahrir Square the passengers in some stations, such as Sayyida Zaynab or al-Malik al-Salih, would find large numbers of boys or youngsters, in early or middle adolescence, getting into the carriages in school uniform carrying bags, though their clothes were very tattered and their bags and shoes were in a deplorable state. They would quickly spread out along the carriages, running down the aisles oblivious of those standing in the way, shouting at each other from one end of the carriage to the other, waving their arms and their bags, exchanging insults, shouts, and vulgar remarks, which terrified the other passengers who were sitting or standing—men and women coming back exhausted from work and unable to predict what to expect from these little devils, who gave the impression that no one could possibly put them in their place.

Just by looking at the faces and the conduct of these young people you could tell immediately that they were lost youth whom no one was educating, neither their families nor their teachers, and whom no one could restrain, neither their fathers and mothers nor their teachers. The only lessons they had received in how to behave were those they saw and heard on television—a mixture of sexually stimulating images, advertisements for products arousing desires they cannot fulfill, and religious lectures and sermons disconnected from the reality of their daily lives.

It was not hard to imagine what was bound to happen to these youngsters as they grew up, whether they went on to get a higher education, work in some workshop, serve food in a restaurant, deliver fast food to people's houses, look after parked cars, or even fail to find any of these wonderful jobs and end up sitting in front of a television in some house, some room in the shantytowns, or some nearby coffee shop.

Then Eid time comes and they have managed to scrape together a few pounds. They go out on the streets or walk along the Nile in Cairo or the seafront in Alexandria, and how can they spend the Eid with their small amount of cash, other than by harassing people? What is there to deter them? What are they frightened of losing? People's respect? The love of their father or mother? The sympathy of a brother, who has tried to travel illegally to Italy or Greece in search of work but has not succeeded and has come back disappointed to sit in front of the television in the coffee shop as well? Or should they be frightened of the brutality of the police, who are no longer much better off than they are?

This seems to me to be the real explanation of the phenomenon of sexual harassment in Egypt, an explanation that reminds us in some ways of Yusuf Idris's famous story, "The Cheapest Nights," in which he describes how an impoverished peasant at the end of the day finds he has no other form of recreation than to lie next to his wife, who is also exhausted. During Eid, these young people in their turn look for the cheapest possible form of relief from a miserable reality, but a form more shocking than the one Idris describes. More than sixty years have passed since Idris wrote his story. The population of Egypt has tripled since then, and millions of people have moved from the countryside to the cities looking for work, though only a small proportion of them had found rewarding work in the first twenty years after the story was written. Many of those found decent jobs in factories, earning reasonable wages and a reasonable degree of self-respect, like the workers who filled the Helwan metro in the 1950s and 1960s. In the following twenty years many of them went to the Gulf and were able to marry with the money they had saved, so they did not think of harassing women at Eid time. But in the last twenty years, while the population has not stopped growing, many doors have closed for those seeking a livelihood at home and abroad—abroad because there is less demand for Egyptian workers in the oil-producing countries and at home because of excessive economic liberalization, with the government withdrawing more and more from intervening in the economy and the private sector preferring to use machines over employing workers, with the remaining jobs available to most young Egyptians no longer of the type that would divert them from harassing women.

Over the last twenty years, under Mubarak, the Egyptian government did not show any serious concern about the fact that the problem was growing worse. It was worried about other things that we don't need to go into here. It did not mind pretending to be working to solve the problem by setting up a Ministry of Youth, for example, or by releasing statistics that showed a reduction in unemployment, but it was glaringly obvious that the problem was growing worse day after day. So the officials must have counted the employed and the unemployed in a way that included the lost youth among the ranks of the employed. When they saw that these figures did not solve the youth problem, they thought of setting up a new ministry called the Ministry of Population and Family Affairs, and in its turn the ministry could not solve the problem because the new minister could not do anything without the cooperation of the minister of economy and the minister of trade and industry, but these ministers in turn were busy with other things that were more important to them than the problem of youth and sexual harassment.

So only one solution remained: for the minister to organize a demonstration somewhere completely safe from any harassment, joined by certain eminent women who were equally immune from harassment, holding banners that called on young Egyptians to refrain from any acts offensive to public decency, provided that some pictures of the demonstration were taken for widespread circulation.

2 Appropriating Public Property

1

Farouk Hosni, the Egyptian minister of culture for more than twenty years under President Mubarak, in his campaign to become director-general of UNESCO, did not behave in a manner befitting a minister from a principled country that derives its political positions from the sentiments of its people, that does not treat its enemies in the same way it treats its friends, and that does not spend taxpayers' money without restraint or a sense of responsibility. On the contrary, the culture minister behaved in this affair as if the ministry and the state were both his private estate or the estate of his father. So the tale of his candidacy and the ultimate election for the post is saddening from start to finish.

Farouk Hosni told the president that he wanted to be nominated for the post and asked him for his support. The president agreed and promised to help him. That was the first we heard of the matter. We never heard that the Egyptian government was thinking about nominating an Egyptian for this prominent position and had drawn up a list of major Egyptian intellectuals of international repute and people known to have taken positions serving Arab culture who attempt to change the educational curricula in Arab countries in a way that threatens this identity and this heritage. All we heard was that Farouk Hosni wanted the job and the president had agreed to his request. So it was rather like the way a landowner deals with his or his father's estate. The spoiled child wants, for example, to marry a beautiful girl who comes from a rich family and has many suitors, so he needs support and assistance. All the people on the estate need to be mobilized to achieve this objective, and all the revenue of the estate is put at his disposal as long as it serves this aim.

The people on the estate, including the poor peasants, spend close to a whole year hearing only about how the spoiled son wants to get married. The son submits his candidature, the son goes abroad, the son returns, the president of Egypt speaks to the American president about it, the Egyptian president asks the Israeli enemy not to create problems for the spoiled boy, the Israelis take the opportunity to ask the Egyptian president for something in return, though we do not know what exactly they requested. The Egyptian foreign minister puts his work aside to make the contacts necessary to win support for the spoiled son. The Egyptian president and foreign minister use the weight of the state to persuade other Arab countries not to put forward a rival to the Egyptian candidate. Senior officials in the Ministry of Culture drop their usual work to devote themselves to the minister's campaign. The newspaper published by the ministry follows the campaign day by day and writes about the minister's glories and achievements. Egyptian intellectuals are asked to write in the newspaper to support him, and so on.

Because the minister is aware of the importance of the Zionist role in publicity in the west and in influencing the decision-making process there, the minister spares no effort to win over Israel and Zionists to his camp, regardless of whether this is in line with the opinions of the Egyptian people. So the minister goes to seminars and meetings in Europe at which he says in various ways how he loves Jews, expresses great regret over what happened to them in Germany seventy years ago, loves peace in general and appreciates 'the other,' whoever that other might be. In remarks to the British newspaper the *Daily Telegraph*, he says that if he wins the post of UNESCO director-general he will have no objection to visiting Israel or having normal relations with it. As the boss of the person in charge of the national translation project, he says he would encourage the project to translate books by Israeli authors and promises to complete projects to restore Jewish antiquities. He gives a prestigious cultural award to someone who has earned not the respect of Egyptian intellectuals but rather the approval of Israelis. A devilish idea also occurs to him: to invite an Israeli conductor to conduct an orchestra at the Cairo Opera House. This was the first time such a thing had happened, which must have made the Israelis happy and distressed any Egyptians who heard of the event. But nothing stands in the way of the spoiled child, so everything is possible. The minister even recruits a number of Egyptian intellectuals to attend the concert on the grounds that they love classical music and love peace at the same time, and he pushes them to write to the effect that there's nothing wrong with that.

All these parties and trips from one country to another must be very costly. And who, I wonder, will tell us how much of these expenses has been covered by the coffers of the state and of the Ministry of Culture? Was the president's support for the minister enough in itself to approve the appropriation of all these funds?

We have heard that some of these expenses were covered by a famous and very wealthy businessman who would travel with the minister from place to place, and on several occasions we have seen pictures of him on television, walking alongside the minister. What advantage, one wonders, did this famous businessman gain from giving his backing? Was the businessman eager to ensure that an Egyptian, or Arab, or Muslim minister became head of UNESCO in order to serve Arab or Islamic culture? Can we be sure that the expenses covered by the businessman from the goodness of his heart will not mean burdens falling on the shoulders of other Egyptians?

No one knows exactly why all these efforts failed. I think it improbable that the reason was Israeli and Zionist opposition, or even the opposition of the United States. Both of them must have been well aware that Farouk Hosni could do them excellent service, more so than the successful Bulgarian candidate, because an Arab who is complacent about his country's rights and ready to cooperate would be much better in Israel's eyes than a European who has no direct connection with the Arab–Israeli conflict. In fact the European might adopt an anti-Israeli position, motivated by general humanitarian principles and ideals.

Whatever the reason for the failure, it was not that the Zionists and the Americans were hostile toward him, as the minister claimed when he came back, because he had done everything he could to win their friendship before the election and had confirmed that he was willing to do more if he won. Of course the minister was bound to say such things after he lost the election because he was trying to win Egyptians to his side now that the Ministry of Culture was all he had left. What is more surprising is the remark the minister attributed to the Egyptian president when he tried to console the minister on his defeat: "Put it behind you!" he supposedly said. In other words, do not let what happened cause you any grief and concentrate on the future, your future in the Ministry of Culture, that is. What is surprising about the remark is that once again the president treated the subject as though it were a private matter involving Farouk Hosni's personal interests. Egypt had failed to obtain an important position in a major United Nations body, one that it could very possibly have obtained if the whole matter had not been handled as if it involved a private estate and the private interests of a spoiled child. This failure deserved to make all of us, including the president of course, feel regret at what had slipped through Egypt's hands. But in this case we find the matter being treated as a minor setback to a dear son who has to be comforted, in spite of everything Egyptians have done and the money and effort they have wasted, and the least that must be done to console him in his sorrows is to leave him in the senior position he has held in Egypt for twenty-two years.

2

When the train heading to Upper Egypt was in that tragic accident in 2002 in which several hundred people (some say thousands) were killed, it was a great shock. But as people began to pick up information about the circumstances of the accident and about how overcrowded the carriages were, with people, luggage, and crates blocking the corridors so that it was not easy to reach the doors or jump out of the windows, and when it was discovered that the cause of the fire was a kerosene stove that a poor man was using in one of the carriages, making a living by selling cups of tea to passengers (this was against the rules, of course, and the inspector must have turned a blind eye to it, again in order to make a living)—when people learned all these details, the accident seemed quite logical and understandable. What seemed strange was that such accidents did not occur every day and that day after day one train after another reaches Upper Egypt safe and sound with all its passengers, without a collision or a fire breaking out.

Similarly, when the Van Gogh painting of the poppies, which is valued at $50 million, was stolen from the Mahmoud Khalil Museum in Cairo in broad daylight in 2010, without the thief apparently using force or any modern technology to prevent the alarms from going off or to deactivate the cameras monitoring the paintings, and without leaving any trace that might lead to his arrest, at first sight it seemed most extraordinary and surprising. But as the details of the incident started to be published and we discovered that most of the cameras were not working in the first place, that the number of guards present at the time of the theft was very small, and that most of them were busy doing something other than protecting the paintings at the time, such as having something to eat or taking an unscheduled break on some pretext or other, and when we heard that the minister was accusing the museum director, and the museum director was accusing the minister, to the extent that the museum director was suing the minister for sending men to search his office for any papers that might help the director prove that he was innocent of any negligence—when we heard all these details and more, the incident seemed quite natural and very logical, and the only strange thing was how such incidents did not happen every day and how Egypt still had so many valuable objects on display in museums or stored in storerooms. How come such incidents didn't occur every day in Egyptian museums, when they were in such a state: the guards and their salaries, the directors and the way they are appointed, the ministers and the ease with which they avoided taking responsibility, and so on?

3

I want to draw attention to one characteristic of the regime that ruled Egypt before the revolution of January 2011, a characteristic that has not received the attention it deserves: the regime's cruelty. I don't mean the regime's cruelty in dealing with the poor and the helpless, those who had no one to support them or intercede on their behalf, because that is familiar and well known. What I mean is its cruelty toward its own wealthy associates, the influential people who were very close to those at the top of the regime.

From time to time we would hear about the downfall of someone who just the day before had been among the regime's lucky few, and then the regime had suddenly abandoned him, almost throwing him out the window into the street. And when the media found such a person alone, with no one to support him, they would start publishing all the dirt they could dig up on him, exposing to the world details of all the bad things he had done since he took on a ministry or some large institution and bringing out into the open details of the state land and state funds he had illegally appropriated for himself, his wife, his friends and protégés during his long career close to the center of power.

What was surprising here was not what people dared to do when they found that the regime had abandoned such a person, but rather all the cruelty the regime showed toward someone who had tried his hardest to please those in power and who had thought he was quite safe as long as he continued his work trying to please them.

One aspect of this cruelty was the way the pillars of the regime pretended they never had a close relationship with this person, as if they had not made vast profits through the corruption of which the man was now accused, and the way they unleashed the investigative authorities on him while turning a blind eye to many others and allowed the government media to delve into his career while saying nothing at all about others like him.

There's only one thing that could protect a man who was suddenly thrown into the street as a result of this excessive cruelty on the part of the regime, and that was for him to be brave enough to threaten those who had abandoned him by saying he would bring the whole house down on everyone's heads if they continued to treat him that way, and that before he was harmed he would create a public scandal and everyone would have to face the same accusations. Only then, and provided the threat appeared to be serious, might the regime have backed off and left him alone.

What helped the regime shirk responsibility for the corrupt deeds of these people was that people have very poor memories. It was easy for people to forget that this minister or official who was now being sacrificed had been in his post for a very long time, that on many occasions he appeared with other officials who showed him the greatest affection and approval, and that throughout that period he sat at the same table as other ministers and the prime minister without any of them paying attention to what people were saying about him. He would even be awarded some great honor after he was asked, for some reason or other, to give up the position where he had engaged in all these corrupt practices.

When hundreds of millions of dollars were wasted on some big project, although senior experts raised objections to it, and the project suddenly came to a halt and started to give off the smell of corruption, it was easy for people to forget that when the project was launched it had been described as designed to "build a new civilization," as being as important to the future of Egypt as the Aswan High Dam was when it was built in the 1960s.

It was easy for people to forget that this corrupt minister or official did not receive his important position because he was already known for his great competence or his unparalleled integrity, or because his widespread popularity made him more deserving of the position than anyone else. The regime chose him for that position for some incomprehensible reason and without making any effort to justify the choice, which of course made it likely that he must have been chosen for the position because he could be trusted to be instinctively willing to act corruptly in a way that spread the benefits among other pillars of the regime. It was easy for people to forget all this and think only that an official who was acting corruptly had suddenly been found out.

What was it that drove the regime to expose one prominent person after another to this cruel treatment?

The reason may simply have been bad luck, that a scandal had come to light that was not expected to come to light. Or the reason may have been that the official committed a serious offense against some pillar of the regime and didn't realize how serious the offense was, and hence earned enmity and was targeted for revenge. Or the reason may have been that the regime reckoned that this official had eaten his fill from corruption and that it would be useful to give someone else a chance who had the same talents but who might be more ingenious and inventive in the way he engaged in corruption. But the real reason may have been that the regime had a fixed policy of sacrificing some pillar from time to time as a smokescreen to protect the others, since it was obvious that this policy offered an advantage that is not to be underestimated: using one corruption case to distract people from many other instances of corruption.

4

Dr. Samuel Johnson was a shining light in the history of British culture in the middle of the eighteenth century because of his contributions to literature and language. But what has brought him even greater renown to this day is the fine book about his life and thoughts written by his friend and disciple James Boswell, under the title *The Life of Dr. Johnson*. Boswell spent several years at Dr. Johnson's side, recording every day his opinions and thoughts about life and about famous English politicians and writers, and giving us a treasure of wise ideas and perceptive insights into various aspects of life.

Boswell relates that one day they were in a carriage traveling through the English countryside when they went past a large country house of great beauty, surrounded by lush gardens, indicating that the inhabitants lived in great wealth and luxury. Boswell remarked to Johnson, "One should think that the proprietor of all this must be happy," to which Johnson replied, "Nay, sir, all this excludes but one evil—poverty."

I liked the remark and saw it as confirmation of what I already believed. Yes, I always believed it, until a Lebanese singer was murdered in a case that fascinated Egyptians for several months and created in me a great unease that I would like to share with readers in the hope that I can find a way out of it.

Here we had an Egyptian man of about fifty who acquired such great wealth that his fortune should be the stuff of legends. Far from owning just a house here and a palace there, this man owned whole cities, and the city he had just finished building had every possible amenity and embellishment. His wealth had enabled him to become influential not just in the economy of the country but also in its politics, and he held a prominent position in the ruling party and in the upper house of parliament, very close to those at the top of the regime. All this we knew and did not find strange, but we knew nothing about his private life. We might have guessed at the various pleasures and delights that his wealth made possible in the way of food, drink, luxury cars, and affairs with women. But the surprise that the murder case sprang on us went way beyond our wildest imagination, because the Lebanese singer, with whom we now know he was totally infatuated, was receiving, apart from gifts and precious gems, a monthly amount of more than a million Egyptian pounds. But even stranger is the amount the man is said to have paid to have her killed just because he was angry with her for some reason or another (I do not think it is useful to know the details). Instead of killing her himself, he hired a man who was willing to carry out the job on his behalf as long as he was paid enough to make it worth his while. In this case the amount paid was more than a million and it was in dollars rather than Egyptian pounds, because the job was difficult and very risky and a man does not usually risk his life for a sum denominated in Egyptian currency.

What would Dr. Johnson have to say about this? What can a man want that cannot be acquired with money? Or what is the evil that cannot be excluded even if enough money is available? Even pangs of jealousy can be appeased with the right amount of money, and this is exactly what the singer's wealthy admirer is accused of doing.

Objections might be raised on the grounds that you cannot guarantee that all the conditions will be right and that something might not happen that had not been taken into account or included in your planning or the planning of the man assigned the murder mission, so that an ordinary murder becomes a big scandal and the murderer is arrested and confesses everything. Similarly, by bad luck, the crime might take place on the territory of a country that has no interest in having the crime committed on its territory and whose ruler is another rich man, in fact a man whose wealth is many times greater than your own and who is extremely angry at the way the perpetrator has shown contempt for the laws of his country. And this man's anger isn't something to be dismissed, because the whole Egyptian regime, which is prosecuting the defendant for murder, is deeply indebted to this ruler, and since the Egyptian regime depends on him for funding, he has to be placated.

This is what actually happened, and for weeks or months it looked as if Dr. Johnson was right in the end. Money can only exclude some sources of evil, but not all of them. So for months the media brought us news and pictures that confirmed this fact: the man was truly crushed, brought to court under tight guard, his hands in chains, looking utterly cowed and wretched, and all that could not have been just for show. The prosecution was calling for the death penalty and succeeded in proving that he took part in the murder through incitement. Not just that, but he was indeed sentenced to death and his famous lawyer expressed his anger and extreme indignation at the sentence, as if he had failed in his defense and had let the defendants down. People thought that this was the end of the matter and that the man no longer had any tricks up his sleeve to escape, however much money he had.

But far from it. We know what happened after that. The verdict was appealed and the sessions were postponed month after month. In any case the man was sitting pretty in a prison that had every comfort. He was brought whatever he wanted to eat and could receive any guests he liked. In the meantime some things were being worked out. The fuss that some of the murdered singer's relatives had made in Lebanon, such as her father and her former husband, was solved by paying another few million dollars, and in exchange the relatives dropped their civil suits, that is, their demand for compensation for their grief and for the material loss they suffered when they stopped receiving what the singer used to send them before the murder. Then came the decisive step: the reduction of the sentence from death to fifteen years' imprisonment with hard labor for the wealthy admirer and twenty-five years for the man who carried out the murder. The sentence evoked great surprise but provided a valuable lesson, fully documented, to the youth and people in general in this country about the importance of money and the insignificance of everything else: life, death, love, reputation, and so on. Anyone who harbors any doubts about this should go back and consider the story of the man's life from its start up until this moment.

Although I know all this, I still like what Dr. Johnson said at the beginning of this story: "Nay, sir, all this excludes but one evil—poverty."

The reason I like the remark, despite the rich man's victories, is that this man's wealth caused so much misery to so many people, known and unknown, and even brought much misery on himself, however much he may pretend the opposite to himself and to others.

3 Bequeathing the Unbequeathable

1

I once read about a Dutch woman who was married to one of the great-est, most popular, and most famous politicians in Holland. Her husband died, leaving her with two young children. The woman made a decision that was unusual but showed wisdom and keen insight. She decided to take her children to another country far away where no one had heard of their wonderful father and bring them up out of the limelight in the belief that their father's fame could well corrupt the children, particularly the boy, in several respects. The boy might be treated in a way he did not deserve, and that in itself would have a damaging effect. People might pamper him and give him too much attention, so that he would start to think he was more important than he really was. And the attention and the pampering might lead him to expect similar treatment from every-one and to get upset when he did not receive it, without his having any right to be upset. People might forgive him the mistakes he made, out of deference to the memory of his great father, so he would persist in his mistakes, and people might worry about hurting his feelings because they liked his father so much, so he would not have to pay the proper penalty for his mistakes, and so on.

I remembered this story while I was thinking about the son of former President Mubarak being named the head of the policies committee of the ruling National Democratic Party. Did the president or his wife have the same worries as that Dutch woman, I wondered?

Of course it had nothing to do with whether the president's son was competent or not, whether or not he was able to handle the responsibility that was entrusted to him. In fact, in this case, the more competent the son was, the greater the loss. If the young man in question had everything it takes to succeed and excel without relying on his father's name and position, the loss that resulted would be immense. Add to that the special circumstances of Egyptian society in particular, where people are used to treating the president, any president, as a demigod, and one is bound to expect such treatment to be extended to the son, because people crave the various rewards that come with proximity to the man in power. If we add that, we can only imagine how great a danger was bound to threaten the son and his future. But in fact the danger was yet greater, because the danger was not confined to the son who was revered and received all this respect; it naturally involved the whole Egyptian political system. What lesson did this appointment teach other young Egyptians? Did it not imply that the best qualification for appointment to the highest and most responsible positions was to be related to the president? Was this the first lesson the president's son would have liked to see taught by the Future Foundation that he agreed to head, with its mission to improve the state of Egyptian youth and Egyptian society?

I like the story about a famous leader who went one day to make a speech and, when he came out on the balcony of his palace to start, saw thousands upon thousands of people gathered in front of the palace chanting his name, carrying pictures of him, and holding up banners supporting him. The man felt a surge of self-importance and thought he really was one-of-a-kind and the genius of his age. One of his close associates came up to him and whispered in his ear, "Remember that you're human!"

It's never easy to take this advice, for people in such situations to remember that they are just ordinary people placed in extraordinary circumstances through no merit of their own, because human beings are weak, very weak, and one of the many aspects of their weakness is their constant willingness to believe what they want to be true, even if it is very far from the truth.

I notice this in myself as much as in others. I am a university professor and I have noticed that if five or six students come to my office on a particular day, one after another, all more anxious than usual because of an imminent exam, and one of them asks me a question and I answer, and another inquires about something related to the exam and I explain, and a third has a request to which I agree out of sympathy, and one after another they say how thankful and grateful they are in a tone that is exaggerated because they are in a weak position compared to me, I have noticed that in such situations I experience for some time a considerable degree of self-admiration and conceit in that I believe what I am told and consider it truthful simply because I want it to be so.

Such thoughts come to mind when I see pictures of many leaders and presidents, especially Third World presidents, since people surround them with numberless forms of adulation and flattery, and from their pictures and their behavior they seem to believe what they hear. Such thoughts were bound to go through my mind when I saw pictures of the head of the policies committee of the National Democratic Party, who was also the son of former President Mubarak, on the occasion of some party conference. It would have been easy for a young man like him to believe that he was one-of-a-kind and a genius of his time, not only because he was young and inexperienced compared to all those around him and to those who held similar positions, but also because from a tender age he had enjoyed treatment quite different from any other child in Egypt, whether in terms of comfort or in terms of the intense interest those around him took in him and their willingness to meet any desire that might come to his mind, since his father had always been either president of the country or vice president. Now the son was walking with ministers behind him, even the prime minister and major intellectuals, listening with great interest to every word he uttered and showing their admiration for everything he said, as if he spoke only words of wisdom, and the government newspapers praised his statements and published them on their front pages because they were bound to be deep and significant.

So it came as no surprise to hear it told that during a party conference he said that he "was not the greatest person in Egypt." The remark was no doubt correct, but it was unfortunate that he should have said it merely out of modesty, and it must have given rise to expressions of approval and smiles of admiration on the part of those around him.

In light of all this, if someone said to him, "You are the person best suited to succeed your father as president," how could he have conceivably objected?

2

I was amazed by the daring of Gamal Mubarak, the son of the former president, when he was head of the policies committee of the National Democratic Party, during his visit to the United States. The visit in itself was strange from the start because his father had not gone to the United States for several years, either officially or unofficially. The timing of the visit was important, occurring just after Barack Obama became president and was starting to meet kings and presidents from various parts of the world. Why did the former president's son go to the United States, and in what capacity? Why was an interview arranged on CNN, the most famous TV news channel in the world, with one of the most famous political editors in the United States, Fareed Zakaria? And why was he asked all those questions about Egyptian and Arab policies and about Egypt's relations with Iran and the Palestinian problem? Was it because he was the president's son? And why should the president's son have a status above that of other Egyptians? Or was it because he was head of the policies committee in the ruling party? What made him head of that committee in the first place? Was it his obvious eligibility? Was it that he had proved himself exceptionally aware of and interested in the affairs of the country? Or was it that his statements revealed a deep understanding of what was happening in Egypt and the rest of the world, without anyone preparing the statements for him or briefing him in advance on what he should say?

None of this qualified him to make the visit or to give such an interview. Was it because he was a nice young man who speaks English well? I thought that was what it was, but how many millions of nice young Egyptian men are there who speak English well? Some people asked, "Why should any young Egyptian, such as Gamal Mubarak, be forbidden to go into politics, since he might prove to have commendable ability and to be better than others?" But that argument made people angry because the simple answer to it was, "Why should we have deprived millions of young Egyptians who are as good as or better than Gamal Mubarak of the wonderful opportunity to be president of their country?"

Some might have argued that the important thing was to ensure that the presidential elections of the time were completely fair and that the referendums were not rigged, and then there would have been no objection to Gamal Mubarak or someone else winning the presidency. But the answer to that was, "How could the elections have been fair when the whole state was working on Gamal Mubarak's behalf for several years to prepare him for this role and the state media were all at his service?" What equal opportunities could there have been in this case?

This is the crux of the matter and it is as clear as sunlight. The whole state was working to serve this plan, especially as its success or failure depended, in the view of the state, on whether or not the United States approved of it. So the visit took place, and the president's son went to the United States to tell the new administration what it wanted to hear, completely regardless of what people in Egypt felt or what they thought about what was being said to the Obama administration or whether what Gamal Mubarak said served the Egyptian public interest.

All this is as clear as the sun, so how did Gamal Mubarak and his father fail to see it? If Gamal Mubarak failed to see it, how could he have been fit to inherit the presidency, regardless of whether or not he had the competence for it? The position that he took by making the visit was contrary to one of the most basic moral principles: that one should not exploit a position one has obtained purely by chance for the sake of personal gain and at the expense of the interests of others (who in this case happened to be 80 million Egyptians). The visit was just one in a long series of violations of this moral principle, a series that began when Gamal Mubarak started to take on official positions without proving that he had the talents that qualified him for those positions.

4 Selling the Unsellable

1

Every now and then, stories of another sell-off drift our way like a poisonous wind we are fated to endure. One industry after another was offered for sale, then department stores such as Omar Effendi, then banks such as the Bank of Alexandria. Then people said, "Why not sell the public utilities as well, such as the telephone company, the railways, the water and electricity companies, the airports, and the highways?" The last we heard was of putting Alexandria University up for sale.

What exactly is the story?

There are some phony explanations that are not credible. They say the public sector has proved it is a failure. See what Abd al-Nasser's nationalizations brought you to? The government has been a hopeless businessman, a useless farmer, and an even worse factory manager. The manager who doesn't have a personal interest in the company cannot work efficiently or be loyal to the company in which he works. In fact he will probably steal from it. Leave these things to those who can manage them properly and protect them from corruption.

They also say to look at the Soviet Union, the leader in public ownership and the pioneer of the public sector. Where did public ownership take it, what did the public sector do for it? Economic stagnation, the waste of resources, and corrupt management, while the country is now back in good health after getting back on the right track, allowing the private sector to own factories and farms, and abandoning forever the system of five-year plans laid down by the state.

Just look at China and the economic miracle it has achieved by allowing investors, Chinese or foreign, to produce for profit and to do what they want with their profits.

Anwar al-Sadat did well, they say, when he saw the light and opened the door to privatization, and Hosni Mubarak did well when he followed the same course and even repealed the articles in the constitution on the public sector and state ownership, and admitted that the private sector was the engine and leader in economic growth.

All these arguments are flawed, and are meant to conceal the truth, because Egypt is still living on the remnants of the public sector that they disparage day after day. The economic stagnation came about not as a result of the public sector but because of the Israeli attack in 1967, which ruined the economy and political life equally. It's not impossible to dismiss and replace the corrupt manager of a state-owned company. People are not motivated only by profit. Private incentives and public incentives can be combined. The Soviet Union was not undermined because of the public sector but because of totalitarian government, and it's not impossible to imagine a system that combines a strong public sector with democracy, as illustrated by the example of Western Europe after the Second World War. Five-year plans are not stupidities, but corruption ruins five-year plans as much as it ruins everything, and corruption exists in the private sector as much as it does in the public sector. In fact it is the private sector that is best able to corrupt the private sector.

Privatization was not a stroke of genius that occurred to Anwar al-Sadat or Hosni Mubarak. In fact it was imposed on both of them and neither had the means or the will to resist it. In any case it would have been possible to encourage the private sector while preserving the public sector without one wiping out the other, as China has done, for example.

So where did this hellish idea come from?

It's amazing how new ideas arise from new circumstances, a fact that has often been remarked on. "Necessity is the mother of invention," it is said, or, "Need creates more new ideas than a dozen universities would ever produce." That's how the idea of privatization arose, I believe, but unfortunately "need" in this case doesn't refer to what I need or what you need but what those with plenty of money need. In the end it's a question of surplus money looking for opportunities for profitable investment, and not a matter of the private sector being more or less efficient than the public sector. The areas for profitable investment change from one period to another, and for now the most profitable is in 'privatization,' that is, the purchase of state-owned assets. It hasn't always been like that. In the third quarter of the nineteenth century—that is, about a century and a half ago—there was also surplus money in England seeking activities for investment, but the money did not find opportunities available in privatization but rather through providing loans to weak rulers who could easily be persuaded to borrow to spend on projects they didn't need, and at exorbitant interest rates. If a prudent ruler did not yield to their pressures and refused to borrow, they replaced him or had him killed to bring in a ruler who did comply.

The khedives Said and then Ismail fell into such a trap in Egypt, as did the Ottoman sultan in Istanbul. In the last quarter of that century and the first years of the twentieth century, surplus European money found a good home investing in our infrastructure projects, and then there was a hiatus between 1914 and 1945 because of wars and the Great Depression. Surpluses built up again after the war but they went to rebuild Europe and Japan and also in the form of what was called foreign aid, most of which was official loans, that is, loans from one government to another. With this we built factories and the Aswan High Dam and equipped our armies. At that time and until about 1970, there was great enthusiasm for the public sector, even among the same international financial institutions whose only concern now is to criticize the public sector and applaud privatization. It began to change starting in the 1970s, when there were surpluses seeking new investment opportunities in our countries. The most profitable they found were through privatization, that is, buying up what the state had built over the previous twenty-five years. So it wasn't a stroke of genius that occurred to President Sadat and that President Mubarak adopted, it was just a hellish idea with the purpose of making a profit. How did Egypt come to swallow this bait, the bait of privatization?

2

When privatization was proposed in the 1970s, they naturally didn't tell us that the intention was that foreigners, the owners of surplus capital, would buy the assets of the Egyptian state. They told us the idea was that the private sector would replace the public sector, and since the private sector is always better and more efficient than the public sector (or so they told us), there was nothing to worry about. They portrayed it to us as though what mattered was that the individual would replace the state and the private the public, while what happened in most cases was that foreigners took the place of Egyptians.

The idea of privatization struck us as very strange when we first heard of it in the 1970s, and when President Sadat said he had decided to sell the Pyramids plateau to a shell company registered in Hong Kong to build golf courses and chalets on top of the antiquities buried around the Pyramids, people were outraged. Sadat quietly dropped the idea and the company sued him for compensation. At the beginning of the 1980s, a well-known lawyer dared to suggest selling off the Suez Canal to pay off Egypt's debts. Egyptian writers laid into him and ridiculed the idea, which he never mentioned again.

At the end of the 1980s, a journalist began a campaign advocating that Egypt sell its paintings and other valuable works of art, such as those in the Mahmoud Khalil and Gezira museums, in order to pay off some of its debts, on the grounds that these objects were worth half of Egypt's total foreign debt. It occurred to me at the time that the idea was not very different from the case of a young man so addicted to drugs that he is horribly dependent on borrowing, and when his creditors threaten not to lend him any more money unless he repays his previous debts, he runs to his mother and, encouraged by the creditors, presses her to give him her jewelry to sell to pay off his debts, including the gold pieces his father gave her when they got engaged and married, because this addict can't tell the difference between an inanimate lump of gold or silver and a pledge his father gave his mother at their engagement or marriage, and can't tell the difference between selling a Gauguin or a Renoir and selling iron bars.

Fortunately there was an uproar that time too and no one dared put the idea into practice. But the idea recurred in the form of selling Alexandria University, and what was odd in that case was that those proposing the idea were not developers but the minister of education, the president of the university, and the governor of the city where the university was located.

3

In the history of the Ministry of Education in Egypt (or the Ministry of Learning, as it used to be called), there have been many ministers chosen for the position because they were great men. It went without saying that education was a major national responsibility so a great man had to be in charge of it. Each of these great men did wonderful things before and after they took on the ministry. Saad Zaghloul became minister of learning a hundred years ago when he was already known for his nationalist activities during the Urabi revolt. Abbas al-Aqqad said of him, "The leadership of Saad Zaghloul undeniably contributed to the whole national renaissance — the launching of factories, banks, trading companies, educational institutes, and political assemblies that had not existed before the renaissance."

Abd al-Razzak al-Sanhouri, before he became minister of learning, was famous as a great jurist, and when he became minister he set up the People's University, which took learning outside the walls of schools and universities to ordinary people. Taha Hussein was a writer and great reformer. When he was appointed minister of learning, he introduced free education.

Then came a time when no one knows where they got the ministers of education or higher education. One hears their names for the first time and their names are hard to remember because they come to the job without having done anything important to justify their appointment and they leave without doing anything worth remembering.

That was until a minister of higher education came along who will no doubt go down in Egyptian history as the one who suggested putting Alexandria University up for sale.

The idea of selling Alexandria University is a very strange one and no doubt requires some explanation. The university, any university, consists of land and buildings, professors and students, deans and the administration, programs and curricula, so which exactly of these various components would go on sale? If only the land and the buildings are for sale, who would gain from the sale? The professors, students, and inhabitants of Alexandria? A development company whose name was often mentioned: Emaar Properties of the United Arab Emirates?

If the objective, other than profit for the company, was to beautify the area around the Alexandria Library, as we were told, is beautifying this area a national priority for Egypt right now, worthy to have state money spent on it, or should priority go to something else, eradicating illiteracy for example? And is the demolition of the Chatbi Hospital to beautify the area, which is part of the proposed sale project, really what we need, or do we need to build another hospital like it or even one less beautiful? And has anyone thought of the inconvenience to the students and faculty if they were moved, because of this beautification project, to land far from the city center?

There are many questions the minister of higher education hasn't answered, nor the president of the university, nor the governor of Alexandria, who have only issued successive statements, sometimes confirming the sale and sometimes denying it, without revealing the justifications for the sale or the identity of the buyer, all of which gives one the right to suspect that there was something quite improper going on.

4

Dr. Muhammad Aboul Ghar wrote an alarming article in one of the daily newspapers about preparatory work for a project that could be given euphemistic names such as "replanning the Alexandria Library area," "developing the eastern harbor," or even "developing the city of Alexandria." Whatever the name, in reality the project involved demolishing important buildings close to the Alexandria Library, including the Chatbi Hospital, the buildings housing the theoretical faculties at Alexandria University, and a number of residential buildings.

The frightening aspect of Dr. Aboul Ghar's article was the implication that meetings were held for the purpose of persuading some prominent Egyptian architects to endorse a dubious project and then using the names of these architects to get the project approved, or, as Aboul Ghar put it, to give it a bogus seal of approval.

One of the suspicious aspects was that when these architects asked who had paid the fees for the international architects to draw up the project designs, the answer was that they had done it free of charge. The architects then discovered that the fees had been paid by Emaar Properties of the United Arab Emirates, a large development company that had chosen a number of international architectural firms to design the project. In other words, it was the developer that had paid these companies!

When the Egyptian architects whose endorsement was sought asked about the funding for this massive project, which includes a 120-story building by the sea, apparently with an enormous hotel, they were told, "The funding is not a problem. We know how to get hold of the money."

The Egyptian architects were also upset that the architectural firms had not consulted the national plan for the urban development of Alexandria, so apparently the project was meant to put into effect only a concept that served private objectives, and these did not need to be consistent with any national concept of the public interest.

Dr. Aboul Ghar also expressed his concern that a decree had been issued "postponing any decision on the projects submitted" after the Egyptian architects rejected all the proposals, and saying he suspected there was "a secret plan to demolish Alexandria University." He called on the university professors "to defend their venerable university."

What was yet more worrying, after reading Dr. Aboul Ghar's article, was that what he described was completely consistent with what has been happening in Egypt in other fields. Projects give the impression of public service though in fact they serve only private interests. Officials in very high positions go along with the climate and, backed by their positions, help to promote dubious projects. Big developers make important decisions that affect the supreme interests of the nation. High-rise hotels and then even taller hotels block the view of the sea, or of anything at all, while earning amazing profits for a handful of people.

5

When the state is lax, as the Egyptian state has been since the 1970s, and sells some of its assets to the private sector, foreign or Egyptian, then it's only to be expected, and probable, that these assets will be sold at less than their real value.

It's easy to twist the arm of a weak state, and it's easy for villains to pay off its officials, because it doesn't have institutions to monitor them and hold them to account. Anyone who monitors them and tries to hold them to account is punished rather than rewarded.

But it's also to be expected, and probable, that such a state will be too weak to impose its conditions on the buyer regardless of the price he has paid. A state that takes its responsibilities seriously should not sell the public sector or state land for the buyer to do what he wants with them. On the contrary, there are important considerations that must be respected. There are workers who can be dismissed or given early retirement only with compensation on terms that respect their rights as human beings and that meet their basic needs. There are also those who consume the commodities that the public sector used to produce, and it is one of the state's responsibilities to protect the rights of these consumers and not leave them prey to a buyer who can do what he wants with them and charge them any price he pleases. The state is also responsible for the interests of society as a whole. The buyer cannot be left to damage the environment, pollute the water, turn a green area into an expanse of concrete, or convert a quiet residential district into a place with noisy bars and restaurants.

International financial institutions, such as the International Monetary Fund and the World Bank, talk much about the benefits of selling off the public sector and how the sales will increase efficiency (financial efficiency, of course), that is, cut costs and increase revenues, but they rarely talk about what the new owners will do with the assets they buy or the need for them to commit themselves to the higher social objectives that, at the end of the day, represent the ultimate purpose of the whole development process.

It might be said that these institutions assume that the state that is selling its property is a powerful state that can impose on the buyer whatever conditions it sees fit to ensure that these higher social objectives are protected. But it's easy to assume something that we know full well is not the case, and these institutions must know the truth about the states they urge to start privatization, that they are in fact soft states that have agreed to sell their property in the first place only because they are weak.

6

There has been endless talk about the corruption associated with privatization, about public-sector companies sold for less than their true value, and about how some of those responsible for the public sector benefited from that through the authority they had and their ability to influence those in power.

We heard plenty of talk about this kind of corruption in the case of the sale of the Bank of Alexandria and then the sale of the Omar Effendi chain of department stores—two deals that actually went through—and then about a deal to sell land in Tahrir Square to a French company, which was said to have been signed. Then we started hearing on and off about a deal to sell some of the land and buildings at Alexandria University and some of the land and buildings around it.

In every sale that went through it was said that the sale price was way below the real value and so the state must have lost out. Since such sales, at prices below the real value, cannot conceivably happen just through negligence or ignorance, then there must have been private interests behind it and so it must have involved corruption. This kind of corruption is of course reprehensible and abhorrent, but I don't consider it the worst variety. In fact I see it as minor corruption compared to what deserves to be called 'major corruption.'

Major corruption in the sale of state property is connected to two questions:

First: What does the buyer do with the state property after buying it?

Second: What does the state do with the money it receives from this sale?

On both counts previous experiences of the sale of state property in Egypt show that what the buyers do with their purchase often involves serious damage, economic, social, or environmental, and that the state does not spend the proceeds of the sale on creating new productive assets to compensate for those it has lost. Both aspects are serious enough to require detailed consideration.

When the idea of selling the San Stefano Hotel in Alexandria came up more than twenty years ago, the word 'privatization' was still new to our ears and we were not fully aware that it could turn our lives upside down. For years we still didn't know what would take the place of that famous hotel overlooking the sea in one of the most beautiful parts of Alexandria.

The hotel carried historic memories for Egyptians, and its demolition was saddening if only for that reason, but we told ourselves we mustn't surrender to our emotions and that if a new hotel was built in its place it might bring Egypt much more hard currency.

We thought it was no more than a matter of a new hotel replacing an old one, but look what emerged: a group of towers of unequaled ugliness, devoid of any human dimension.

Endless blocks of concrete, followed by similar blocks one after another, hiding the sea and the sky and all the beauty and air God had given to the people of Alexandria, all so that a group of investors could make more profit. I'm not especially interested in whether some of the profits also went to certain public-sector officials who facilitated the sale and didn't set conditions for what could be built in place of the hotel, but if they exist they will no doubt go to hell when they die. What matters to me is this hell they are responsible for creating for us in this life.

In the matter of the sale of the Bank of Alexandria, whether it was sold at or below its real value is less important than what the bank's policy will be after it is sold, who will be given loans, and what they will be used for. As for Omar Effendi, much has been said as well about its being sold for less than its real value, and this is very regrettable of course, but what worries me most is what will become of Omar Effendi in its new guise.

Whatever is said about the incompetence of the management at Omar Effendi and other public-sector enterprises and about the poor incentives given to workers there to encourage them to make an effort to provide a better service to customers, Omar Effendi did perform two significant services for the Egyptian economy: providing an outlet for the sale of many Egyptian-made products and making these products available at reasonable prices to a broad band of the Egyptian middle class, which cannot pay higher prices, whether for the same products or products of higher quality. Will Omar Effendi become an outlet for imported goods rather than Egyptian-made goods? Will this sector of the Egyptian middle class be forced to look elsewhere to buy the clothes, household appliances, and furniture it needs and lose another part of its income, which has started to erode?

7

A few years after the defeat of June 1967, Egypt began a wretched phase of its history during which it was run not in the interests of Egyptians or Arabs but of an alliance of American and Israeli interests on one hand and of a very small clique of Egyptian businessmen and politicians associated with them on the other, a clique that saw its own private interest in serving American and Israeli interests. This phase lasted for more than a third of a century, since it was unaffected when President Mubarak took the place of President Sadat.

Everything the regime in Egypt did throughout that period confirmed this fact: that Egypt was not being run in the interests of Egyptians, elections and referendums were constantly rigged, the control of the media continued, freedom of opinion was curtailed, the emergency law was extended again and again on the grounds of combating terrorism, and successive prime ministers were chosen without relying on free elections and without even exploring what people wanted. Ministers were selected in the same way, and anyone who gave evidence of any commitment to serving the interests of the people rather than the interests of that alliance of interests was disposed of at the first opportunity. The regime constantly ignored the Arab nationalist movement, adopted one political position after another that was not in favor of the Palestinians but rather of Israel, and carried out the wishes of the U.S. administration and served its interests in the Arab world, as it did toward U.S. intervention in the Gulf in 1990, the blockade of Iraq, and then the U.S. occupation of Iraq in 2003.

The regime backed the U.S. position toward Iran, contrary to Egyptian and Arab interests, and so on.

The privatization policy President Sadat launched in the mid-1970s and Mubarak then adopted, which accelerated in the early 1990s, especially in the last four years of Mubarak's rule, was part of this "running Egypt against the interests of Egyptians." Although there was no objection to denationalizing some public-sector enterprises that had been nationalized in the 1960s for political reasons that were no longer valid, privatization as an overall policy definitely did not distinguish between successful and failed enterprises, between whether it was or was not possible to turn an enterprise from loss to profit without renouncing public ownership, or whether it was or was not related to the state's strategic interests. It did not distinguish between a sale to Egyptians and a sale to foreigners and did not receive assurances to prevent a state monopoly becoming a monopoly held by individuals and so on. This type of privatization was definitely part of "managing the Egyptian economy against the interests of Egyptians."

In 2004 an important change took place in the Egyptian government, even if the way it came about was no aberration from the usual way the prime minister and ministers were chosen. The new government took a course different from its predecessors in several respects, even if the new course was no more favorable to the interests of Egyptians: it adopted accelerated privatization, accelerated normalization of relations with Israel, and more active steps to pave the way for Gamal Mubarak to succeed his father as president.

The change was evident in the choice of new ministers and the increased emphasis on the personality of the heir and the way he or his name was involved in the measures taken, while the role of President Mubarak and the men closely associated with him gradually diminished. It was also evident in the signing of a Qualifying Industrial Zone (QIZ) agreement with Israel and the U.S. a few months after the new government took office, in the natural-gas agreement signed with Israel on terms that were unfair to Egypt, and in the speed with which privatization proceeded and the way doors were opened wide to foreign private investment without subjecting it to adequate conditions to protect Egyptian workers and consumers.

Then, less than two months after the international financial crisis of September 2008, the National Democratic Party announced a new plan called "managing state-owned assets" that included giving away equity in eighty-six public-sector companies in the form of vouchers to be distributed freely and indiscriminately among all Egyptians aged twenty-one and over. The operation was to take place within a year and a half and the new owners would have the right to dispose of their shares as they chose—selling them or keeping them, collecting the dividends, and taking part in the management—though the state would retain either 30, 51, or 67 percent of the equity of these companies without ceding it to citizens and the value of any land these companies might own would not be included in the value of the vouchers distributed.

In light of the regime's dishonorable record of managing the country against the interests of Egyptians, serious doubts were bound to arise about the real purpose in launching this proposal so suddenly and without preparation, hurrying to promote it through the media and announcing the government's intention to put it to the People's Assembly in the form of legislation and to finish the process off in such a short time, especially given the international financial crisis, which should have prompted anyone wanting to sell to proceed cautiously. This all also occurred just weeks after the prime minister had announced that the government was abandoning the idea of selling Banque du Caire on the grounds that the moment was not conducive to a sale in light of the international crisis. The idea of selling Banque du Caire had previously been vigorously promoted, and the name of Gamal Mubarak had come up as one of the main advocates of the sale, while President Mubarak's role in the announcement and promotion of the plan was much reduced.

This sudden and unusual activity was bound to raise suspicions that the new project was just a continuation of the same well-known practice of running the country against the interests of Egyptians, but this time at a pace that was thought necessary for one reason or another, perhaps related to the imminent end of President Hosni Mubarak's term in office and the desire to facilitate the succession of his son, perhaps by winning complete support for a succession from the U.S. administration, which had so far been evasive on the subject. Or maybe the reason also had something to do with the international financial crisis, since proposing this project now would make it easy for some people to obtain Egyptian public-sector assets at the lowest possible price.

These suspicions became near certainties when people followed the way the project was presented in the media, some of the details that were announced, and the arguments the government advanced to justify and defend the plan, especially in remarks and statements by investment minister Mahmoud Mohieddin.

I asked several people who follow such economic and political developments in Egypt what they thought of the proposal, and although they have a solid knowledge of economic conditions in Egypt, they told me that they didn't understand anything. I interpreted this as proof not that the proposal was mysterious but rather that it was too obvious. But the obviousness was coupled with a blatant contradiction between what the government was saying about it and the regime's usual behavior for the past third of a century, and similarly the contradiction between the objectives the government claimed to be seeking through the proposal and the results to which it would inevitably lead—all of which would lead one either to describe what one hears as outright charlatanism or to admit politely that one doesn't have any idea what is happening.

The government said the aim of the proposal was "to expand the scope of ownership," but what is wider than public ownership? The public sector is the property of all Egyptians, including children, so what kind of distribution would this be if it involved giving free vouchers to those over twenty-one, without the government stipulating that the owners of the vouchers could not sell them to others, without providing serious guarantees to prevent the vouchers from ending up in the hands of a very small number of monopolists, and without uttering a single word in opposition to ownership passing to foreigners?

If expanding ownership was such a cherished goal that the government was using it as the title for its proposal and repeating the phrase to us day and night, why didn't it occur to the government to pursue it throughout the last eighteen years of privatization? Was selling one enterprise after another in the past to what were called "principal" or "strategic" investors just a mistake that the government wanted to correct? Or, more plausibly, were there several ways to put the public sector into the hands of principal or strategic investors, and the easiest way at the moment was to distribute it initially for free to all Egyptians?

The government said that distributing ownership of the public sector in the form of shares for citizens would help to strengthen their sense of belonging or loyalty, or used other words that had the same meaning and sounded much the same as all the empty slogans the government was accustomed to using. If people's sense of belonging and loyalty was so important to the regime, why for at least the previous eighteen years had it committed acts the most important effects of which had been to weaken that sense of belonging and loyalty to the country, so much so that young people preferred risking their lives in the Mediterranean to staying home and older people, with the exception of a small minority who benefited personally from the regime, preferred to distance themselves from participation in any political activity?

So the real motive for launching this proposal could not have been to expand ownership or strengthen Egyptians' sense of belonging and loyalty. What might the reason have been?

When Mahmoud Mohieddin, investment minister at the time, was asked about the connection between proposing the voucher plan at that particular moment and the international financial crisis, and whether it would be wise to put the assets of the Egyptian state on sale, as poor people with vouchers were expected to do, in an economic climate that was so bad that selling would favor the buyers rather than the sellers, Dr. Mohieddin answered in two different ways. First, he asserted that thinking about the plan had begun before the international crisis, saying once that it had started in 2006 (his interview with *al-Ahram* newspaper on December 6, 2008) and another time that it had started in 2004 (seminar at the Opera Cultural Salon on December 15, 2008). Whenever the thinking started, whether in 2004 or 2006, the question still stands: Why didn't the government change its position on this plan after the financial crisis struck? In fact there is evidence to suggest that the international crisis really was connected with the sudden launch of the plan and the way it was advanced in such haste and promoted with such insistence. Whether the idea was born before or after the crisis, there is strong evidence that the enthusiasm about it began after the crisis, which also reinforces suspicions that certain international parties gave hints or put pressure on the Egyptian government, after the international crisis began, to carry out this idea in the interests of certain probable investors abroad who were looking for cheap assets they could easily convert into profitable and rewarding assets after the crisis ended.

But Dr. Mohieddin gave a different answer on another occasion when he was asked how the proposal was connected with the international crisis. First, he said something to the effect that the international crisis was ephemeral, in other words that it would come to an end sooner or later. That's true, of course, but it's not a good answer to the question, "Why are these companies being offered for sale sooner rather than later?" In other words, why were they going on sale during the crisis and not when you're sure that it's over?

Second, he said that the companies included in the voucher plan (and which might be sold later) would be affected by the international crisis just as much as any other company, whether the plan existed or not. But that, too, was not an acceptable answer to the question of why the companies were going on sale at a time when they were vulnerable to the international crisis and why we didn't wait until the companies were back in good health.

In response to those who said that giving out vouchers would end in them being sold, he said, "That would be to underestimate the prudence and intelligence of the average citizen, because they are more intelligent and more conscious of their economic interests than we think. That means they might prefer to save the amount, or invest it to obtain a return or spend it on consumption. If average Egyptians decide to sell their vouchers instead of keeping them, or sell some of them and keep the rest, what's the harm in that? Everyone can make a decision based on their own needs and we shouldn't deprive them of their right to decide what to do with the vouchers."

On the danger that the operation might end with vouchers being sold to monopolists, the minister said, "There's no need to worry about monopolies because the government will retain a stake in every company and there are rules for takeovers, such that if anyone owns more than 5 percent of the equity, the Capital Markets Authority will be notified, and if the stake were to exceed 10 percent, it would need to obtain approval from the authority."

Anyone reading this would be in no doubt that the minister was speaking in his capacity as minister and not in his capacity as a former professor of economics, because it may be true that Egyptians, however poor and badly educated, are prudent and intelligent, but prudence and intelligence would not stop them, if they are poor, from selling a voucher worth four hundred Egyptian pounds and spending the money on essential goods. In fact prudence and intelligence might dictate such behavior, because when one is extremely poor, holding on to a voucher in the hope of receiving a dividend of 30 pounds or less at the end of the year might be utter stupidity when the prices of basic necessities are constantly rising and when selling the voucher now might be a precondition for the owner surviving another year.

To say that monopolies would be prevented by the legal guarantees that the ministers mentioned and by the state's retention of a 67, 51, or 30 percent stake in the assets of the companies would be to underestimate the importance of two factors:

First, the state's 100 percent ownership of the public-sector companies that were in fact sold to a principal or strategic investor had not previously prevented them from being sold to monopolists, and hence the state's retention of these percentages of the remaining assets would not prevent them from being sold to monopolists in the future and sooner than we might expect.

Second, the Egyptian regime's attitude toward monopolies over the last quarter-century, especially after the new government took office in 2004, did not incline one to believe it when it said it had provided sufficient guarantees to prevent the creation of new monopolies. This disinclination was corroborated by the stipulation of a mere "notification" if a shareholder bought more than 5 percent of the vouchers, which meant that a family of five people could own one-quarter of a company's shares with only a notification to the Capital Market Authority and could raise its stake to half the company's equity if the wife's family were included.

"Notification" was supposed to be less onerous than applying for approval, because the Capital Market Authority cannot object to a notification, whereas it can reject an application for approval. But approval was required only when an individual's stake exceeded 10 percent of the shares. Given the excessive leniency the regime usually showed people with assets, the requirement that they obtain approval would not have been much more onerous than the requirement of mere notification. For people with assets in Egypt, there hadn't been much difference for some time between expressing a desire for something and actually obtaining it.

What would have given the requirement of "approval" any value would have been the existence of a real democracy in the Egyptian political system. But, in the absence of democracy, and in light of the widespread manipulation of the law, the requirement for government approval was merely a smokescreen, like talking about "expanding the scope of ownership" and "increased public participation in the management of the country's assets." In fact if there were real democracy such a proposal would never have been made in the first place or promoted so extensively.

If one followed the statements by the minister of investment and other officials about the plan to distribute ownership of the public sector to Egyptians in the form of vouchers, it was clear they were anxious not to deny that some of the vouchers, and perhaps all of them, would be sold, and that some of them would be sold to foreigners. They were also anxious not to emphasize this fact, so they talked about selling to foreigners only if they were asked about it, and when asked they gave short and brusque answers.

I interpreted this as an attempt to conceal the real object of the plan: to sell the state's remaining assets to foreigners by first putting them in the hands of ordinary Egyptians so that the regime could avoid political and moral responsibility for selling Egypt's assets to non-Egyptians.

Dr. Abd al-Moneim Said, the head of the al-Ahram Strategic and Political Studies Center and one of the theorists of the Mubarak regime, wrote an article in which he wondered sarcastically why there was so much talk about "selling Egypt" when it was just a matter of selling companies and physical assets. He also asked daringly what exactly the harm was in selling to foreigners, as if he could see no difference between the public-sector companies remaining in Egyptian hands, even if sold to the private sector, and ownership passing to foreigners.

What Dr. Abd al-Moneim Said said on the subject and the way he ridiculed those who criticized sales to foreigners implied that insisting on Egyptian assets remaining in Egyptian hands means clinging to antiquated and obsolete ideas and a type of national chauvinism inappropriate in the wonderful age of globalization, which makes no distinction between the national and the foreign. But in fact Dr. Said was mistaken if he imagined that the age of globalization requires us to be indifferent to whether the owners of economic enterprises in Egypt are Egyptian or foreign. The phenomenon of globalization has advantages and disadvantages, and a prudent state is one that maximizes the advantages and reduces the disadvantages to a minimum. It is not in the interest of any state, whatever its economic strength, to let the wave of globalization sweep across its territory, allowing freedom of ownership with no distinction between the national and the foreign, or to let foreigners transfer profits and capital as they see fit and without controls. The states that are strongest economically and most supportive of the phenomenon of globalization, including the United States, intervene to set limits on foreign ownership of their land. The Asian crisis of 1997 showed that it is a mistake to give foreign capital too much freedom to move from one country to another. The countries that placed more restrictions on capital movement, such as Malaysia, were less affected by the crisis and quicker to recover than the countries that applied fewer restrictions, such as Thailand and Indonesia.

A few days after the voucher plan was announced, finance minister Youssef Boutros Ghali appeared on a television program and said that the companies included in the new plan were not very important, or something to that effect, and that they were companies that produced things like biscuits and underwear. He repeated the examples of biscuits and underwear in a deliberate attempt to give the impression that the companies were insignificant and did not deserve any attention, although they did in fact include some of the biggest and most important Egyptian industrial companies, such as the iron and steel company and the aluminum company.

The plan that was announced did not list in full the names of the companies, but merely mentioned examples. In light of this obfuscation, despite the large number of companies included in the plan and considering this new method of privatization—that is, distributing the assets for free, initially to forty million Egyptians—and the assumption that their decision to sell, if and when these forty million people took it, was bound to be in their best interests provided they took the decision freely, it would be easy to add to the list of companies that would end up being sold other assets that would be more strategic and more crucial to national and Arab interests and to national sovereignty, such as the Suez Canal, universities, state-owned newspapers and publishing houses, and banks that had not yet been privatized. In selling these new assets, the justification would always be "expanding the scope of public ownership" and leaving people free to make the decision to sell by themselves, while the state merely played the role of spectator.

This is what drove me to describe the plan as "fiendish" and to believe that it was neither patriotic nor moral. It was fiendish because it tried to exploit a weak spot in most Egyptians, that is, their poverty, which would have driven them to sell while pretending that they were expected to do otherwise. It was unpatriotic because it permitted the sale of assets that should be kept in the hands of the Egyptian state, or at least in the hands of private Egyptians. And it was immoral because the decision makers did not have the courage to take responsibility for their decision, but instead put the responsibility on others.

8

Those who work on development matters and follow political life in the Third World are familiar with the following phenomenon, which is somewhat amusing if also rather lamentable.

It is noticeable that senior officials responsible for economic policy in Third World countries—ministers, their senior aides, the presidents of banks, and even prime ministers—are anxious to have good relations with senior officials of international financial institutions such as the World Bank and the International Monetary Fund. They always treat them with respect and hospitality and are very receptive to their advice and requests when it comes to the economic policy these international institutions advocate without distinction between one Third World country and another.

The reason they are so anxious to have good relations has less to do with the Third World officials believing that the advice is sound or useful to their countries and more to do with the influence these institutions have in Washington, and with another important factor: the fact that ministers or senior officials in the Third World are well aware that if they lose their important jobs in their country, the only alternative that would make up for it would be a senior position in an international institution. Both jobs offer material privileges and great prestige, and these Third World officials know that things are never stable in their countries, that there are many grudges and intrigues, and that it's impossible to be confident that the status quo will last. So it's desirable, even imperative, to make provision for the future, and so they have to have strong relations with the senior staff at international institutions. These international institutions, for their part, think it is in their interest to maintain these close relations because that makes it easier to secure implementation of their recommendations and directives, since what could simplify implementation of the economic policy desired more effectively than giving those responsible for implementation a personal interest in it?

Another factor that helps to ensure implementation of the policies promoted by international institutions is the way their staff is accompanied by manifestations of grandeur and ostentation. They always travel first class on planes, sit in VIP lounges, stay in the best hotels, and enjoy various tax-free privileges, as well as having large salaries that end with an excellent pension of course, all of which means that if you happen to be at an airport you can tell the international civil servants from the others just by looking at the material of their suits, the shine of their shoes, the type of briefcase they carry, and perhaps also from the way they talk, move, and look around them, so much so that they almost seem to belong to a different species from the rest of humanity, set apart by God in a way that suits their lofty mission.

This is a truly lofty mission in one sense, but a real assessment of it requires a full discussion, because international institutions, even if they appear to transcend all countries, have in fact, since they were founded more than sixty years ago, been fundamentally subordinate to the will of the U.S. government and the governments of the other big western industrial countries, joined in the last thirty years by the interests of the giant corporations and the financial institutions. So international organizations, especially the two big financial institutions (the World Bank and the International Monetary Fund), have come to draw their policies and basic decisions from the interests of these two parties: the U.S. administration and giant corporations, usually referred to as multinational corporations. Although all or most of the countries in the world are represented in these organizations and the staff of these organizations claim to be entirely impartial and show all countries the respect appropriate to this broad representation of all countries, in fact they serve only those interests, which are often opposed to the interests of small countries.

So these jobs are undoubtedly grand for all the reasons I have mentioned related to external appearances, but they are not necessarily jobs that deserve all this reverence and honor when we recognize the reality of the interests they serve.

Many people have written analyses of the real motives behind the policies the World Bank and the International Monetary Fund recommend or stipulate, but I don't know many people, especially among government officials, who are ready to admit these real motives. One of the few senior Egyptian economists who have shown a surprising willingness to act on the basis of this admission, although they have held ministerial positions in Egypt, is Dr. Zaki Shaf'i, the first dean of the faculty of economics and political sciences at Cairo University. This man was known for his independence of opinion and his indifference to ostentation and high office, so no high offices were offered him until the unexpected happened in the mid-1970s, when we saw him suddenly appointed minister of economy. It was no surprise that he didn't stay in office long, but I heard from a source close to him that when he had a visit from an official of the International

Monetary Fund, an Indian who bore all the traits of an international civil servant as I have described them, and when the official tried to impose the will of the fund on the Egyptian government, of course with the same perennial prescription that the fund presses on every Third World country, regardless of its circumstances and particular social problems, Shaf'i laid into him and almost threw him out of his office. Shaf'i is said to have shouted out angrily, in front of his aides, "How can a young Indian who has no knowledge of the state of Egyptian society come to me and, just because he has a few statistics, a degree from an American university, and the name of a big international institution behind him, try to teach me what economic policies I must apply in Egypt?"

So an Indian economist goes off to steer the economic policy of the Egyptian government, a Brazilian economist to guide the Indian government, and an Egyptian to guide the government of the Congo, and so on. The message is always the same, regardless of the differences between Egypt, Brazil, and the Congo, and the argument is always that these policies come from an impartial international body that transcends all countries and, for that reason, is invested with every appearance of reverence and respect.

Suddenly we heard that Dr. Mahmoud Mohieddin, the Egyptian minister of investment, had been offered a senior position in that great international body, the World Bank, and that he had accepted the position, and everyone was happy with the news: the minister, the bank that nominated him, and the president who agreed to the nomination. Although the news was a surprise, it wasn't difficult to interpret in light of what I said earlier, because the minister was known to be ready to adhere to the International Monetary Fund's policies and had proved his loyalty to those policies in a way that left no room for doubt. The position was grand in all the senses I mentioned earlier and the president had no reason to object, because despite the loyalty Dr. Mohieddin had shown to the regime throughout his six years as a minister, it would be easy to find someone else to play the same role, since it really required nothing more than carrying out what the International Monetary Fund and the World Bank requested, along with considerable rhetorical skill at professing to believe that these requests serve the Egyptian economy.

5 Spurious Nationalism

1

Like millions of other Egyptians I was naturally delighted when Egypt won the Africa Cup of Nations in Angola in 2010, but I'd like to admit two things to the reader.

First, I didn't sit and watch the final match as millions of other Egyptians did, but just asked what the result was when I reckoned enough time had elapsed since the match started. It wasn't because I had important work that stopped me from watching the match, but just that I wasn't as interested as many others in following what was happening minute by minute, as well as the fact that I wanted to spare myself the nervous tension I would inevitably have felt if I had followed it live.

Second, my happiness with the result was more like relief that Egypt hadn't lost than pride in the victory. That's because I disagree with the many who see in soccer an important gauge of progress or backwardness and who see winning matches as a wonderful thing that entitles one to feel proud of oneself.

At the end of the day I see it as just a game, and on top of that not a very difficult game. Yes, it requires certain skills, some of which can be acquired only through much practice and effort, as well as a minimum of cooperation between the members of the team, discipline, some cunning in handling the members of the other team, plus of course a considerable amount of physical fitness. This is all true, but it all seems completely disproportionate to the degree of importance so many people attach to this sport and the degree of enthusiasm they show for the result that emerges, whether joy or grief. There must be something else to it that isn't quite obvious.

Add to that the amazing connection between winning in a sport like soccer and feelings of nationalism and loyalty to the country. We can imagine a surge of nationalist enthusiasm on victory in a war for a cause that people support, or at success in conquering space or landing on the moon, or if some compatriot had made an ingenious discovery or invented something of benefit to the whole world, or even if some compatriot had won a Nobel Prize for literature or science. All these could conceivably arouse nationalist zeal, because they might prove that the soldiers fought heroically or were bravely prepared to sacrifice themselves for the country, or that a major advance in science had led to the discovery, the invention, or the prize. But how does winning a soccer match compare to all that?

Frankly I believe that passionate excitement about winning a soccer match is attributable to the mass appeal of this sport more than to any other consideration. In my opinion it's very similar to the passion for popular film stars. The actress may be beautiful and the actor may be an excellent actor, but it's not her beauty or his acting skills that are responsible for the degree of enthusiasm, merely their fame. Fame brings more fame, and enthusiasm brings more enthusiasm. You become more passionate about a cause when you are one of millions marching in a demonstration, chanting for the cause, than you would be for the same cause if you were hunkered down alone at home. So just as television is without doubt largely responsible for the interest in soccer matches and the rising level of passion for them, it is also responsible for the high degree of enthusiasm for expressing one's "loyalty to the country" when "the country" is taking part in a match.

We must also recognize that opportunities for arousing enthusiasm for the country are now much fewer than they were in the past, not just in the case of Egypt and the Arabs but as a general phenomenon in the whole world, for reasons we don't have time to go into now. But if there are fewer opportunities to express one's loyalty to one's country, the need to be chauvinistic and to assert one's sense of belonging to a group of people remains deep-rooted, whatever the object of the chauvinism or the group of people involved. If one is not going to be chauvinistic about an ethnicity, a piece of territory, or an army, then why not be chauvinistic about one soccer team opposed to another?

If that's the case, it's no surprise that our politicians exploit soccer matches to increase their popularity or even to obtain a popularity they did not enjoy in the first place. If the ruler has come to power by force rather than based on the will of the people, it will benefit him (or so he thinks) to have his name or image associated with those great players who won the soccer match, in the hope that their popularity might have some effect on the way people feel toward him. So the ruler receives the players with great acclaim and bestows on them various accolades and honors in an attempt to give his people the impression that he feels the same way as them, rejoicing when they rejoice and lamenting when they lament. In this case one finds the ruler trying to link the name of the country closely with the triumph of the soccer team, in the hope that it will sink into people's minds that this soccer victory is an achievement that has as much importance as people attach to political and economic achievements, and also that it will sink into people's minds that this victory must have something to do with the fact that the ruler is in office at the moment and so deserves some of the credit (perhaps all of the credit) for bringing about this great triumph.

We are not living in the age of the triumph of capitalism (or of socialism, of course) or of democracy or human rights. We are also not living the end of history, as some writers claimed twenty years ago, nor the age of the clash of civilizations, as someone else said a little later. We are living "the age of the great masses": the age of television, satellites, satellite channels, and mobile phones that include cameras, email, and the Internet. This is the age of television programs that are seen simultaneously by hundreds of millions of people even if they don't deserve to be watched by even ten people, newspapers that have a daily circulation of millions but half of whose pages are advertisements, broadcasters some of whom earn monthly salaries of a million or two million Egyptian pounds and some of whom in a previous age would not have deserved to get jobs as broadcasters in the first place, and films that don't contain a single intelligent idea but are stunning commercial successes because they feature the face of an attractive actress, and so on. What's responsible for all that is not the age of untamed capitalism, but the age of the great masses.

This of course explains the phenomenon of soccer as we see it today. It's an old game, known in various forms to all peoples in all ages, but it didn't become such an exciting game until the age of the great masses. It didn't become more exciting because the players grew more skilled but just because they grew more famous. And the players became more famous not because they were unusually intelligent, fast, or alert, or more willing to cooperate with the other members of their team, but because they appeared so often on the television screen or in the pages of the newspapers seen or read by millions of people every day. In other words the players have become famous simply by being famous.

It all seems very foolish, even without any violence or squabbling between competing teams. But if the intense passion for a soccer team is accompanied by the level of hysteria, delirium, and aggression that we see every season, then it would seem extremely regrettable.

In this hysterical climate everyone who can use it to his own advantage is bound to try to do so. The unemployed carry colored flags to sell to people with cars who don't have anything better to do than to drive around the streets honking their horns, and newspaper owners compete over how to convey the happy news to the masses. (Should they make the result of the match into a banner headline in red ink, or make do with the word "Congratulations" on the grounds that everyone will understand what is meant? After all, is anyone thinking about anything other than the amazing 2-0 result?) Ministers who haven't done a single thing to win people's affection go to congratulate the victorious team, standing next to them to appear in the same photograph, and once even congratulated the president himself as one of the reasons for the stunning result. Gamal Mubarak, the young man with ambitions to become president, his father's position, found no better way to win people's hearts than to be photographed congratulating a winning team so that people would think he felt the same as other people feel and that his heart beat to the same rhythm as the Egyptian street.

When you have hysteria of this kind, it's so easy. Everyone has been drugged and so you can do what you like with them. You can get anything from them before they come to their senses.

No one should be deceived when they hear that this is a form of patriotism, proving that Egyptians are strongly attached to their country and unanimous in their love of it, on the grounds that men and women, Muslims and Copts, old and young, rich and poor have all set their hearts on one thing—that Egypt should beat Algeria. The intense excitement before, during, and after the match does not stem from strong patriotism but from the same phenomenon I am speaking about: the phenomenon of the great masses. The excitement grows simply because you are part of a very large group, you shout louder because you can see and hear thousands of people shouting like you, and you blow your horn louder because you know you are one of thousands blowing horns and beating drums. You can't love your country more just because you kicked the ball in the right direction twice, whereas your Algerian brothers didn't manage to do that even once.

In my opinion this hysteria, and not patriotism, is also the reason why some soccer players and their coaches break down in fits of sobbing as soon as the match is over. It's the sudden relief from the high tension and the frenzy generated by thousands upon thousands of people chanting and shouting at the same time.

There may be no great harm in all this, and it might even bring some benefits, just as exorcism rituals and *moulid* celebrations have certain benefits. But we should be cautious about confusing these hysterical outbursts with the growth of patriotism and a sense of belonging.

Because of all this I, like others, was most upset at what happened between Egypt and Algeria on the occasion of the soccer matches in 2010. The fighting, the insults, the beatings and stabbings by young Egyptians and Algerians were upsetting enough, but I think what happened between the two governments was even more disgusting.

It was not the first or last time that fighting has broken out between two groups of people of different nationalities, religions, or even colors, but that this should lead to a quarrel between two governments, each of them supporting its own nationality, religion, or color, is something that rarely happens unless one state has declared war on the other. Even that doesn't usually happen because of a fight between ordinary people, but for much deeper reasons connected with the history of relations between the two countries or because of a covert enmity that goes back to old problems or differences. If an argument like this arises between two Arab countries that have a long history of friendship and cooperation and are linked by strong ties of religion, language, culture, and common interests, then this is really upsetting and very shameful.

I read much of the commentary written on what happened, some of which unfortunately stoked the fire and inflamed people's feelings. One of the motives for the regrettable attitude taken by some writers and journalists, and also some politicians, was their desire to make personal or political gains by posing as patriots defending the rights and dignity of their compatriots.

But even if the writer's motive was just the instinctive wish to stand with the people of his country against the people of the other country, then I think that too is not a commendable attitude, because a writer who comments on public affairs should be more sensible than other people and more able to reflect on what has happened and see it in its wider context, through his wider knowledge of the history of relations between the two countries and their common problems.

Those who commented on the 2010 events should have been able to grasp the grave consequences that a deterioration in relations between Egypt and Algeria might have, such as preventing them from taking a united position on problems that are much more important than the problems of soccer and the World Cup—the Palestinian cause, for example. It might have obstructed greater economic cooperation that could help speed up the development needed in both countries, or deprived citizens living in the other country of the treatment and protection they need. Realizing how important these things are compared to winning or losing a soccer match should have prevented a writer or journalist from helping to inflame people's feelings and add fuel to the fire.

The writer or journalist should also have realized that in an argument of this kind, however violent and bloody it might be, it really isn't very important to know who attacked first and who acted in response to that attack, because in such matters it's very difficult, if it's even possible in the first place, to define the starting point, and equally difficult to judge whether the reaction was proportionate to the original action. In my opinion both sides were at fault, and it's very easy, by finding out the circumstances of the media frenzy and the ages and social and economic circumstances of those fighting, to discover why they made this mistake. But definitely their parents or guardians should have been expected to behave more sensibly than what we saw. It would be stupid if a father and mother came and fought with the father or mother of another child and exchanged insults just like their children, so that the conflict, which started as a quarrel between two naive kids, turns into a battle between two governments that should be grown up and realize that their quarrel could do grave damage to everyone, old and young.

2

One of the inevitable disadvantages of having a president stay in office for a long time, such as twenty or thirty years, is that the president is bound to grow weaker as he advances in age, leading to reduced vitality, loss of dynamism, declining receptivity to new ideas, an aversion to making important political or economic changes, and the possibility that the president may submit to what his associates tell him, even if it is harmful to the public interest.

But there is another inevitable disadvantage that is no less serious and may even be more serious, and that is the inclination to consider the whole state as if it's the president's private property for him and his family to do what they like with, so that decisions are made on the basis of personal whims, however harmful that might be to the supreme interests of the state. A long term in office may entrench in the president's mind the sense that he and the state are the same thing and that his private interests and those of his family are no different from the interests of the state as a whole.

In the case of Egypt, where President Mubarak was about to complete thirty years as president, this phenomenon started to become more and more evident and with increasing frequency, such that in a period of no more than two months we saw two glaring examples of how the state had come to be treated as though it were private property.

The first example was the president's behavior in the case of the nomination of culture minister Farouk Hosni for the post of UNESCO director-general, starting with how he went along with the minister's desire to be nominated regardless of whether he was the best Egyptian for the job or the one most likely to succeed, how state money and the time and effort of government officials were spent to support the minister, and how Egyptian diplomacy was mobilized for the same purpose to the extent that some important interests were sacrificed, including through the fulfillment of certain Israeli demands.

When the sorry story ended in the pampered minister's failure to achieve his wish, the minister did not offer to resign from the ministry, if only to show his regret at all the effort and money wasted and at the concessions it had cost the state. On the contrary, the president assured him that he would stay in office.

Then we were surprised to find the same thing repeated on the occasion of the soccer matches between Egypt and Algeria. In my opinion the president and his sons probably treated the soccer matches as part of their efforts to improve the image of the son who wanted to take his father's place as president, and also to improve the image of the presidency as a whole, by associating the image of the president and his sons with the image of the Egyptian soccer team, and by showing the soccer team and its coach special honor as though they were about to fight a military battle. But the country also sacrificed foreign policy considerations and national interests in the attempt to win the match, and made relations with an important Arab country, Algeria, dependent on winning or losing the match.

We were told that the players and their coach would be paid fantastical bonuses if they won the match, bonuses way out of proportion to the means of a poor country such as Egypt, which needs to have this money spent in much more important ways and which should be showing more generosity in encouraging young Egyptians to develop their abilities and talents in fields that would make a greater contribution to a national renaissance than soccer ever could.

Then the match ended with Egypt losing, so what happened? Instead of leaving the team and the coach to think about what happened and try to learn from the experience and discover their mistakes in the hope of winning next time, the president and his sons gave them a reception worthy of great conquerors, honoring them as if they had won for Egypt the greatest victory in its history, although they didn't win at all. Then they were promised the bonus for losing, just as they had earlier been promised the bonus for winning, and no doubt they were told the same thing the minister of culture was told when he lost: "Put it behind you." In other words, ignore everything and don't let what happened put you in a bad mood, because what matters is not that people are disappointed but rather that the president should continue to be pleased with you. It didn't matter that Egypt and Algeria were at odds; what mattered was that the president and his family stay in power.

The fact that the same president had been in power for close to thirty years undoubtedly played a role in all this. The president was used to acting in affairs of state, whether to do with culture or soccer, as though they were his private possessions. But in the soccer case there was a new development that wasn't evident in the case of the minister of culture: the president's younger son, who headed the policies committee in the ruling party, played a considerable role when it came to the soccer matches, and the elder son joined him after the match was lost, severely insulting the Algerians and in effect suggesting the Algerian ambassador be expelled from Egypt, although this elder son held no political office and had no authority to expel the Algerian ambassador or any other ambassador. So he was acting as if he were evicting the ambassador from his private estate, and no doubt this development was also one of the consequences of the father staying in office for such a long time.

6 A Police State

How can we explain the strange attitude the regime of President Hosni Mubarak took toward the opposition and public opinion in Egypt, which was quite different from the attitudes of presidents Abd al-Nasser and Sadat?

What's the secret behind the indifference the regime showed toward what people felt?

It's very possible that each of these periods had different ambitions. Abd al-Nasser was a politician in every sense of the word. He had a project and his political ambitions were fundamental. Of course he wanted to retain power (what ruler wants power to slip from his hands?), but Abd al-Nasser used authority for a purpose, and that purpose was primarily political.

Sadat was also a politician, even if politics didn't dominate his life as much as with Abd al-Nasser. Sadat in his turn loved power, but he also loved and enjoyed a life of luxury, which I don't believe was ever part of Abd al-Nasser's ambitions.

The regime of Hosni Mubarak brought to power a group of people of a different kind. Although some of them had shared in power in the time of Abd al-Nasser or Sadat, as soon as the Mubarak era began, their aspirations and ambitions changed into something quite new. Apparently things that were impossible to do in Abd al-Nasser's time and that were difficult but possible to do in Sadat's time became very possible and very easy to do in the time of Hosni Mubarak. By that I mean rapid and unlimited enrichment without the least effort. That was the aspiration and ambition of the majority of senior officials in Mubarak's time, and when you have aspirations and ambitions of this kind, indifference to people's feelings and to trends in public opinion starts to appear and grow.

What exactly was there to upset them? People talked about politics, while they talked about finance. People talked about loaves of bread, while they talked about cake. People talked about the problem of private lessons, while they talked about the profit to be made selling Alexandria University.

Of course people created a distraction and could be tiresome but things that mattered to the regime went ahead without delay. All the regime needed for dealing with public opinion was some riot police, and they saw no need to waste valuable time entering into discussion with the opposition.

I remember a particular incident that occurred at the end of the 1960s and shook the Abd al-Nasser regime. A bus ran into a tree on the bank of the Nile in Agouza and some of the passengers were killed. There was an uproar, and officials tried to find out if the cause of the crash was that the bus wasn't roadworthy, the driver was negligent, or the road wasn't wide enough. One of the results of the accident was that the whole street was redesigned in the hope that the accident wouldn't happen again. How does this compare with the almost total silence on the part of officials when a pickup truck crashed toward the end of Mubarak's time, killing fifteen girls on their way to school in the town of Atfih? Or when Egyptians drown from time to time trying to reach the shores of Italy or Greece because they can't find suitable work in Egypt?

The difference may be due to the different ambitions and aspirations of the rulers in the two periods, but I think there are other reasons. Abd al-Nasser felt that he derived the legitimacy of his regime from people's approval of his socialist project and his development initiatives, and Abd al-Nasser couldn't rely on any foreign aid, whether from the Americans or the Soviets, if Egyptians were angry with him. Yes, Abd al-Nasser received economic aid from both sides, but the Soviets wouldn't have lifted a finger if Egyptians rose up against Abd al-Nasser, and the Americans weren't prepared to protect him from his people if the people turned against him. In fact, starting from the mid-1960s, Abd al-Nasser might have been worried the Americans would push some opposition elements in Egypt to overthrow his regime.

But President Mubarak's regime was completely different. American approval seemed to have become so assured, even guaranteed, that the regime could do without the approval of Egyptians, or that's how those in power in Egypt apparently saw it. So if a ferry sank, buses or trucks crashed, or Egyptians drowned off the coasts of Italy or Greece, they didn't need to bat an eyelid.

2

Former communications minister Tarek Kamel made a surprising statement in October 2009 that hasn't received the commentary it deserves. He said that the Egyptian government naturally eavesdrops on telephone conversations because if it didn't, foreign investment wouldn't come to Egypt.

The statement was surprising in more than one way: in that the government eavesdropped on telephone conversations, which we thought was part of an era that had ended, and in that a government minister admitted it as though it were normal and unobjectionable, whereas we thought it was shameful and did no government any honor. The minister then linked this eavesdropping to the flow of foreign investment, but what does the one have to do with the other?

I have read several comments on this statement, but everything I have read has been sarcastic and intended to make people laugh, as the statement did provide fertile material for speculation about what could take place in a telephone conversation between Egyptians that might persuade a foreign investor to go back on his decision to invest in Egypt. But the statement also deserves some serious thought, especially as the minister was completely serious when he made it.

The first thing that might strike one when one hears this statement is great surprise at the extent of the change that has taken place in Egypt in the past forty or fifty years (in fact maybe also in the whole world). Yes, there was telephone bugging in Egypt in the 1960s, on a large scale, and no one doubted it happened unless they were completely unaware of the nature of the political regime in Egypt at that time. It wasn't just telephones; taxi drivers eavesdropped on their passengers, some students on their professors, and some university professors on their colleagues, and so on. But this would all take place in secret, and when it was discovered it always created a scandal for the person doing it and for the person who induced them to do it. What had happened since then to make a respectable minister declare that the government was eavesdropping on people without his appearing to have admitted anything important?

In fact we thought this eavesdropping had ended when Anwar al-Sadat announced in the early 1970s that he had eliminated the "centers of power" that seemed to be responsible more than anyone else for the police-state mentality that governed Egypt in the 1960s, when he issued orders to burn many of the files the intelligence services had saved and the phenomenon known as "the dawn visit" had come to an end. This last referred to the police's practice of coming to arrest political activists at home during the night and taking them to the police station without the detainees knowing the charges against them. It would emerge that their only crime was saying something, on the telephone or somewhere else, that suggested hostile feelings toward the regime or some important regime figure. We thought all this had come to an end in the Sadat era. And what had happened, one wonders, to make this eavesdropping not only desirable but also, as the minister of communications put it, essential?

A little reflection is bound to make us believe what the minister said, at least as far as the government eavesdropping on people is concerned, whether or not it had anything to do with foreign investment.

For a start, developments in communications technology over the past fifty years have brought great progress in the ways one can eavesdrop on people without their knowing. In the 1960s, for example, a person speaking on the telephone sometimes felt that a stranger had come in on the line, which might persuade him to be cautious. This is no longer necessary in light of modern eavesdropping techniques. It's now possible to bug a telephone in complete confidence. More importantly, all modern governments without exception now have a powerful argument for various types of eavesdropping, without needing to justify it on the grounds that someone is suspected of being hostile to the regime's policies or hostile to those in power. The person who is monitored doesn't need to be a communist or a leftist or any kind of extremist. It's enough that there be suspicion that the person might be intent on carrying out a 'terrorist' act. 'Terrorism' is now used with multiple meanings, without the perpetrator, or the possible perpetrator, necessarily belonging to any political organization or embracing any ideology that is hostile to the regime. All it takes is for the person to be found, before boarding a plane, with a small penknife, a pair of scissors, a razor blade, or even an ordinary bottle of water big enough to make explosives if certain other chemicals are added. Anyway, the term 'terrorist' is now used in so many different senses and so widely that it can apply to almost everyone. In this case everyone can be assumed to be a terrorist until they prove they are not, and hence eavesdropping on anyone can be justified without recourse to any of the traditional justifications.

Such thinking must have been behind the way the communications minister made such an astonishing statement without seeing how strange it was. But what does all this have to do with foreign investment? Does terrorism frighten foreign investors more than it frightens other people? It struck me that the answer may lie in what I read many years ago when there was much talk about the phenomenon of multinational companies and their investments outside the borders of their countries of origin, and how they moved their activities from country to country whenever they found the 'investment climate' in one country more attractive than in others. I read that the first thing these giant companies asked about before deciding to invest in a particular Third World country was "the personality of the interior minister." What they meant was how strict and decisive he was, how prepared to use an iron fist to deal with any unrest or strikes by workers demanding higher wages or complaining about working conditions or layoffs. Of course the political climate matters to these companies, and from time to time they reassess it to see how favorable it is, because violent political upheavals can endanger their investments and might lead to new legislation that is not in their interests, or to sudden restrictions on the transfer of profits abroad. They have to be confident of 'stability,' and in order to guarantee this stability, phone tapping might be essential.

But let's assume that this was all true: phone tapping was needed to ensure stability, and stability was needed to ensure the influx of foreign investment. Why should we attach so much importance to the influx of foreign investment that we were willing to sacrifice one of the most important personal freedoms and one of the most important human rights: the freedom to criticize and express your opinion, the right to express yourself without restraint, and freedom from fear that you are constantly being monitored, that your doings might be held against you, and all your secrets and mistakes known and even recorded for use against you if and when necessary?

Did encouraging foreign investment justify all this fear and so much loss of freedom? How much money would the country have needed to attract from foreign investors, I wonder, to make such restrictions on people's freedoms justifiable and legitimate? At what price, I wonder, would people have been happy to give the communications minister free access to their secrets, to do what he likes with them?

Has the world changed so much in the last forty or fifty years that a respectable man such as the communications minister could defend the restriction of freedoms with an argument based on the foreign money the country would receive, without appearing to have any doubts about the rightness of this kind of thinking?

3

I'm not a great fan of the word 'transparency' and I don't think I have ever used it in an article or a book I have written. The reason for that is that I can scarcely detect a trace of transparency in our political life or that of others. We live in a world dominated by opacity and deception, circumlocution and pretense, the concealment rather than the exposure of facts, and all this is the complete opposite of transparency, which suggests a clean pane of glass that reveals the truth rather than hides it. I have started to believe that the repetition of a certain word or slogan time and again usually means that what is happening is quite the opposite, and that the constant repetition of a certain slogan is probably part of an attempt to distract people's attention from the fact that it isn't being put into practice in the real world. So in time of war there's plenty of talk of peace, there's talk of concern for those on limited incomes when the concern is in reality confined to those on inflated incomes, and talk of concern for the 'social dimension' when this social dimension couldn't be further from the government's mind, let alone the use of the slogan "For Your Sake" by the National Democratic Party when you were the last person anyone was interested in.

But all that is one story, and the talk about presidential candidates in the few months before the revolution is another story. Everyone was talking about the succession and was apprehensive about what the government would do to bring it about. Every day they noticed a new report, a new photograph, or a new visit that could only be intended to make it easier for the president's son to take the place of his father. His pictures were all over the front pages, and the inside pages were full of his interviews and statements, linking his name with good news such as village development or reforms to the pension system. He was photographed kissing a young child tenderly, or listening attentively to the complaint of an old farmer, just as we are used to seeing with presidents and other leaders, and before them with kings and princes. And he, the president's son that is, was treated by ministers, and even the prime minister, as though he were already president. He would travel with ministers on trips to major countries, meeting senior officials in those countries in the hope of winning their approval for the plan to have him succeed his father.

As all this went on, people could see it daily, and they found it depressing and humiliating that their government was treating them in this way instead of the president's son leaving people to choose whom they wanted as their president and meanwhile going about his own private business, as he should do in any really democratic country.

What was worse was that when they were asked to explain what they were doing to enable the president's son to succeed, they pretended to be surprised. "Succession?" they said. "Who said anything about a succession? Has anyone said that the president's son wants to stand? Anyway, it's much too early to be talking about the presidency. Who said that the presidency is vacant and needs to be filled? President Mubarak is in excellent health and has said himself that he will stay in office as long as his heart is beating. Anyway, the whole question depends on elections and referendums, which will of course be just as clean as previous elections. Besides, who said that people are interested in the question of the presidency? Egyptians are so poor they're only interested in their daily bread, and whoever's responsible for their poverty they don't have time to think about whether the president's son will succeed his father or not. Anyway, supposing the son does succeed, haven't Egyptians been passed on from one president to another since the 1952 revolution without being consulted in the matter? It's true that since the proclamation of the republic in 1953 it hasn't happened that a president has passed his office to his son, but this is a minor difference, and the important thing anyway is that the subject isn't on the table in the first place, and no one's thinking about it except for a few people who love to snipe at the regime. The decisive proof of that is that when the president himself was asked on his last trip to the United States whether his son was thinking of standing as president after him, he replied that his son hadn't spoken to him on the subject."

In summary, regardless of the subjects the president talked about with his sons when they met, people didn't have the right to know anything about them or even to wonder what was behind all the disinformation propagated by the media to pave the way for the president's son to succeed. Orders must have been issued and there must have been an agreement to impose a complete blackout on this subject until, at the right time, people would suddenly find he had been appointed as their president. This disinformation and this blackout were what are now called transparency in current political parlance.

4

It's time to admit that the opposition in Egypt was going through a serious ordeal when the January 25 revolution broke out. Yes, the opposition was so large and widespread that I could almost say that it included the overwhelming majority of the Egyptian people. Most Egyptians, men and women, were indignant and aggrieved and looked forward to the day when God would put an end to their torment and relieve their distress, fully aware that responsibility for their distress lay with the regime in power.

Apart from its being large and widespread, we can also describe the Egyptian opposition as vociferous. Everyone could hear its voice, other than a very small handful of privileged people who sat near the summit of power and lived off the fat of the land. This small handful didn't want to hear the loud voice of the opposition. But this loud voice often sounded more like a hysterical scream than criticism and demands for reform, and this hysterical scream was itself evidence of the serious ordeal the Egyptian opposition was going through. The Egyptian opposition had been through a phase when it really did call for reform and make specific demands, when it was calmer and less vehement (that's how I remember the opposition in the 1970s and 1980s, that is, thirty or forty years ago), but the Egyptian opposition had changed and its way of speaking was not what it had been.

The severe ordeal the opposition was going through in Egypt is not hard to explain.

First, the regime's opponents had lost the last glimmer of hope that they could come to power or even share power in order to carry out reforms they believed were essential. Democratic states have what is known as 'rotation of power,' whereby no individual or party monopolizes power forever. But Egypt ran on the principle that power was eternal and that whoever came to power would do everything in his power to stay there forever.

When power rotates, it's possible to have a reasoned debate about policies, and both sides try to mobilize public opinion to their side of the argument. But when there is a monopoly of power, the opposition gives up and people gradually lose confidence in the value of having any opposition at all. When the opposition and its supporters lose hope, it's easy for criticism to change into slander and for the demand for reform to turn into hysterical screaming.

Second, insisting on monopolizing power made those in power crude and cruel in the way they treated their opponents and everyone suspected of being on the opponents' side. The cruelty and crudeness of those in power grew as time passed because they became accustomed to holding office and to the privileges and luxuries that power brought them, and they could not imagine how anyone else could come and take their places or how they could move into the ranks of the opposition.

The longer they stayed in power, the more people were prepared to serve them, if only to obtain lavish material rewards. In fact they ended up with a large number of people willing to carry out the task of beating up the regime's opponents, even torturing them if necessary. This frightened the regime's opponents and their sympathizers and they grew even weaker.

Third, the rule of law hardly existed. The regime even gave up pretending that it existed. The police protected only those with power and arrested only those who angered the rulers. The judiciary carried out their orders, or that's how it gradually developed, and if the judiciary happened to obstruct those in power, its rulings were ignored as if they had never been given.

Yes, there were human rights organizations and foreign correspondents, but the organizations had limited capacity and few resources, so the government habitually ignored their protests. The foreign correspondents had their particular preferences, depending on the importance foreign governments and media attached to particular members of the opposition. In their eyes the importance of the regime's opponents did not depend on how faithfully they expressed the feelings of the people but on whether foreigners approved of them. If an opposition figure objected, for example, to the Egyptian government's position on the way the Israelis treated the people of Gaza and the Egyptian government treated him unusually harshly, this wouldn't appear in the foreign newspapers or radio stations out of deference to the feelings of the Israelis. So it was a lucky opposition figure who could win the approval of his people and of the foreign media at the same time, and this rarely happened.

Fourth, in its harsh treatment of the Egyptian opposition, the regime received strong support from some foreign governments, in money, weapons, and training in ways to deal with opponents, including methods of torture. What really worried the regime was not the anger of its people but the anger of the foreign power that was its patron, and that was the reason why this regime existed in the first place. This foreign power might pretend that it favored democracy and freedom of opinion, and would occasionally issue statements protesting politely at the repression of the opposition or at rigged elections and referendums, and calling on the regime to be more democratic in the future. But the regime was well aware of what these statements were worth and knew that the people who made them did not really mean what they said. So the regime's men grew accustomed to treating these statements with the indifference they deserved. They knew their real function serving this foreign power, what it really liked and what it didn't like, what they might be rewarded for, and what would arouse the foreign power to anger against them.

Fifth, all this made the Egyptian opposition weaker and weaker. Its adversary was powerful and cruel, backed from abroad by a power that was no less cruel, and arguing with it was pointless, whether in the domestic courts or in the court of foreign public opinion. But what made the ordeal of the Egyptian opposition even worse was the change that the Egyptian population itself had undergone. For some time Egyptians had been suffering severe economic crises: incomes were low and grew only slowly while prices rose rapidly, unemployment was growing and spreading among the educated, and finding a job that suited a young person's education had become most difficult. The education, health, and transport facilities that the government provided were of constantly declining quality, which meant that people had to set aside a growing proportion of their income, which was only rising slowly in the first place, to compensate for this decline—in education by paying for private lessons, in health by going to private clinics, and in transport by running the risk that they, their sons, and their daughters might be the victims of accidents in buses or trains driven by men (and sometimes boys) who were suffering as much as they were.

All these worries didn't leave people, whether educated or not, with energy they could direct toward national affairs or politics in general. Most Egyptians had neither the time nor the inclination to think beyond their daily problems, which constantly recurred and which required massive effort and sometimes acts of heroism to tackle. So the regime's opponents found themselves talking to people who might in fact sympathize with what they said but couldn't summon up the strength to support them and stand alongside them. So the opposition, on top of facing the cruelty of the regime, could find only a few supporters among the people, and these supporters were overwhelmed by the hardship of daily life and expended all their energy trying to provide necessities for their sons and daughters.

Sixth, let's also admit that the Egyptian opposition, besides all this, was afflicted with a weakness and a malaise of another kind that it did not want to admit, and that was intellectual malaise, because what the opposition was saying was old and hadn't kept up with changing circumstances. Although the opposition appeared to consist of many parties with different ideological positions, in fact not a single one of them was saying anything it hadn't been saying for more than forty years.

5

One is at a loss to reply when asked about the state of political thinking in Egypt before the revolution. In the first place, was there political thinking in Egypt that can be identified and analyzed?

I don't mean original political thinking that Egyptians might have added to the world's stock of political thought, because Egyptians gave up that kind of innovation a long time ago. I mean something much more modest: just a debate on the political ideas on offer in the world.

Where would we look for political thinking in Egypt? In the political parties and their newspapers? Or in books by political analysts and university professors? Wherever we looked, we would find the haul meager, and it would be difficult to describe it as "political thought."

Egypt had many parties, many more than necessary. But few of them can claim to have had a political ideology, although the Egyptian law on parties stipulated that any party seeking legal recognition must have ideas that distinguish it from other parties.

Let's take, for example, three Egyptian opposition parties (or blocks) that existed before the revolution and that might be seen as those closest to having or offering a distinctive political ideology—the Tagammu' Party, the Nasserist Party, and the Muslim Brotherhood—and see to what extent any of them really offered people a distinctive ideology and kept up with developments in the rest of the world.

The Tagammu' Party, since its creation a third of a century ago, had been associated in people's minds with Marxism, after the school of thought its founders adhered to (or used to adhere to) and because it emphasized the idea of class struggle. But as soon as it was founded, the Tagammuʿ Party decided to open its doors to people who were not Marxists, people who believed in national independence and secularism and were sympathetic to the call for social justice. For its first fifteen years, until the end of the 1980s, the party enjoyed considerable popularity, and its newspaper, *al-Ahali*, enjoyed widespread respect and esteem because it reflected the interests of the less fortunate classes in society, as well as its high professional standard, its many talented writers, and its exceptional sensitivity to what people thought and felt. One could cite the columns by Philip Gallab and Salah Eissa, the cartoons by Bahgat Osman, the articles by Abd al-Azim Anis, and so forth.

When the party was forced to tone down the language of its weekly newspaper in response to government pressure, and it set up alongside the weekly newspaper the monthly magazine *al-Yasar*, this magazine, led by Hussein Abd al-Razeq, played a very distinguished role in activating political thinking in Egypt. Despite the financial difficulties it faced and its status as a monthly, the magazine flourished, with its Marxist and non-Marxist writers and Higazi's wonderful cartoons. The old issues are now a surprise to read when you compare the rich articles and debates it published with what was published toward the end of the Mubarak era in any newspaper or magazine, monthly, weekly, or daily.

The party was greatly weakened in the subsequent twenty years, and no doubt one of the reasons for that was the collapse of the Soviet Union at the beginning of the 1990s and the weakening of socialism throughout the world. But there is also no doubt that one of the reasons for the decline of the Tagammuʿ Party and the serious deterioration of its weekly newspaper, let alone the closure of *al-Yasar* magazine, was the severe pressures it faced from the regime, until the party and the government reached a full truce.

The Nasserists didn't have a political ideology as clearly defined as that of the Egyptian Marxists because Abd al-Nasser was not so much a thinker as a practical politician. Abd al-Nasser undoubtedly brought about an upheaval in the social and political reality of Egypt for two whole decades (the 1950s and 1960s) and won masses of followers in Egypt and the entire Arab world, and many of them still believe that what Abd al-Nasser did and what he advocated is the best platform for political action, whether in economic policy, social policy, Arab relations, or foreign policy.

It's impossible to deny the great popularity that Nasserism continues to enjoy in Egypt and other Arab countries, but I would claim that Nasserism has become, in Egypt as in the whole Arab world, more like nostalgia for a beautiful past than an intellectual attitude. Every year Egypt's Nasserist newspaper, *al-Arabi*, celebrates Abd al-Nasser's birthday and commemorates the day of his death, as does the newspaper *al-Karama*, which is published by another Nasserist party that does not have legal recognition. The name Abd al-Nasser is surrounded by a halo of reverence and respect that scarcely any other Arab leader enjoys, old or new. But the reality that Nasserists apparently insist on ignoring is that it's been more than forty years since Abd al-Nasser died, not at all a short period in the life of the world or any country, especially as the rate of change in the state of the world is rapidly increasing as time passes. It's important to remember that in the forty-five years since the military defeat of Abd al-Nasser in 1967 the world has seen the growth of the policy of detente between the capitalist and socialist blocs (and perhaps it was this very detente that led to the defeat of Abd al-Nasser in the first place), then the return of the Cold War, then the collapse of the whole socialist camp and the disintegration of the Soviet Union, Russia's opening to the world, the transformation of China into a market economy, the growth of globalization, the growth of consumerism, the acceleration of the information and communications revolution, the declaration of war on what is called terrorism after the events of September 11, 2001, the obvious decline in the relative position of the U.S. economy in the world, the declaration and then retraction of what was called the New Middle East project, the sharp decline in Arab nationalism, the escalation of Israeli violence in dealing with the Palestinians, the emergence of new economic powers in Asia, and so on. In light of all these very significant developments, can we talk about Nasserism as though we were still in the year 1970, when Abd al-Nasser died, or in the year 1966, just before his military defeat? Yes, Abd al-Nasser was a great patriot and reformer in Egyptian and Arab politics, but can we continue to repeat his words and his slogans as though nothing has happened in the meantime?

Yes, political and economic dependence is always offensive and unacceptable, but does dependence mean the same in 2010 as it did in 1970? Is the way to tackle it the same as the way Abd al-Nasser tackled it? Doesn't the question require more political and economic thought, as well as analysis of what has happened and is happening in the world?

The Muslim Brotherhood is no less dependent on stirring up people's emotions than the Nasserists. On the contrary, in fact. Raising the slogan "Islam is the solution" always succeeds in stirring up the emotions of Egyptians, more than any other slogan. But is this slogan really useful as an alternative to political ideology? Doesn't this slogan itself need to be constantly renewed and reinterpreted as circumstances change? Yes, Islam is a constant and will remain so through the ages, but can the solutions derived from Islam also be constants, however the times may change? Whenever the slogan "Islam is the solution" is raised, shouldn't an explanation of this slogan be provided, an explanation of how it might be applied in a way appropriate to the circumstances in which it is raised, tackling clearly the developments that have taken place and the events that are now underway in the world?

Yes, the political thinking of the Egyptian opposition was definitely impoverished at the end of the Mubarak era. But again I say: Is there anything strange about that? Can you ask anyone to hone their thinking skills and come up with new ideas when they have lost their freedom to speak? Is it really possible to think when your mouth is gagged? Doesn't creativity, and even thinking, require the ability to express oneself in the first place? For the past thirty years haven't we been just like frightened schoolchildren the teacher insults and hits whenever they open their mouths to speak? In the end would one expect such children to do more than repeat what they've been told? Should we expect them to show any aptitude for independent thought?

6

Forty-five years ago Egypt went through a cruel ordeal because of an appalling military defeat. The 1967 defeat wasn't expected because for a number of years Egyptians had been subjected to a powerful media campaign that promised them certain victory and portrayed Egypt's military might as much greater than it really was. Even after the defeat the media campaign continued to repeat things that could no longer deceive Egyptians after what had happened, such as the slogan "What has been taken by force can be recovered only by force" or "No voice speaks louder the sound of battle," and so on. It wasn't difficult for Egyptians to see that this last slogan meant only that people were forbidden to talk.

At that time the regime faced severe criticism and ridicule in what people said in their daily lives, and jokes that were more bitter than sarcastic. But public criticism rarely went beyond what people were telling each other in private. People were very frightened to speak because of the prevalence of informers everywhere. That went on until a talented man appeared who could express the sadness and bitterness Egyptians felt in their hearts and who became their spokesman overnight, at a time when the newspapers and radio and television stations couldn't reflect in any way what people felt. This man was the poet Ahmad Fuad Nigm, a man of startling appearance and character, who spoke and behaved in an astonishing manner. He would wear only the peasant *gallabiya*, wherever he was appearing. He was tall and lean with a very dark complexion and authentic Egyptian features. But most importantly, he had an extraordinary ability to write colloquial poetry. It was very fine poetry, and very witty, using an unusual range of Egyptian colloquial expressions, proverbs, and sayings. It was also amazing that this man, despite his modest origins, followed what was happening in Egypt and the rest of the world closely and fully understood the motives behind political events and the behavior of rulers.

This poet soon found a blind Egyptian singer, Sheikh Imam, who shared his nationalist feelings and his sense of the oppression suffered by the poor and by Egyptians in general, and who picked up his lute and composed simple but touching songs based on the poems the poet would recite to him, to an enthusiastic reception by those who were angry and disgruntled with what was happening in Egypt. As people began to repeat the poet's songs, the pair's fame spread even beyond the borders of Egypt because foreign journalists and many foreign intellectuals were amazed to find two men with such a simple lifestyle generating such excitement among Egyptian intellectuals and the politicized classes.

Only then did those in power take an interest in the matter. At first they tried to tempt the poet and the singer with money in the belief that they were like most people, ready to change course in order to obtain a certain level of comfort. They offered to play their music on radio and television provided they stuck to love poems and songs and didn't bring up any social or political subjects. The two men found the offer quite laughable because they instinctively understood that God did not create them to write or sing love songs. They went on doing what they did, and in the end they were arrested and put in prison, time after time, until the time they spent in prison was longer than the time they spent outside, yet they continued to write poems and songs, even producing some of their most beautiful songs while locked up.

As time passed, and as things grew worse and injustice spread, the number of people who were angry and disgruntled increased and there were too many of them to be placated by two men reading poems and singing songs inside private houses. In 1995, this inspired a smart man with an idea of genius: that in such a climate there could be no doubt about the success of a new newspaper that reflected what was going on in the minds of these hundreds of thousands of people, as long as it was expressed boldly and with humor. This man had no political ambitions, not even any obvious political affiliation. He was just a clever man looking for a good project to invest in, and he found what he sought in these disgruntled Egyptians. He invited one of them—a man known for his skills as a journalist and organizer, for his attractive writing style and his rare dynamism, as well as his sound understanding of what was happening in Egypt and his sympathy for people's needs and feelings—to lead this team of nationalist journalists in producing this new newspaper, *al-Dustour*, and to join them in this amazing experience.

The newspaper met with success from the first issue even though it was more expensive than any other newspaper. People snatched copies from the hands of newspaper vendors, as if they couldn't believe how deprived they had been of real journalism and had suddenly discovered that it was possible to publish a newspaper that didn't have headlines every day about the president's meetings and doings. And as usual when the stage exists, hidden talents were discovered. On the pages of this newspaper shone the names of many young journalists who had an instinctive talent that had also been honed by many years of suffering and oppression.

The regime tried various methods to stop this newspaper but it didn't succeed. When the newspaper reported that the president was ill, the editor went on trial on a charge of endangering the investment climate in the country and was sentenced to jail. The newspaper continued as it was, however, while his appeal proceeded and he was finally pardoned. The government tried to deprive the newspaper of any advertising and the newspaper was forced to hold the salaries of journalists working there to the minimum. Even so, the journalists didn't leave their newspaper, despite the temptation of high salaries at other papers. Then the government finally hit upon the only remaining solution.

The solution was as simple as it was malicious. Since the owner of the newspaper was still an investor and not a politician, the only way to proceed with him was to buy the newspaper from him outright. If the owner was rich, then there was someone in Egypt richer than him, and this man who was richer and who could buy the whole newspaper had his own political ambitions, but fortunately for the regime they were not incompatible with its own interests. This seemed the best way to silence this group of rebellious journalists and shut their leader's mouth forever.

The plan went into effect and the newspaper was bought. The new buyer began by trying the usual method: offering staff double their salaries in the hope that they would go along with the paper's new policy of making peace with the regime. This method didn't work, as these journalists proved to be of tougher mettle than usual. Only force remained, and the regime was impatient for results because there were only a few weeks to go before the parliamentary elections of 2010 — important elections that would decide the success or failure of the plan to arrange the succession of the president's son the following year, or some other even worse plan of which we were not aware. So speed was essential, however great the shock might be. The mutinous editor was fired and the new owner claimed that the dispute between them was over his salary and not over the newspaper's politics. The editor packed up his papers and left, and with him went every single one of his colleagues. The new editor then faced the task of filling the empty pages, and his only option was to rely on sex and scandals. So suddenly the newspaper came out with whole pages full of pictures of beautiful actresses and other pages full of news about celebrities, where they had dinner, and who attended the engagement party of the daughter or son of some big financier. When the new management reckoned that all this would not be enough to keep the paper's many readers, they had an idea in very poor taste: to claim that the great writer Naguib Mahfouz, who died in 2006, had been murdered. They gave this pathetic story a banner headline and took pictures of Mahfouz's daughters, who had no experience of appearing in the media.

That was how matters stood between Egyptians and the regime a few months before the fall of the regime. I have found that going back in history provides some useful lessons. In the case of Ahmad Fuad Nigm and Sheikh Imam, there were unsuccessful attempts to tempt them with money, and force and violence were used, also without success. Then the same methods were used again, and they proved not to succeed. So I remembered Ahmad Fuad Nigm's beautiful poem entitled "Uyoun al-kalam," which he wrote in Qanatir prison in 1970.

If the sun sinks in a sea of troubles
And a wave of darkness sweeps the world
And we can no longer see or understand
And the way is lost in lines and circles
Then, all you wise and experienced ones,
Your only guide is the eyes of words.

٧

Although the morning newspapers every day keep bringing us news
stranger than the news they brought us the day before, I couldn't believe
it when I read in the papers a few weeks before the fall of the Mubarak
regime that a young Egyptian doctor who was also an assistant lecturer at
Qasr al-Aini medical school had disappeared after saying goodbye to his
wife and children at the Cairo airport and going through the gate leading
to the departure lounge. His wife waited for him to call before embark-
ing but he didn't do so. She tried to call him but found his phone turned
off. The mystery about him continued and no one knew where he was for
thirty hours (some say thirty-six hours), until we discovered that State
Security (or some organization with a similar name) had taken him out
of the airport blindfolded after confiscating his mobile phone and driven
him in a car with tinted windows to an undisclosed location, where he was
questioned about his activities in support of Mohamed ElBaradei in his
campaign for free elections in Egypt.

What makes the incident especially outrageous is that the man was
going to London to sit a Royal College of Physicians exam. In other words,
not only did the man have such a sense of patriotism that he felt it his duty
to work for a democratic system in Egypt, but he was also a young scientist
on whom Egypt might pin great hopes for a national renaissance.

A variety of thoughts crossed my mind when I read this appalling and
astounding report. But the same day I read in the newspapers that the
council of Cairo University had agreed to award Suzanne Mubarak, the
president's wife, an honorary doctorate in appreciation of her services to
society and culture.

I wondered whether it ever occurred to the president of Cairo University as he was thinking about the arrangements for receiving the president's wife to think what he might do to save a teacher in his medical
school from injustice and oppression at the hands of the security people.
Did it occur to the president of the university that his responsibility to

defend the dignity of his people at the university was more important than his responsibility to arrange the reception ceremony for an official figure?

Then I wondered whether the president's wife had heard what happened to the young man who was studying at the same university that would award her an honorary degree. And if she had heard of the incident, did she try, I wondered, to link it with the award of the doctorate? Was one incompatible with the other? Should she accept this honor from a university president who didn't do his duty toward the staff of his university? If the honorary degree she was being awarded was a reward for services to science, culture, and society, was what had happened to the university lecturer the same day likely to contribute to science, culture, and society? Did the security men's great enthusiasm for arresting and questioning the university lecturer, and their deep concern over anything that could help Mohamed ElBaradei in his campaign for democracy, have anything to do with the active preparations to install the president's son in the presidency? And were these preparations for a succession likely to contribute to culture, science, and society?

These thoughts probably never crossed the mind of the president's wife or the mind of the university president because it's almost certain, I believe, that what was published in the opposition press didn't reach any members of the president's family. An impregnable wall had probably been built around the ruling family, not just to prevent anything from upsetting them or disturbing their peace of mind but, more important, to protect those outside the president's family who would be the real beneficiaries of the succession plan, because frankly I greatly doubt that the president's family would have benefited, either in the short or the long term, from the success of the plan, even if the real beneficiaries convinced the family that it was essential. The isolation imposed on the ruling family must also have made them imagine that such things as the president's wife being awarded an honorary degree could add to their prestige and raise their status in the eyes of Egyptians or the world.

In short, then, the people who arrested Dr. Shadi al-Ghazali Harb, who stopped him from traveling to London to sit his medical exam, by which he would have benefited himself and his country, and who instead wasted his time questioning him about what he knew about Mohamed ElBaradei, were the same people, or very similar people closely linked to them, who thought of and arranged for Suzanne Mubarak to be awarded the honorary doctorate. Those people who spent their time on security and giving honorary doctorates said that the award to Suzanne Mubarak was in line with university regulations and that the fact that she was also the president's wife had nothing to do with the award, as if it were pure coincidence that the Suzanne Mubarak who won the honorary doctorate was Egypt's first lady. This was very similar to the argument that Gamal Mubarak, the head of the policies committee in the ruling party, had the right, like any other young Egyptian, to stand for the presidency and that his candidacy had nothing to do with the fact that he was the president's son.

8

Everyone who has known Egyptians and lived among them will testify that they have a sense of humor. All the Arabs and non-Egyptians I have known assert this without reservation. In fact I have often noticed that people from other countries, Arab or non-Arab, are amazed and full of admiration for the way Egyptians are instinctively prepared to see the funny side of any situation and to discover something to make fun of in even the most serious situations.

I had an American friend who loved Egypt with a passion and spoke colloquial Egyptian at a level that you rarely find among foreigners. He wrote several books about the economy and politics of Egypt, and for one of them he put together a collection of photographs he thought reflected life in Egypt and the character of Egyptians, adding suitable captions under each photograph. One of these photographs was of a bus driving down a Cairo street, leaning steeply to the side with the doors for getting on and off, as you see on many Egyptian buses, because of the large number of passengers standing on the stairs at the front and the back. One of the people standing on the stairs was visible, with most of his body hanging out of the bus because it was so crowded. The man was miraculously hanging on to a handle and had managed to keep his balance, but anyone who saw him might think that the body of the bus contained some magnetic material that made the passengers stick to it without their needing to hang on to any part of it. The amazing thing about the photograph was that the young man, who appeared to be of modest income judging by his clothes and the situation he was in, and whose body was both inside and outside the bus at the same time, was smiling broadly at the person taking the photograph, as though he were the happiest man in the world, which led my American friend to give it a caption reading: "What exactly is making him laugh?"

I well remember how Egyptians received the news of the appalling and unexpected military defeat of June 1967. I remember the deep sadness and disappointment felt by Egyptians of all classes. But I also remember how this terrible event made Egyptians tell many jokes and make sarcastic remarks that were full of bitterness but drew a laugh from everyone who heard them.

So laughter is a natural reaction for Egyptians, and the instinctive readiness to see the funny side of any situation is one of the traits of the Egyptian character. How, I wonder, did this trait come about?

I think that behind this sense of humor lies an awareness of the contrast between two opposites, and the laughter usually comes when attention is drawn to this contrast. The joke always contains irony, drawing attention to a contrast that wasn't fully clear to the person hearing the joke for the first time, which the joke serves to bring out. A classic example of irony that always succeeds in producing laughter can be found in the silent films of Charlie Chaplin. In all these films Chaplin plays a small, thin, poor tramp, and in scene after scene this poor tramp faces either the hostility of an enormous policeman with a thick stick or a giant boxer whom Chaplin manages to defeat with one trick or another. The plays and films of Naguib al-Rihani are also based on these glaring contrasts, and always draw laughs because of them.

Are Egyptians always ready to make fun of things because their social and daily lives are full of these obvious contrasts, between rich and poor, between intense hunger and eating to excess, between the overbearing policeman and the feckless peddler, between the arrogant civil servant and the simple citizen who desperately needs a rubber stamp, a permit, or a signature, that is, between someone in authority and the helpless citizen?

That might be the reason, or at least one of the reasons. That theory might be corroborated by the fact that this wonderful trait (a sense of humor or constant readiness to make fun of things) is an urban rather than a rural phenomenon. In other words, it's more pronounced among people who live in cities than among peasants. Egyptian peasants laugh deep and loud but they rarely make up jokes, and when they do make them up they are usually not as clever or pointed as the jokes made up by street-wise people accustomed to the cut and thrust of city life.

⌒⟋⟋⟍⟍⟋

So the parliamentary elections of 2010 inevitably provoked witty comments and constant laughter among Egyptians because of the unprecedented contrasts they presented. Months before the elections the government set to work eliminating any possibility of debate, so the only choice on offer was between two hardly distinguishable candidates. The government insisted that all other parties, whether they were former Marxists, Nasserists, Wafdists, or independents, had to change their names and their identities or else they would be beaten and detained, their newspapers would be closed down, their television programs would be canceled, or they would be labeled 'banned,' as was done with the Muslim Brotherhood, which means prevented from entering the fray because they insisted on keeping their names and their identities. All journalists who wanted to cover the election process were also banned unless the security agencies were confident that they would not describe what really took place, and photographers were prevented from approaching the polling stations as if they were military positions. Despite all that, the ruling party wasn't content to announce quietly that it had won a majority and that was that. It also described the elections as "a fierce battle" that the ruling party had won because of its overwhelming popularity and because people loved it so much, and so on.

Egyptians rightly saw all the preparations for the elections as the height of absurdity and as evidence that the authorities were making fun of them, so they preferred to stay at home as long as they were not forced to go and vote. The turnout was lower than in any previous elections, yet pictures appeared in the newspapers and on television to give the impression that men, women, and children had flocked to the polling stations in their eagerness to vote. The photographs showed not only the president, his wife, and his sons, the prime minister, and the ministers as they voted, but also a poor woman who went to vote carrying her baby on her shoulder, insistent on doing her national duty, and a decrepit old man, leaning on his stick, walking into a polling station eager to express his preference for one candidate rather than another.

The next morning the newspapers came out with the news that everyone knew in advance, but the newspapers pretended they contained new and exciting information. They expressed their surprise that, in spite of everything that had happened, the ruling party had won in a landslide and that the opposition parties had hardly won a single vote, as though it was surprising that "the banned organization," that is the

Muslim Brotherhood, which is banned from doing anything or winning anything, had indeed been unable to win anything.

The scene was really silly and should have been more annoying than funny, but Egyptians as usual could not stop laughing. If one Egyptian met another on election morning, he would ask him with a smile, "Who are you going to vote for?" The other would burst out laughing without replying. Or someone would ask his friend, "Have you gone to do your patriotic duty?" and both of them would break into laughter.

Amid all this, the pictures of officials putting their votes in the ballot boxes and looking up with every sign of seriousness looked totally contrived to newspaper readers, but, knowing what I know about Egyptians, I have no doubt that those officials themselves, when they were alone with each other, far from journalists and photographers, must also have burst out laughing. Given that all these officials knew full well that what they were doing was making fun of people's intelligence, could any one of them try to fool a colleague who had joined him in the same absurd charade?

9

Any dictatorial regime needs two things: a strong security apparatus and a collection of intellectuals and journalists. The security apparatus frightens people by detaining, beating, and torturing them if they think of challenging the system, while the intellectuals and journalists do the propaganda for the regime in a constant attempt to embellish its image or, in other words, to disguise its ugliness and to claim repeatedly that, contrary to what people believe, the regime is democratic and wonderful, seeking only the interests of the people.

I must admit, however, that I sometimes have some doubts about how much a dictatorial regime needed intellectuals and journalists as long as it had a powerful police force. Why do you need to convince people or influence their minds when you can constantly intimidate them? In fact, what was the point of all those efforts to embellish the regime and convince people of something that wasn't true when we could see that all its media efforts, all its newspapers, radio stations, and television channels, didn't appear to have changed people's opinion of the regime one iota? The people knew, and the regime knew they knew, so what was the point of all those publicity campaigns?

It was just a case of, as the proverb goes, "the bullet that doesn't hit you still makes a loud noise." In other words, even if all that propaganda couldn't change the way people saw the regime, it did at least perform the function of scrambling opposition voices or at least, and maybe this is more important, achieved the following propaganda function: giving everyone in the opposition the sense that he or she may have been alone, that there was no one who shared their poor opinion of the regime. "Can't you see that the television, the newspapers, and the radio never stop praising the regime? Is it possible that all these people are wrong, and I'm the only person who's right?" Whatever the real usefulness of the intellectuals and journalists who tried to make the regime look good, it's clear that all dictatorial regimes use them, including the regime of Hosni Mubarak, of course. There were a considerable number of Egyptian intellectuals who devoted their writing to improving the image of the regime and defending it from its opponents and critics. These intellectuals naturally varied in competence and talent, but among them I was struck by a handful of no more than ten who were very close to the top of the regime and had one element in common: they were all well-educated, having traveled abroad in their early youth and obtained doctorates from respectable universities in the political or social sciences or law. It's also noteworthy that they had the opportunity to study abroad because in the 1960s the government expanded its program of sending students abroad at the state's expense in the hope that they would come home and use their learning in the service of their country.

In the 1960s and the early 1970s we had high hopes that these people would truly serve their country, but we were disappointed. As soon as they saw the prospect of earning large amounts of money, starting with the era of the Open Door policy in the mid-1970s, they did not hesitate to change their attitude and show themselves fully prepared to serve those in power, first in the 1970s and then in the 1980s, the 1990s, and into the new century.

This handful of intellectuals was greatly alarmed by the phenomenon of Dr. Mohamed ElBaradei, who had the courage to declare his resolve to stand in the presidential elections of 2011, because they realized that if this was destined to succeed, then they themselves, and not just those in power, would be in great danger. The fall of the regime would mean their fall, and its exposure would expose them. So they started writing in evident desperation to refute the arguments of ElBaradei and his supporters, and to ridicule the call for change, so much so that they denied the value of democracy and started looking for other arguments that might serve them, however contrived they needed to be—a task that only intellectuals of their caliber could do well, because their education at the best universities had given them practice in the use of logic, both sound and twisted, to defend any point of view and its opposite.

One example was an article by the editor of a government daily refuting the arguments of Dr. ElBaradei and his followers. One point he tried to rebut was the assertion that we needed to change the constitution, for which he saw no need. The articles of the constitution that everyone, the educated and the uneducated, understood to exclude all presidential candidates other than two—the president and his son—did not, in the view of this well-known intellectual, exclude any candidate, and Dr. ElBaradei could easily stand as an independent and would have a great chance of success without the need for any constitutional change.

Even worse, this well-known intellectual saw no real need for the democracy that ElBaradei and his supporters extolled so highly, and he tried to prove this scientifically. How did he do that? He resorted to the methodology of questionnaires and statistics he had learned at his distinguished university abroad—a methodology that is of course unobjectionable except when used by intellectuals of this kind. He said that in a recent survey of Egyptian public opinion by a respected research center (which he headed at the time of the survey), the proportion of Egyptians who were interested in democracy was no more than 1 percent. Is that plausible? Yes, but only by using certain euphemisms. He said that Egyptians, according to this survey, believed that the most important problems they faced were unemployment (46 percent), poverty (27 percent), and corruption (13 percent). Those who said the government should give priority to "strengthening political reform" were only 1 percent. Of course he wanted us to conclude that the percentage of Egyptians who might support ElBaradei's demand for democratic reform was insignificant.

This intellectual failed to see that using the expression "strengthening political reform" for democracy might be misunderstood as meaning simply that the government would continue to trick people by claiming that it was endeavoring to bring about political reform and greater democracy, and that the question was whether people wanted to see the government "strengthen these endeavors."

Let's assume that the questions in this survey had been phrased differently and had included, for example, the following question: "Do you believe that passing the presidency from one person to his son, and then to his son and so on, is useful, desirable, and compatible with democracy?" What, one wonders, would have been the proportion of Egyptians who agreed with that?

This writer naturally saw no point in wondering whether the Hosni Mubarak regime, to whose service he and his colleagues were so dedicated, bore any responsibility for all the other problems to which Egyptians attach importance, other than "strengthening political reform," that is, such as unemployment, poverty, and corruption, let alone the regime's responsibility for the growth of religious extremism and irrational thinking, which the man invoked in an attempt just to frighten us.

Part 2

Reasons for Hope

7 Harbingers of Revolution

1

I left the Cairo Book Fair in January 2010 ecstatic, and I cannot deny that at the time I felt that Egypt may be on the threshold of a cultural renaissance, the latest of several over the past two centuries, each of which followed a period of despondency and disappointment.

This sense of optimism that something good was starting to happen in Egypt was unfamiliar, of course, because just before the 2011 revolution people in Egypt, either in what they wrote in the press or what they said in television or in daily conversations, seemed to be competing with each other to find something bad that no one else had yet discovered and to talk about these bad things more candidly and more poignantly. That's easy to understand, because in Egypt there are plenty of reasons to be indignant. But is it not also possible that there were important developments taking place under the surface, which were hidden behind a vast number of irritants but which did in themselves inspire optimism, great optimism, that very welcome things were about to happen in Egypt?

These included what I call the harbingers of a cultural renaissance, but to explain that requires going back forty-two years to when an international book fair was first held in Egypt and comparing what happened at the fair in those days to what happened at the book fair in 2010.

It's hard for young people today to imagine how things were in the late 1960s. Egypt was amazingly isolated from the world and very few things could be imported, not even clothes or foodstuffs (other than wheat), no furniture or toys, no refrigerators or cars. In theory it was possible to import these things but the customs duties were so high that it was almost impossible to do so. There were very sound economic justifications for that, but there was no acceptable reason for the severe restrictions imposed on the importing of books and magazines. There were exceptions to everything, but the exceptions were few and the lucky intellectuals or book lovers were those whose work required frequent travel. But even if one traveled, the maximum amount of money one could convert into foreign currency was five Egyptian pounds, and it wouldn't have been wise to spend all your ten dollars, which was what you got for your five pounds, on books and magazines, instead of on more pressing things such as meeting the demands of your wife and children.

Under these circumstances UNESCO took pity on us and issued coupons with which Egyptians could buy books, paying for them in Egyptian pounds, but this required tiresome procedures that few people had the patience for.

Then the government had the good grace to set up the Cairo International Book Fair in 1969, inviting foreign publishers to display their latest books alongside those of Egyptian and Arab publishers. Educated Egyptians and those in search of knowledge stood in lines to see what the world was writing and thinking, but without the right to buy except by going though many tedious procedures. That was because the foreign publishers wanted to be sure they could convert the Egyptian pounds they received into their currencies, and this required the approval of the currency control authorities. So all you could do was see the book and maybe browse through it, then register your name as wishing to buy a copy and pay for it. Then you would wait for weeks, maybe months, in the hope that the currency control authorities would give their approval, whereupon the publisher would send you the book from abroad.

This discouraged Arab publishers outside Egypt from bringing their books to Cairo, to avoid problems and complications they could do without. Egyptian publishers, on the other hand, had their books in their bookshops all year round anyway, so the main reason why Egyptians went to the book fair was just to look, even from a distance, at what the world's talents were producing in the hope they might have a chance, some way or another, to get hold of a book behind the backs of the censors and the currency control authorities.

Yes, the picture had completely changed by 2010. It was easy to buy foreign books and many Arab publishers brought their books to the Cairo fair. The censorship of books and magazines was much less strict, in spite of the complaints we heard from time to time, and the Egyptian pound was freely convertible into other currencies. As a result the Cairo Book Fair has become a real party or festival every year, celebrated by intellectuals and students. Many Arab tourists come for the event, trying to combine visiting Cairo and visiting the book fair. The number of books on display and the number of visitors have grown many times over, and the sight of so many young people standing in line at the windows to buy entrance tickets is a real joy.

The fair is no longer a Cairo phenomenon, with large numbers of people now coming from the provinces and from villages outside Cairo, easily distinguishable as they walk though the fair. The men come with their wives and children to buy books, sometimes Salafist books but also books on modern subjects, many of them on learning foreign languages and how to use computers, as well as cut-price versions of the books their sons and daughters need for school and university.

All this is no doubt gratifying, but what I and many others have also noticed at the fair in recent years is the extraordinary increase in the number of young Egyptians who are eager to read new books by new Egyptian writers, books of various kinds—literature, politics, society. The successful books sell tens of thousands of copies, whereas once a book was deemed to be a stunning success if a print run of three thousand copies sold out in a year, even with authors as important as Naguib Mahfouz and Tawfiq al-Hakim. This has led to many more bookshops, and we hear of new ones opening every day.

What exactly happened that brought this about? The phenomenon is as difficult to explain as it is gratifying. The expansion of education may play a role because, however much we complain about the falling standards of education, the mere quantitative increase in the number of educated people is bound to bring about an increase in the number of intelligent readers and talented writers. But I believe that cultural openness to the world must have played a role in the growth of this desire to read and this drive to write, whether the openness comes about through travel, more contact with foreigners who visit Egypt, more access to new books and magazines, or through television and the Internet, of course. All these forms of openness to the world have harmful or dangerous aspects, but in my view it would be wrong to deny that contact with the rest of the world must stimulate the mind and add to the passion for knowledge.

This led me to expect a cultural renaissance soon in Egypt, the fruits of which our children would harvest, even if it wouldn't come to the surface until the political barrier was broken, just as the revolution of July 1952 broke the barrier behind which highly talented Egyptians were waiting, men such as Yusuf Idris, Kamal al-Tawil, Baligh Hamdi, Salah Jahin, and Salah Abd al-Sabur.

2

When I was a law student about sixty years ago, the overwhelming majority of students were male. For every thousand male students, there were no more than ten females.

This small handful of female students was naturally very shy, and we would see them walking together in tight groups and disappearing completely as soon as lectures were over. They would not speak to anyone without blushing, and none of us dared to speak to them, except for those whose courage all the others would envy.

I remember that in March 1954 we staged a sit-in at the big hall in Cairo University in protest at the removal of Muhammad Nagib as president because of his disagreement with the other army officers, in that he wanted democracy and most of the others wanted the officers to stay in power. We decided to spend the night in the big hall and to keep up the sit-in until Muhammad Nagib was reinstated. The Revolutionary Command Council sent us someone to try to persuade us to call off the sit-in but we refused, and the astounding result of the sit-in and of the overwhelming public outrage from various groups that supported Muhammad Nagib was that Nagib regained power.

The story is well known, but what I want to mention now is that among the hundreds of people at the sit-in at Cairo University there was not a single woman student, and in fact it never occurred to us that it would be possible for a woman to join the sit-in. The women themselves would have seen the idea as a kind of insanity that neither they nor their families could imagine. Public affairs was a task for men, while women should make do with watching from afar. As soon as there was any sign that a demonstration might take place, the female students would rush off home to keep away from any acts of violence by either the students or the police.

I recalled all this as I followed reports that Egyptian women were taking part in the April 6 movement in 2010 and had joined demonstrations calling for freedom, constitutional change, and an end to emergency law. In the newspapers I saw pictures of women challenging the riot police, attacking them as the police hid behind their shields, and the women's faces showed signs of intense anger. Then I read what the police had done to them and their young male colleagues: beating them with clubs, dragging them along the ground, viciously insulting them, and then throwing them into police trucks.

Yes, the sight was shocking for its extreme and unjustifiable brutality, but I also felt proud of what Egyptian women had achieved over the past sixty years in the way of psychological and intellectual liberation. Egyptian women, or at least very broad swaths of Egyptian women, were no longer prisoners of the belief that they were just bodies. Egyptian women had discovered that on top of that they had minds and hearts, had the same feelings toward their country as men, were as aware as their male colleagues of the state their country was in, and bore the same responsibility.

Egyptian women are everywhere these days, doing all kinds of jobs and filling all kinds of positions. The proportion of women in lecture rooms at universities is close to half and maybe more, they hold leading positions in government and in companies, they have made a worthy contribution to literature, they have excelled in journalism and film production, they have shone as television producers and broadcasters, and they have sat as ordinary judges and almost won the battle to sit on the bench at the Council of State. And now, their heads held high and full of dignity, they were standing their ground against policemen who would view them with pride and respect if the officers in command were not standing nearby to monitor them.

3

For ages we heard only bad news, and then news arrived of the revolution in Tunisia, bringing joy and hope that it might be possible, in spite of everything, for the people to force their oppressive rulers to flee. At the same time the news must have struck fear in the hearts of despotic rulers everywhere, who were surprised to find that however mighty the security forces might be, there were limits to what could be done when the people's anger reached a certain level. Calling in the army to help suppress the people meant assuming that the commanders would approve of the army switching from its task of protecting the people from foreign aggression to that of protecting a very small clique of people from the anger of the people, something the Tunisian army could not conceive of doing.

The contrast was amazing between what happened in Tunisia toward the end of 2010 and what happened in Brazil two months earlier, when a very popular president, Luiz Inácio Lula da Silva, refused to meddle with the constitution so that he could stand for another term in office, and his people elected as his successor a woman who belonged to the same party and shared his principles. The Brazilian people said goodbye to their great president with the same love they showed him when he was elected, while the Tunisian president and his family had to run away and found it difficult to identify a single country that would agree to receive them.

But the Tunisians revolted not only against the monopolization of power but also against an unjust economic policy that benefited only a very small proportion of the population. What ignited the Tunisian revolution was a horrific incident that was a direct result of that economic policy. A young Tunisian with a university degree who had failed to find a job to make a living decided to sell vegetables from a street cart, but the police prevented him on one or another of the pretexts well known to us in Egypt when the police harass poor peddlers in the street. In fury the man poured gasoline on his body, set fire to himself, and later died in the hospital.

Widespread unemployment, especially among the educated, together with arrogance and harassment by the authorities, made people so angry that they came out into the streets determined to change the regime.

This conjunction of an unfair economic policy and dictatorial rule is no coincidence, because it would be really impossible for a democracy to allow such an economic policy, and such an economic policy could be sustained in a poor country only under a dictatorship. It's amazing that the international institutions that call on so-called developing countries to apply these unfair economic policies, without making the necessary distinction between what is good for one country and what is good for another, are the very same institutions, with the same countries controlling them, that advocate for democracy, transparency, and respect for human rights. This contradiction between their two missions is truly surprising. But what is not surprising is that these institutions and the governments that sponsor them show unlimited patience toward the dictatorial regimes that implement these economic policies and give them political and economic backing on the grounds that the political system is an internal matter in which they cannot interfere, while they know that this political system and this economic policy are inseparable, and that one is the twin of the other.

It's useful to remember this when we consider the evolution and effects of Egyptian economic policy and compare them with what happened in Tunisia. The policy known as 'structural adjustment' began to be applied in Egypt when the government of Atef Sidqi came to office in 1986, a year before Zine El Abidine Ben Ali came to power in Tunisia. So this policy is about a quarter of a century old in both countries and people are still being promised that sooner or later it will achieve the desired economic objectives, and so it is often referred to as 'economic reform.' The policy consists of the following elements: liberalizing external trade (imports and exports), taking measures to encourage foreign investment, transferring public-sector enterprises to the private sector (privatization), ending government interference in the free market, for example by allowing prices (including the exchange rate) to move freely, and reducing or abolishing government subsidies on goods and services.

Tunisia carried out these demands rapidly while Egypt did so slowly, so Tunisia won the praise of the International Monetary Fund and other international institutions while Egypt received praise tinged with reservations. That was until the government of Ahmad Nazif came to office in 2004 and the Egyptian government's steps to implement the fund's demands gathered speed. In fact I think this was the basic purpose behind Nazif's cabinet replacing that of Atef Ebeid. From then on, Egypt began to receive the same expressions of admiration from international institutions as Tunisia.

In both countries there was an improvement in the indicators to which the International Monetary Fund attaches importance and by which it measures success and failure, along with a deterioration in the indicators the International Monetary Fund avoids talking about and doesn't pay much attention to when doling out praise or criticism. The growth rate of gross domestic product (GDP) was higher, along with that of average incomes, and foreign investment increased (that has happened in Tunisia for the past twenty years and started to happen in Egypt in 2005). But three other things occurred that the International Monetary Fund and the other international financial institutions don't like to talk about unless they are forced to: higher unemployment, a growing gap between rich and poor, and the economy's greater exposure to changing world conditions and hence its greater vulnerability to fluctuations that take place abroad. The result was that in Tunisia, after more than twenty years implementing International Monetary Fund policies, GDP rose at more than 5 percent a year, about a fifth more than in Egypt, but the unemployment rate also rose sharply, to a level about 50 percent higher than the rate in Egypt (14 percent of the workforce in Tunisia, compared with 9 percent in Egypt, according to the official statistics, which probably greatly underestimate the real level of unemployment in both countries). The gap between the rich and the poor also widened significantly and became greater than it was in Egypt (the richest 10 percent of Egyptians earn eight times what the poorest 10 percent earn, compared with thirteen times in Tunisia), according to United Nations figures for 2007/8, and the reality is probably much worse here as well, since much of what the rich earn is invisible and cannot be calculated.

Similarly, the international financial crisis that started in 2008 had a more severe effect on Tunisia than on Egypt. GDP growth in both countries fell from about 5 percent over the ten years before the crisis to 3 percent in 2009 in Tunisia and about 4 percent in Egypt.

So there are statistics to explain why a popular uprising broke out in Tunisia before one broke out in Egypt. But of course these statistics don't tell the whole story, especially when it comes to the question of when revolution will break out. Unemployment and the gap between rich and poor are only two of the reasons for anger and revolution. There is also the level of corruption, and even here the situation in Egypt apparently wasn't as bad as in Tunisia. After Ben Ali fled it was reported that during his years in power he had accumulated a fortune worth more than $13 billion in the form of deposits in foreign banks and ownership of an airline in Tunisia, luxury apartment blocks in Paris, and hotels in Brazil and Argentina.

Dictatorship and restrictions on freedoms are two other causes of revolution, and here again I believe we'll find that the Tunisians had more cause than the Egyptians, because the Ben Ali regime in Tunisia was crueler and rougher in the way it treated the opposition and restricted freedoms than the Mubarak regime in Egypt.

But there are other reasons for indignation in which Egypt was ahead of Tunisia. Zine El Abidine Ben Ali didn't try to install his son as his successor, as the Egyptian regime did for several years. There is also the level of poverty itself. If poverty goes beyond a certain level it makes the poor feel that they have nothing to lose and that however dangerous it is to protest and however severe the penalty for rebellion, it cannot be much worse than doing nothing. In this respect Egyptians had more reason to be angry than the Tunisians because the average income in Egypt was about half what it was in Tunisia, and the proportion of people below the poverty line (living on less than $2 a day, that is) in Egypt was seven times what it was in Tunisia (44.6 percent in Egypt compared with 6.6 percent in Tunisia).

So there were many reasons to be angry, and the statistics point in multiple directions. In the end what was decisive is not the result of adding and subtracting but psychological factors that are difficult to measure, such as the intensity of the anger and the obstinacy of those in power, not to mention the level of support that external forces gave to the rebels at home.

8 January 25

1

Something very important happened on January 25, 2011, something that I believe to be unprecedented in the history of political activity in Egypt and that reflected important developments that had built up in Egyptian society over the past twenty or thirty years and were bound to produce such an event. The masses that came out on the streets that day, chanting, making demands, and expressing their anger at the whole situation in Egypt, made up a movement characterized by a number of phenomena that were new to Egyptian political life.

First, the vast numbers of people who took part in the demonstrations and protests were unprecedented. Demonstrations began in central Cairo on that day with gatherings around the High Court building, which then marched to Opera Square, to Abd al-Moneim Riyad Square, and then to Tahrir Square, and some people estimated that at some time that evening Tahrir Square contained thirty thousand people of all ages, determined to stay in the square until their demands were met. They brought blankets and some gave out food and water to those who needed it. People embraced each other, even those who did not know each other, in jubilation at what they were doing. To see such large numbers of people working together on a single political project is not only unfamiliar but also unprecedented in Egyptian history.

One reason of course is that there have never been so many people as there are today, but another reason is their greater ability to communicate and mobilize in a way that wasn't available at any time in the past. One of the most common slogans among popular movements in the first half of the twentieth century was "Long live the struggle of the students with the workers," since the sectors of society most willing to voice popular demands were indeed university and secondary-school students and factory workers. One reason why these sectors came together was that it was easy to gather them in one place. Demonstrations would begin either inside universities or from factories. Things have greatly changed since then. Physical assembly is no longer essential as a starting point because now there are mobile phones and the Internet, so organizing and arranging to meet no longer require being in one place. This can be done among people in different places with different jobs or professions. Many of those who took part in the demonstrations of January 25 kept in touch with their friends and colleagues by mobile phone, telling them what was happening and inviting them to join them in a particular street or at a particular intersection, where they would come and join the demonstrators.

Second, the demonstrations took part simultaneously in many provincial cities and towns, in Suez and Ismailiya, Mansoura, Damietta, Tanta, al-Mahalla al-Kubra and Baltim, in Beni Suef, Asyut, and Aswan, Rafah and Sheikh Zuweid, and so on, apart from Cairo and Alexandria. This is something that the history books record only for 1919. Communications must have played a role here, too, but another factor was the rise in political awareness that had taken place outside Cairo and Alexandria, and the diminishing gap between the two big cities, on the one hand, and the other cities, on the other, in the level of understanding of political and economic conditions in Egypt and the rest of the world.

Third, this time we noticed the significant participation of educated people from various social classes or sectors. They all gathered in the same places and chanted the same slogans. This phenomenon must have been connected with the spread of education in Egypt in recent decades. We never stop complaining about the declining standard of education in Egypt at all levels, from primary to university level, and this complaint is well founded, of course, but we must recognize the benefits that have come from the sheer quantitative expansion of education. The rate of illiteracy is still shamefully high (still affecting more than a third of the population), but it is no longer 80 percent as it was at the time of the 1952 revolution.

Provincial universities, whatever their educational standards, must have played a positive role in spreading political awareness across the country, because that awareness is no longer confined to a small social class as it was until the middle of the last century. It has extended, with the expansion of the middle class, to include a much higher percentage of Egyptians. It was this middle class, with its upper and lower subdivisions, that provided the people who demonstrated on January 25. They included both highly educated nationalists and nationalists with only a basic education, yet they rallied around the same slogans that gave voice to the same demands.

Fourth, there is a striking difference between the causes of the January 25 revolution and the causes of previous revolutions and uprisings in Egypt. Demands for the evacuation of foreign forces and protests against foreign occupation were the basic driving force behind most Egyptian uprisings until the early 1970s. There were protests and uprisings against the French occupation (1798 to 1800), the British occupation (1882), and the Israeli occupation of Sinai (1972); economic motives were not an important factor in protests by Egyptians until the 1970s.

That was because the 1970s brought economic policies that were completely new to Egyptians and that led to a reduction in state interference in the economy and successive cuts in government subsidies for goods and essential services. The uprisings and protests driven by economic motives began with the uprising of January 1977, followed by protests by factory workers and street demonstrations by various groups of employees over the past twenty years, culminating in this last uprising on January 25. In this last uprising economic motives went hand in hand with political motives: the demand was for bread and dignity, and the protests were simultaneously against high prices and the plan to install Gamal Mubarak as president. The demand for political freedoms, a change of regime, unrigged elections, and the elimination of corruption went hand in hand with the demand for an economic policy that served the interests of the broad masses and narrowed the gap between classes.

The economy was usually absent as a factor in Egyptian popular uprisings until the 1970s and then the economy came to dominate protests, until the Kefaya movement appeared in 2005. Since then, anger for political reasons has come together with anger for economic reasons—a trend that took shape clearly on January 25.

Fifth, it's striking how small a part political organizations and trade unions played in the uprising of January 25. The role of leaders was also very small, if not nonexistent. Some of the parties completely disappeared, even some that had once been revolutionary parties. One of them declined to take part on the grounds that January 25 was an official holiday, while another said its members could take part "on an individual basis"; in other words, it was up to them as individuals to decide whether they wanted to do so. We were scarcely aware of any role played by the Muslim Brotherhood as a political organization. No well-known party leaders took part and we didn't hear anyone chanting the name of a serious leader. It's not hard to explain, because the decline and atrophy that had afflicted party life in Egypt over the past half-century had prevented the emergence of any political leaders, just as the regime's policy had succeeded in reducing all the parties, including the ruling party itself, to dwarfs with little or no influence, and in weakening the professional associations and trade unions until they no longer carried out any effective mass actions.

At the same time it's surprising and admirable that young Egyptians managed to organize an uprising (or revolution) like the one that began on January 25 without leaders of any kind, which is decisive evidence that the Egyptian people have not lost their dynamism in spite of all the various forms of oppression they have suffered over past decades and although they have been deprived of the opportunity to discover new leaders and push them to the fore. If we add to that the unprecedented contribution to the January 25 demonstrations by women, veiled and unveiled, of various social classes and levels of education, we can clearly see how seriously wrong many people were when they said they had lost hope in the Egyptian people's ability to come back to life.

2

When the Egyptian people rose up on Tuesday, January 25, it was not a revolution of the hungry, as many expected, but of an angry people. The anger was clearly evident in the expressions on the faces of the demonstrators, in the words they wrote on their banners, in the voices of those chanting, and in the way they spoke to radio and television stations.

Yes, there were strong reasons to be angry, connected to prices, the standard of living, and unemployment, but the political and social reasons were no less important.

The demonstrators came out calling for the overthrow of a regime known for injustice, corruption, and dictatorship, and these were important factors in why people were angry. But in addition to that there was another factor that contributed to the anger, and that was the arrogance and disdain the regime exhibited when people could see no justification for arrogance. The regime treated the Egyptian people as though they were minors so stupid that they were unable to make decisions for themselves, so they deserved their poverty and subjugation. Prime minister Ahmad Nazif once made remarks to the effect that Egyptians were not fit for democracy—something any ruler in any country had not dared to say of his people in a long time, at least since the end of the period when the king was seen as "God's shadow on Earth," more than two centuries ago. The minister of education treated teachers and schoolchildren as though they were scum sent by God to be disciplined, while the minister of culture treated intellectuals as servants whose job it was to sing his praises and justify his mistakes. The president and his wife thought it was their right that news about them, however insignificant it might be, should take precedence over the most important news about Egypt and the rest of the world, and that their travel arrangements should bring traffic to a halt for all other Egyptians, even when they were going to have a break in Sharm al-Sheikh. The government newspapers and other media spoke about the regime's opponents with contempt and disdain, either ignoring news of them completely or misstating their names, for example by calling the largest political organization in the country, the Muslim Brotherhood, the 'banned group.'

The election rigging that took place immediately before the revolution, in November 2010, was of a crudeness unprecedented in the history of Egyptian elections, reflecting indifference toward and gross contempt for the people and their wishes. It resulted in a parliament with no dissenting voices. When some opposition politicians thought of setting up an alternative parliament, the president's comment was, "Let them amuse themselves," illustrating his indifference toward how people felt about the electoral farce.

Then came the explosion, one of the reasons for which must have been people's anger at this level of arrogance and indifference, because among the men running the regime people couldn't see any who had unusual intelligence, rare wisdom, or exceptional competence in administering the country: education was in decline, obtaining health care at a reasonable price was becoming more and more difficult, unemployment was rising, and the country's foreign policy did not stem from any patriotic impulse. So what was there to justify all this arrogance? Egyptians were well aware that their country is full of people who could run things more competently and less corruptly, so why would their anger not grow until it brought them to an explosion of the kind that happened on January 25?

But nothing could persuade the regime's men to abandon their arrogance. When five Egyptians killed themselves or tried to kill themselves outside parliament and in the streets of Alexandria, saying they were fed up with living in unemployment, poverty, and humiliation, all the regime's men could say was that they were a bunch of mental cases who should have been treated in the mental hospital in Abbasiya. When angry demonstrations started on January 25 and continued day after day, the head of the ruling party's policies committee, who also happened to be the president's son, didn't consider it his responsibility to make a statement or give a speech defending the 'policies' that people thought had unleashed all this anger, or to explain to us the 'policies' that might be adopted to calm people down, as if the job of the head of the policies committee was only to work on becoming president. All the regime did was to refrain, temporarily, from publishing the photographs of the policies secretary that they had been in the habit of publishing in less heated times—photographs in which he appeared to be deep in thought, without his having uttered a single word to suggest he had ever had a worthwhile thought in all the years that he had held this important post.

After three days of tempestuous demonstrations the president appeared on television to speak to the people, and suddenly we discovered that the most he was prepared to favor us with was a cabinet change of the kind we had seen and grown tired of time after time, replacing one old face with another and appointing one of the ministers in the old government as the new prime minister, although the new prime minister, having been a minister for the past six years, was also responsible, along with the other ministers, for what people were complaining of. If now he could meet the wishes of the masses, why hadn't he made an effort in the previous government to avoid angering the masses? As for the other new ministers, they were just ghosts of the old ones. One was an obedient subordinate to the hated minister of culture, and now he was the new minister of culture. The old minister had insisted that people refer to him as "the artist minister," so what might the new minister ask people to call him? The new minister of trade and industry was the right arm of the previous minister, so what change could she be expected to achieve?

Then the president repeated his old refrain that "the priority is to combat poverty," but why, one wondered, hadn't he been able to reduce poverty in the thirty years he had been in power? What, one wondered, did he plan to do to reduce poverty in the coming months that he hadn't already thought of?

So the regime seemed determined to treat the people with the same arrogance and indifference, as if the demonstrators, hundreds of whom had been killed, came out to protest because they couldn't find anything else to busy themselves with.

The crisis deepened after the mass rallies in Tahrir Square and the streets of Alexandria on Friday, January 28, but the regime remained silent for four days until Tuesday, February 2, when it had the good grace to announce that the president did not intend to seek reelection when his current term expired. Was this the most the president could offer us at the age of eighty-two years, more than a third of which he had spent as president? The only outcome was angry demonstrations in protest, because even if he had announced he didn't plan to go on until he was ninety, what about his son? Did he also not plan to stand for the presidency? There was no answer.

The president's only other promises were to ask parliament, which was fraudulently elected through and through, to comply with some court rulings on appeals against the election results and to change one or two articles of the constitution on the number of terms a president can serve and on the requirements a president must meet. But he didn't explain to us why this should give us any hope that a parliament that was based on rigged elections and not on the true desires of the electorate would comply with the real wishes of the demonstrators.

3

Several weeks before January 25 I received a telephone call from a woman I didn't know, saying she was a student in her final year at the medical faculty at an Egyptian university and that a group of students in her faculty wanted to meet me to discuss a number of matters related to the present state of Egypt, especially the common phenomenon of young people who are determined to emigrate as soon as they graduate, in despair at their chances of finding suitable employment in Egypt and at the quality of life in Egypt in general. I told her I was willing and we agreed on a day, but she said she would call me back to confirm as soon as she had obtained the approval of the security office in the faculty.

She called me back two days before the date set for the session and said she was sorry but the security office had told her that orders from above meant I couldn't come to meet them in the faculty, that she was arranging to hold the session somewhere outside the faculty, that she had chosen a bookshop in Heliopolis, and that she would put up notices in the faculty advertising the event. I agreed and we fixed a day. But she called back and said the security office refused to let her put up notices in the faculty because the notices were for a talk by someone that security had already refused to let speak on campus.

A few days later she called back to say she could arrange the meeting without putting up notices in the faculty and relying solely on personal contact with the students and on the Internet. We agreed, and a colleague of the woman came to take me to the bookshop. It was a long way and we got into a long conversation. The young man impressed me with his personality, his culture, his enthusiasm, and his candor. He was also in his final year at the medical faculty, and I discovered that he and the woman were both from Minya, that he was twenty-two, that his father taught Arabic at a school in Minya, that he (the student) had read most of my books, and that his father encouraged him and his brother to read. His father would promise them rewards for certain achievements and the rewards would be books by Naguib Mahfouz or Taha Hussein. He also told me he planned to emigrate as soon as he graduated and that he had already applied for a green card at the U.S. embassy.

When we reached the bookshop and I met the woman student for the first time, I was equally impressed—a woman 100 percent Egyptian, in hijab, with a brown complexion and fine features. I was struck by her strong personality (I had already noticed that from the decisive way she spoke in our phone conversations), which won immediate respect from anyone who met her. I said to myself, "So is this the kind of young people Upper Egypt produces when they are given the chance to be educated and to discover the world? Here we have a young Egyptian woman who has been well brought up, who combines the traditions of her family with public activity, including organizing seminars and defying security offices."

The meeting was a success. The young people present, about evenly divided between men and women, expressed themselves well and were also good listeners. The last question I was asked was whether I was optimistic or pessimistic about the future of Egypt, and I answered without hesitation that I was optimistic. That was always my answer in such seminars but my optimism was reinforced this time by meeting these two fine young people and by the way the participants in the seminar had behaved and spoken. I explained why I was optimistic, saying:

"First, things in Egypt are now so bad that they can only change for the better. It's impossible to imagine anything worse than this.

"Second, the history of Egypt for at least the past two hundred years is a history of rises and falls, cycles of progress and decline, but each period of progress starts at a point that is better than the point at which previous periods of progress started. It's true that the current period of decline has gone on rather long, at close to thirty years, and some might say more than forty years, but it has to come to an end soon.

"Third, the last few years strongly remind me of the four years between the defeat of the Egyptian army and the other Arab armies in the Palestine war of 1948 and the revolution of July 1952. During that period Egypt saw an astounding level of political incompetence, a noticeable increase in corruption, and growing decadence on the part of the king, so people grew very frustrated and thought their suffering would never end, then suddenly the army staged a coup that overthrew the king and the feelings of frustration turned to joy and optimism for the future.

"Fourth, we shouldn't underestimate the psychological changes that can take place overnight as soon as people recover hope that things will improve. Despair kills off enthusiasm, but hope can revive it and can make people capable of miracles. That's what happened in the days and years after the 1952 revolution. That can happen again as soon as there is positive change in the system of government in Egypt.

"Fifth, beneath all the bad things we see and all the difficulties we complain of, there are very positive changes taking place below the surface that can't be seen easily, and these are paving the way for wonderful things that are bound to appear above the surface one day. These changes include the expansion of education, however much the standard may have declined, the fact that women are going out to work and are more active in social life, and the fact that young Egyptians are more in touch with the world."

That's what I cited at the seminar as reasons to be optimistic about the future of Egypt. Then came the amazing sequence of events that started on January 25 and continued until Hosni Mubarak stepped down on February 11. During that period we heard that some of the worst and most hated members of the regime had been dismissed and that Gamal Mubarak would not be standing for the presidency after all the questionable efforts the regime had made to promote him. Suddenly the clouds cleared from the sky and everyone looked more cheerful. They started to sing and dance in the street. The frustration suddenly ended and hope was restored. We saw signs reading "Lift your head up, you're Egyptian," and young Egyptians of all classes sweeping the streets and washing statues, as if Egypt had suddenly heard something that made it wipe away its tears, spruce itself up, and give the world a radiant smile that proclaimed the start of a new page in its history. I said to myself, "I was right to be optimistic," but what happened in those eighteen days redoubled my optimism and added new reasons for optimism to the old ones.

Even before January 25, I already felt that the new generation of young Egyptians had very positive qualities, way superior to how our generation was when we were their age, but I didn't realize that these qualities were so widespread throughout Egypt, rather than confined to a particular social class.

I knew that Egyptian women had achieved real intellectual and psychological liberation, whether or not they covered their hair, but I didn't realize that this intellectual and psychological liberation was so widespread, geographically or in terms of class, or that this psychological liberation combined with the endearing reserve that has always been a trait of Egyptian women had created such a wonderful new mix. This had a positive effect even on the behavior of young men, making them more exuberant, more confident in themselves, and more respectful of the opposite sex.

I knew that the incidents of sexual harassment that had recurred in recent years on public holidays had something to do with the widespread sense of frustration and with the fact that large numbers of young men had lost their self-confidence and their self-respect. But then we saw young men behave in a completely different manner in places packed with young men and women: they treated each other with respect and goodwill, and the young men acted with maturity, offering all the help they could to the young women taking part in the demonstrations.

I still believe there's a need to explain and explore the reasons for this extraordinary change in young Egyptians, which wasn't at all evident and then suddenly emerged into broad daylight. I have some hypotheses that need testing. Is openness to the world the reason? Are the economic problems themselves among the reasons, as if the problems had melted them down and then transmuted them from base to precious metal? Is it the spread of education, which must have reached many young people who were intelligent by nature and had an innate disposition to learn, so that fine fruit grew from soil that was barren until it received even a few drops of water? In fact I sometimes wonder whether in the end the reason has something to do with the nature of Egyptians, fundamentally latent in those who live in rural areas and who are the repositories of centuries of Egyptian civilization, a nature that suddenly comes to the surface as soon as it is relieved of some of the burdens weighing down on it.

Whatever the reason, what those eighteen days brought to light was something wonderful and astounding, and it was bound to give us new reasons to be optimistic.

4

Throughout the ages the scope for mobilizing the masses to take part in a concerted activity such as demonstrating or rebelling against those in power has been extremely limited, dependent on the technologies available. As long as communications technologies were simple and primitive, the possibilities for mobilizing and influencing the masses were also basic and limited.

So for centuries revolutionaries and agitators could bring supporters together only to a very limited extent, depending on their capacity for effective oratory, that is, the extent to which they were articulate, eloquent, and able to speak clearly and forcefully. In the history of modern Egypt, up until the middle of the twentieth century, there were few people who had those skills, the most prominent of whom were Abdallah Nadim, the orator of the Urabi revolt, Mustafa Kamel, Saad Zaghloul, Mustafa al-Nahhas, Ahmad Hussein, Makram Ebeid, and Fathi Radwan. All these men were extremely articulate and eloquent, with a command of the Arabic language, clear enunciation, and strong delivery. They did not need loudspeakers to amplify their voices, and loudspeakers were unknown in Egypt anyway until the beginning of the twentieth century and were then not much used, even when available, until the middle of the century.

There were newspapers, of course, even before the beginning of the twentieth century, and historians relate how people would rush to buy newspapers even before the First World War to follow certain issues and scandals. Broadcasting appeared in the early 1930s but the impact of newspapers and the radio remained limited in a society where the vast majority of people were illiterate and lived in villages that did not have electricity.

The situation began to change in the middle of the century, but it's important to remember that in order to mobilize people and arouse their enthusiasm the only methods available to the 1952 revolution were not much different from those available in the uprising of 1919. There were still few newspapers in light of an illiteracy rate above 80 percent and the fact that people in the countryside (who accounted for about the same proportion of the population) did not have electricity and had so little purchasing power that they couldn't buy a radio or the batteries it needed. The number of radios in the villages was very limited and, apart from the headman, only a small number of people owned them.

When the Free Officers who carried out the revolution of July 23, 1952, sent one of their number to the radio building to broadcast their first communiqué telling the people that the officers had seized power, the man they chose was Anwar al-Sadat, based no doubt on the fact that he had a strong voice, read well, and was better able than the other officers to avoid horrible grammatical errors. But the radio's impact on people remained small, confined to those in cities for some years, even after the revolution. One of the first songs to appear because of the revolution, a song that won wide popularity, was a beautiful song with the opening line, "To the guesthouse, to the guesthouse, there's news on National Radio." The words alone show how the only radio or one of the few radios in the village was in the headman's guesthouse. But the revolutionaries soon discovered the importance of investing in radio to mobilize people to support the revolution, and they were helped in this by the appearance of the small portable transistor radio, which made it possible for the new station that the revolution set up, called the Voice of the Arabs, to be heard in remote villages in Egypt and in other parts of the Arab world. This made a major contribution to the wide popularity of Gamal Abd al-Nasser, and made the director of the station, Ahmad Said, an important figure in the history of the 1952 revolution.

Egyptian radio did everything it could to mobilize people behind the Free Officers and it inevitably recruited the most popular singers, such as Umm Kulthum and Muhammad Abd al-Wahhab, to contribute by singing songs in praise of the officers. The radio also helped to create a wide following for new young singers such as Abd al-Halim Hafez and Faida Kamel, whose names were long associated with inspirational songs lauding the leader of the revolution and everything important he did, from nationalizing the Suez Canal to uniting Egypt and Syria and supporting new revolutions everywhere.

The revolution also set up new newspapers such as *al-Sha'b* and *al-Gumhuriya* to compete with traditional newspapers like *al-Ahram* and *al-Akhbar*, and new magazines such as *al-Tahrir* and *al-Risala al-gadida* to rival established magazines such as *Rose al-Yusuf*, *al-Musawwir*, and *Akhir Sa'a*. It soon became clear, however, that it would be difficult to rely on journalists who had started work and established themselves in the time of the monarchy and the old parties, so the revolutionary government suddenly took a step that was extremely bold and rash: nationalizing all newspapers and magazines and substituting people they trusted for people who were competent, in the sense that what mattered was said to be one's loyalty to the revolution rather than the standard of one's performance as a journalist.

People accepted all these changes in broadcasting and the press as long as they were sympathetic toward the revolution and as long as they continued to feel that the new system of government, in spite of being dictatorial, was translating people's real demands into realities and laws. But this sympathy declined little by little and people felt the impact of restrictions on the media more and more when the media seemed to be working solely to legitimize the rulers.

So we find that people sympathized with Salah Jahine's song celebrating the nationalization of the Suez Canal and Abd al-Halim Hafez's song criticizing the World Bank for refusing to finance the Aswan High Dam much more than they sympathized with the propaganda that went with the defeat of 1967. People made fun of the way the media described the defeat as just "a setback" and didn't believe what the media said about "the economics of war" and about how "no voice should be louder than the sound of battle," and so on.

The rapid introduction of television by the revolutionary government was completely understandable from a regime that was new to governing and was trying to change the way people thought and to create a following for rulers of a completely new kind. But the effect of television remained limited by the purchasing power of most Egyptians throughout its first ten years, through the 1960s, and it did not become overwhelming until emigration to the Gulf countries from the early 1970s enabled millions of Egyptians to buy televisions. As one would expect with people who were unenthusiastic about newspapers because of widespread illiteracy, when men, women, and children who had rarely stepped foot outside their village or their small town were offered an irresistible device that brought them sound and enticing pictures instead of only sound like the radio, from the mid-1970s television became the regime's basic tool for gaining the support of the people and shaping their ideas.

It's very important to note the big difference between the role of the media in how the 1952 revolution began and developed and its role in the revolution of 2011. The difference can be summed up by saying that while the role of the media in the 1952 revolution was basically revelatory, in the 2011 revolution it was dynamic and productive.

What we now call the 1952 revolution began as just a movement (it has sometimes been called al-Haraka al-Mubaraka, or the Blessed Movement) started by a very small number of officers who told the people what they had done after they finished the job without asking for any mass action to overthrow the king and his regime. Although anger against the monarchy was widespread among all sectors of the people, the most that was possible in the way of mass action under the monarchy was for student groups to link up with worker groups, carrying banners and shouting slogans such as "Long live student solidarity with the workers" and "Down with this or that," or marching down the street until the police dispersed them.

Mass rallies were possible only on one or two university campuses, at some secondary schools, and at some factories that employed a large number of workers, and so they were rare. The number of newspapers and magazines that opposed the regime was also very small, and they were even less able to mobilize people than speakers at universities or factories, despite the strident tone used in attacks on the king and the regime and the eloquence of the opposition, because of the low newspaper circulation previously mentioned.

There was no way other than a military coup by a group of officers who were confident of public support but could not mobilize people behind them in advance. That's what I mean when I say that the media in 1952 basically played a revelatory role rather than a creative or revolutionary role. The movement turned into a 'revolution' not by mass mobilization but through what the movement did, the measures it took, and the laws it promulgated. That's what made it truly worthy of the title 'revolution' after being at first merely a 'movement.'

What happened on January 25, 2011 could be described as a revolution the same day and a very few days later, not because of what the revolutionaries had done and the slogans they raised, but simply because they managed to bring so many people together in what has been fairly described as a million-person rally. This was only possible, of course, through media. Those large numbers who could not have been mobilized in 1952 through rallies in universities, schools, and factories could be mobilized by cell phone, the Internet, and Facebook—media that could not be muzzled by government control, as newspapers and broadcasting could—and as soon as the young people and their supporters had gathered in public squares, television played an important role in adding to their enthusiasm and doubling their numbers. It's true that the government controlled the official television channels, but these channels had lost their monopoly and much of their audience years ago, replaced by private channels, Egyptian, Arab, and foreign, that had won people's trust more and tried to maintain this trust by reporting what was really happening in the street.

To the voice that radio conveyed and the words that were printed in the newspapers, television added pictures, which multiplied the impact of the news reports, especially if they were about something like a popular uprising. Pictures in the media can easily be manipulated in a way that enhances the effect. Merely arranging pictures in a sequence, giving some pictures more time than others, choosing pictures that produce a certain effect, and excluding others can increase or reduce the effect of any given news story, and the story may become an inspirational piece of rhetoric or a work of art, hitting the target more powerfully than any story published in the newspapers or heard on the radio. If carefully chosen music is added to the words and the pictures, the polemical effect is multiplied, attracting new numbers every day to the revolutionaries gathered in the squares.

Some of the television channels that came to us from abroad seemed to have their own objective to fan the flames of revolution, not just to increase their advertising revenue, since some of them don't broadcast any advertisements anyway, but for other unknown reasons possibly connected to the politics of the countries that finance them. They not only broadcast pictures of the demonstrations as they happened minute by minute but also brought in commentators to explain and interpret them, and they chose commentators they knew would favor the revolutionaries, while not inviting those who would not be supportive. In this way the role of the media went way beyond merely 'covering' the revolution. They did in fact make an effective contribution to making and steering the revolution.

In the days following the January 25 revolution Egyptians grew accustomed to seeing ministers and the prime minister on their television screens as soon as they were appointed, announcing to people what they intended to do. Then the military men who had taken power felt it was essential that those in power appear on screen in their turn in order to win public opinion over to their side. We saw some members of the ruling military council face to face and we saw their facial expressions, by which we could judge how sincere they were in what they said and how good or bad their intentions were. We also saw a prominent writer on television, sharply criticizing and embarrassing the prime minister in a confrontation that was followed a few hours later by the prime minister's resignation and replacement. A few slips of the tongue on television were the downfall of a deputy prime minister, damaging his reputation and contributing, along with other similar mistakes, to his departure from government. The meetings that senior officials held with politicians or writers and intellectuals started to take place on camera and were broadcast live on television.

So with the January 25 revolution television became a basic tool on which the revolutionaries relied, on the one hand, and those in power used to appease them, on the other. The two sides competed to control it in the belief that it was the most important influence on public opinion, instead of old methods such as making speeches, publishing articles in newspapers, or talking on the radio. Whom to select to head a television channel and whether to keep or dismiss a certain broadcaster were now important decisions that called for political acumen and had to be made carefully and cautiously. But using television also became an important way to get out of major political predicaments. It could be used with success to solve a major problem, or used badly, making the problem more complicated.

The trial of the deposed president and his sons was apparently one of these major political predicaments that they sought to resolve by resorting to television. People were insistent that the former president and his sons must rapidly go on trial, and they took this as a test of how loyal the new rulers were to the objectives behind the revolution. But the new rulers found themselves under intense pressure, from abroad and domestically, to treat the former president and his family in a completely different manner, possibly to the extent of saving them from any punishment. So the best course of action was to string it out as long as possible in the hope that the problem would solve itself with the passage of time. But people repeatedly demanded a trial and would not stop. The way out was to hold a trial that was broadcast live on television, with the deposed president lying on a stretcher and his sons appearing behind bars in the courtroom, but the session was very short and was soon brought to an end.

It was said that there was not a single house in Egypt that didn't watch those scenes and there was no one walking on the streets while the trial was being broadcast. It was also said that people calmed down after seeing the television images. If that is true, then important decisions are now being made based on what can and cannot be done through television. So the media are no longer merely a means to inform people of events that are happening, but rather they define the course of events, including, for example, whether the deposed president will be punished or not.

5

Revolutions have many positive effects, including exposing hypocrites. Because they strike like powerful and unexpected storms, revolutions take everyone by surprise—those in power, their retainers, and their lackeys—just as a storm takes by surprise the passengers on a ship on the high seas, some while they sleep and others while they are up to no good behind the scenes, whereupon they make futile attempts to cover their naked bodies as quickly as possible and rush in every direction trying to find a way to escape.

When the storm breaks there's no time to hide the stolen loot or to make a pretense of dignity and piety. That's also what happens when an unexpected revolution starts: what was hidden is brought to light and those who were pretending to be serious and imperturbable are shown to be big buffoons in reality. Those who were acting as public exponents of the official line turn out to be parrots repeating what they were told. The advocates of 'new thinking' turn out never to have had a bright thought in their lives, and senior officials turn out to have been thieves just like the junior officials. A media official had been busy taking in and paying out thousands of pounds to some prominent person and the man in charge of the police was distracted from his job providing security because he was busy arranging for Copts to be murdered as they came out of church, and then procuring camels and mules for "thugs" to ride into Tahrir Square, and so on.

The revolution in Tunisia, which happened a few weeks before the revolution in Egypt, enabled us to see the fascinating sight of secret cupboards hidden behind bookshelves, with stacks upon stacks of banknotes of various currencies, and boxes full of assorted jewelry accumulated by the deposed Tunisian president and his wife during a twenty-three-year reign throughout which they repeatedly lied about their concern for the interests of the poor. In Egypt the January 25 revolution enabled us to find out things we could not have found out otherwise. Could we have imagined that Hosni Mubarak's family had really accumulated such fantastical amounts of money, or that the members of his retinue owned so many palaces everywhere, or that ministers had really obtained so many millions of square meters of state land? The revolution brought all this to light for us overnight, and in the future we will no doubt hear many more tales on long evenings or read about them in history books and scandal sheets.

But revolutions also expose many hypocrites, large and small, just as a violent storm throws up dead bodies to be found by people walking along the beach in the morning—insects, small fish, and enormous animals that have breathed their last.

Yes, there are many small hypocrites, people who were forced by difficult circumstances to do the regime's bidding and not to speak about the injustices they saw in front of their eyes. We might forgive them more than the others and, because they were poor and in need, overlook the small acts of deceit they committed. But there were also many outrages by ministers, senior officials, writers, and artists—people who didn't need more money or positions that would bring them only spurious authority and more money, of which they already had enough to keep them, their children, and their grandchildren for hundreds of years. Some of these people were stunned into silence by the shock and had nothing to say. But others showed a remarkable ability to adapt, suddenly trying to pose as supporters and advocates of the revolution. This latter group of hypocrites might have amazed people by the way they changed sides so quickly were it not for the fact that those who had experience of them and knew their history knew full well that they had done the same thing several times before with different rulers. Some of them had lived in the time of the youth organization that a socialist ruler had set up and sung the praises of socialism, and had then strongly defended the Open Door policy launched by a capitalist ruler. They were once famous for their intense hostility toward Israel when the ruler was intensely hostile, but later for advocating prudence and opposing fanaticism when the ruler agreed to reconciliation and negotiations, whereupon they sang his praises as the hero of war and peace. Then, when the socialist ruler and the capitalist ruler were gone and a ruler came who didn't believe in either socialism or capitalism or in anything at all other than rapine and plunder, they went along with his rapine and plunder and sang the praises of his calm, his prudence, and his dislike of the electric shock method. They gave him new titles such as "the bomber pilot who struck the first blow" and changed the history books to make him, rather than his predecessor, the hero of war and peace.

All these people were taken by surprise by the revolution of January 25, but some of them maintained enough composure and self-control to change their stance quietly and sedately. Some said they had been defending the previous regime out of sincere conviction, but democracy was naturally superior and the will of the people must of course be respected. Some performed acrobatics to forge new friendships quickly with senior opposition figures. But there were some hypocrites who saw no need to offer any defense or to pretend that they had long been part of the struggle. They immediately slipped into the new revolutionary discourse, relying on the fact that most people had not read what they had written only two days before the downfall of the president, or relying on people's poor memories or simply on repetition, since repeating a lie is in itself enough to make the lie sound true and to make a professional fraudster look like a respectable man.

I won't say more about such people because no doubt we will hear all of them tell many stories in the future, but I now want to speak about another category of people, not usually classified as hypocrites although it includes individuals who are more hypocritical and much more harmful. I mean those rulers of major countries who lie endlessly to serve the interests of their countries and who heaped praise on our despotic rulers, provided them with the money and weapons they used against their own people, and treated them with great affection and respect. Yet when the interests of those countries changed and they needed other rulers, they turned against their old friends, accused them of the most heinous crimes, acted as if they had suddenly remembered the benefits of democracy and the evils of despotism, and joined those calling for freedom as if they had never helped to deny it to the very same people.

The United States supported the Hosni Mubarak regime throughout the thirty years he spent in power. It gave him more military and economic aid than it gave any other country in the world other than Israel and provided his police state with the equipment it needed to face down the Egyptian people, trained officers to use the equipment, and allowed, in fact encouraged, international institutions to give it financial help without any objections related to democracy or human rights, whereas it often used that pretext to prevent aid to and even impose economic sanctions on other countries it didn't like. The man, his sons, and his entourage were welcomed to Washington time after time. Then the United States suddenly turned against Hosni Mubarak. Its praise turned to censure, and instead of offering aid, it threatened to cut it off or reduce it. The United States had done the same to despotic rulers before, suspending aid as soon as it realized that their downfall might be more useful than propping them up. It had done that with Marcos in the Philippines, the shah in Iran, Saddam Hussein in Iraq, and so on. Dictatorship suddenly ceased to be a blessing and became a curse, and what could be more hypocritical than that?

Let's look at the attitude of all western countries toward Muammar Qadhafi, whom they befriended and flattered for more than forty years. The Italian prime minister lavished praise on him and didn't object to his recruiting Italian girls when Qadhafi thought it would be useful to Islam to shower money on them if they announced that they had suddenly discovered the greatness of Islam. Then Italy and the other western countries suddenly announced they were distancing themselves from Qadhafi, as if they realized only that day that he had been governing his people with an iron fist and squandering his country's money on crazy projects, driven by a degree of megalomania rarely encountered in history. The western world was patient with this man and continued to humor him for forty years, while it would have been the easiest thing in the world to get rid of him in any of the hundreds of ways they use to get rid of rulers who are loved by their people and known to be honorable and patriotic when it is in their interests to get rid of them.

In short, while it is important to expose all the forms of hypocrisy practiced by our small-time hypocrites throughout the thirty years that the deposed president ruled Egypt, it is also important that we don't pay homage in gratitude to big hypocrites simply because they happened to support us in overthrowing him, because it really was just a coincidence, a temporary convergence of their interests with our hopes, without there being any real change in their hearts or their intentions.

6

The Egyptian revolution started in the wake of a successful revolution in Tunisia and was followed by uprisings in other countries that promised similar success. Encouraging signs in one country reinforced the reasons to celebrate in the other countries. The world spoke about an Arab spring, after a long, miserable winter. Many official circles in foreign countries, including great powers, spoke of how they supported what had happened in Egypt and offered us aid. The two prestigious financial institutions, the International Monetary Fund and the World Bank, joined the side in favor and in their turn offered generous support for the Egyptian economy.

Yes, Egyptians were killed, the Egyptian economy suffered a severe shock, mistakes were made choosing some of the new officials, some of those mistakes were corrected and others were not, but all this could not destroy the spirit of optimism until five months after the removal of the president, when suddenly clouds gathered in the skies and people began to wonder whether they were right to be optimistic.

It was quite understandable that in the wave of jubilation people might overlook the immediate reality, which was that a revolution like this in a country like Egypt was bound to have important and powerful enemies, and that they would not let matters proceed in the way Egyptians hoped without putting obstacles in the way. Yes, it was understandable that people would overlook this but, to be honest, I was astonished and I remain astonished by how little has been said or written to try to define who exactly is hostile to the revolution, to analyze their motives and what positions they are likely to take. We have seen everyone carried away by emotional expressions of support or condemnation, as if the events were so momentous that they relieved us of the responsibility to think and analyze. I was also quite astonished, and I still am, that people could keep talking about what was happening in Egypt as if Egypt were alone, an island isolated from the rest of the world, and as if what was happening there depended solely on the outcome of an internal struggle between the supporters of the new system and the supporters, or remnants, of the old regime, while the world looked on like a spectator awaiting the outcome.

In the first days of the revolution and before Hosni Mubarak stepped down, U.S. President Barack Obama and his secretary of state made some amazing statements, all of them including overt support for the revolution and appeals to the Egyptian president to respond promptly to the revolution's demands. The U.S. president even used the word "immediately" to describe how Hosni Mubarak needed to act. When a former U.S. ambassador known for his strong links with Hosni Mubarak returned to Egypt and announced after meeting the president that he thought Mubarak should stay on in the presidency, the U.S. secretary of state soon said that he was expressing only his personal opinion and not the opinion of the U.S. administration.

This U.S. position in support of the revolution continued even after the revolution succeeded, and this represented a surprising development in the attitude of the United States toward Egypt. Analysts had a responsibility to set about trying to understand and explain it, but this is something I haven't seen reflected in the Egyptian and foreign commentaries I have read. This reluctance to explain the change in the U.S. position cannot be explained by saying that it's unimportant, because it's self-evident how important what happens in Egypt is to the whole Arab world and to the Zionist project, and also how important it is whether the United States favors or opposes it. I'm inclined to attribute this reluctance in the Egyptian media to the fact that emotions were running so high that people shied away from an attempt to analyze. In the case of the foreign media, I have long been accustomed to the fact that it is not inclined to highlight the role of the great powers in developments in Third World countries. On the contrary, it is excessively inclined to attribute what happens purely to internal factors, so that responsibility always falls on the shoulders of these countries, which rarely enjoy free will to do what they want, and in this way the great powers can evade responsibility.

I have read some Egyptian and foreign commentaries that express the belief that the U.S. administration must have been frightened and sorry at what happened in Egypt, since Hosni Mubarak had been a loyal ally throughout his presidency. These commentaries ignored official U.S. statements that suggested exactly the opposite. It's true that official statements often say the opposite of the truth but the U.S. statements I refer to didn't suggest that, because in them the U.S. administration supported the revolution insistently and repeatedly in a way that it wouldn't have needed to do if its real wishes were different.

In fact I don't find this development in the U.S. position at all surprising because this was not the first time, and of course it will not be the last, that the United States or any other great power has abandoned a loyal ally as soon as it decided it no longer needed his services and that he had become more of a liability than an asset. Explaining such a shift in U.S. policy after the event is easier of course than predicting it before it happens, but I do see some strong reasons to explain this U.S. shift in policy toward the regime of Hosni Mubarak.

Corruption is of course a significant element in any regime that provides essential services to a superpower, since a superpower cannot depend on patriotic politicians to carry out policies that are not in the interests of their countries. It has to rely on politicians who put their personal interests ahead of the national interest, and this is the essence of corruption. But corruption can reach a level that the superpower considers too damaging to tolerate. International capital is interested in seeing a certain level of corruption in order to achieve its objectives, especially in the first stages of the transformation from a closed to an open economy, but the foreign investor is also interested in seeing a certain minimal level of stability and respect for the law, which might be compromised by too high a level of corruption.

Perhaps more importantly, the world is changing, and what served the interests of the superpower in one period may not serve them in another. Look, for example, at the U.S. attitude toward King Farouk in Egypt in the 1940s and how it changed after that. During the Second World War, it was desirable that such a regime should survive, and among the Americans and the British who were occupying Egypt no one dreamed of abandoning their support for the monarchy amid a grueling world war fraught with great dangers, including the danger of a German occupation of Egypt. That was no longer the case after the war was over. It's no wonder that there was a succession of military coups in the Third World after the war and that many of them (including the 1952 coup in Egypt, which later changed into a revolution) had the support of the Americans.

In the changes that have started to take place in the world in recent years, it's very possible to see the need for a change in the U.S. position toward a regime such as that of Hosni Mubarak. The twenty-first century began with the United States in a situation quite unlike the situation it was in half a century earlier. For a short time, in the wake of the collapse of the Soviet Union and its satellite regimes, we thought we were entering a long phase of unilateral U.S. domination of the world, and there was much talk of a unipolar system (with one American pole) replacing a system controlled by two superpowers, the United States and the Soviet Union. But it soon became clear that the United States, despite its military superiority over all other countries in the world, was too weak economically to rule the world.

As the economic competition heated up between the United States and the European Union, and between the United States and new powers in East Asia with amazing growth rates, especially China, it became clear that we were on the threshold of a new age based on multiple poles rather than a unipolar age, and that each of these poles would inevitably work to establish a foothold in one part of the world or another at the expense of the other poles in preparation for a new age of competition. It is most unlikely that this competition will reach the stage of war (or at least overt war), as was the case until the middle of the twentieth century, but there will be intense economic competition, maybe no less fierce than military confrontation. In the new era the competition might take the form of struggle between international companies rather than between countries, but governments, with their armies, their diplomats, and their intelligence agencies, will inevitably be mobilized to serve their companies, as they were when the companies were exclusively owned by citizens of one country.

In readiness for this new confrontation with new poles, and with old poles that are recovering their vigor, the United States was bound to rearrange its relationships with its old allies or dependents, including of course the Arab governments. From the perspective of the new age, the Arab regimes, from the Atlantic to the Gulf, must have looked obsolete and lamentably, even ridiculously, decrepit. Can America face its competitors in the new era with allies such as Mubarak, Ben Ali, and Ali Abdallah Saleh? Such people may have been useful in the time of Soviet rivalry, when victory depended on the type of activities practiced by intelligence agencies, such as terrorist acts, to intimidate and threaten, but in an era that basically relies on economic competition, greater economic efficiency was required, and less corruption and more respect for the law. From that perspective many of the Arab regimes seem to belong to a bygone antediluvian era, so it would be useful, essential in fact, to do away with them.

We can find a precedent for what is happening now in what happened to the Arab system sixty years ago, at the end of the 1940s. The United States was equally planning for a new era after the economic collapse of the two old imperial powers, Britain and France, although they had emerged victorious from the Second World War. The United States was planning to inherit their possessions, but America could not rely on old politicians like Nouri al-Said in Iraq, Mustafa al-Nahhas in Egypt, or Camille Chamoun in Lebanon. Military coups seemed more appropriate. In the mid-1950s the U.S. president made a famous statement announcing what became known as the Eisenhower Doctrine. He said that after the era of traditional imperialism in the Middle East, a vacuum had arisen that had to be filled, and he suggested filling it by forming alliances between the United States and the new governments in the Middle East. Abd al-Nasser objected to the Eisenhower Doctrine and offered Arab nationalism as an alternative to alliances with the West, and in that way the Arabs achieved significant successes, until the United States and Israel overcame them with the attack of 1967.

How, one wonders, does the U.S. administration envision filling the void that arose with the fall of the Mubarak regime and other Arab regimes? To what extent does this American vision match or diverge from our own hopes? What exactly are those hopes in a world that is radically different from the one we were used to? What can we do to fulfill those hopes, even if they are at odds with the expectations of powerful foreign states?

Part 3

Reasons for Concern

9 A Revolution or a Coup?

1

There was plenty to rejoice about in what happened in the few months after the January 25 revolution in Egypt, but also plenty to worry about.

The reasons to rejoice were obvious and well known: suddenly seeing a new generation of young Egyptians who combined loyalty to the country with vitality, intelligence, and willingness to make sacrifices and who combined new skills and ideas derived from their openness to the world with confidence in the country's traditions and cultural heritage. It was also gratifying to see Egyptian women daringly taking part in public affairs, revealing no less intelligence, dynamism, and self-sacrifice than their male counterparts.

All this was novel, and it still gladdens me whenever I remember it. The political developments were also heartening, as if a nightmare had ended and a heavy weight was gone from our chests. Those at the top of the regime had been removed, the diabolical plot to put the son in his father's place was done forever, hated ministers and officials were also gone for good, and new ministers and officials had come in—people known to be patriotic and honest—and it was expected that more patriots would replace corrupt officials in various sectors, such as the media, education, culture, the economy, and so on.

How could one not rejoice at all that after decades of misery and frustration? How could all that not make one optimistic about a brilliant future for this country, which had waited long for a single piece of happy news?

But there was also anxiety.

Watching some television program I was taken aback to hear a journalist say "separating ownership from management," an expression I hadn't come across as a way to describe what happened in the January 25 revolution. In economics we talk about separating ownership of a joint-stock company (a company owned by the shareholders, that is) from the company management when the managers don't hold any equity in the company they are running. What the journalist really meant was that the people who carried out the revolution, or created it out of nothing (and therefore deserve to be called its owners), were not the people who were making the crucial decisions on running the country: they didn't choose the prime minister or the other ministers and they didn't make the basic decisions relevant to the country's future after the revolution.

What would seem normal in revolutions is that those who carry out the revolution are the ones who make the crucial decisions and run the country after the revolution succeeds. That was the case in the French and Russian revolutions, the Egyptian revolution of 1919, and its revolution of 1952. So what are the implications of this split between "ownership" and "management"? There are aspects that are reassuring, and others that are troubling.

It is reassuring that the army, whose commanders took on the management, complied with the wishes of the revolutionaries, not just by protecting them from the might of the regime and hence enabling them to keep up the pressure until the downfall of the president and his senior aides, but also by replacing certain ministers who had stayed in place even after the deposed president had stepped down, and then again by replacing the prime minister who had taken his oath of office in front of the old president with a new prime minister who had the approval of the revolutionaries. After that it looked like the revolutionaries might calm down. But it was disturbing to note how the revolutionaries remained distant from the management or decision-making process.

Questions arose, for example, about the delay in preventing the shredding and burning of files in State Security premises until protesters moved in to secure them, and about the delay in getting rid of certain people who still held very important and influential positions, some of them in the presidency, others in the civil service, the media, and economic, educational, and cultural institutions.

One could excuse all that on the grounds that it was still only a short time since the former president had stepped down and it was not possible to do everything overnight. But among the positions I mentioned there were some of the kind that did require decisions that could be, indeed must be, made overnight and not of the kind that could take weeks or months.

On the other hand, it could be excused on the grounds that those who carried out the revolution did not have leaders to speak in their name, so it wasn't easy to discover the demands of the revolutionaries or their wishes with any clarity or certainty, and that anyway the Supreme Council of the Armed Forces had tried after taking power to find out what these demands and wishes were by meeting representatives of the young revolutionaries or sitting down with opinion makers who were close to them. It might also be said that this revolution was the work of individuals or groups that didn't belong to political parties or known ideologies and only rallied around general undefined slogans, such as demanding bread, freedom, and dignity, and that this made it difficult to guess what would or would not satisfy them or to choose the figures they would accept or reject.

Both of these excuses are perfectly understandable, but there were ways to deal with these problems and overcome the difficulties they created that didn't happen. Many people called for a presidential council that would make fundamental and pressing decisions on behalf of the revolutionaries, who had no known leader to speak in their name and did not follow the banner of a party with a clear political platform. This presidential council could include civilians and military men, and there could be a referendum on the names of the members, and it wouldn't be difficult to choose names that were generally accepted and enjoyed broad popularity, to be put to the public in a referendum.

If this presidential council had been formed, it would have been necessary to let it perform some of the crucial and urgent tasks, including removing from office some of the officials who were unacceptable to the public and who nonetheless still held important and influential positions, and appointing others who were acceptable, as well as forming councils or committees to start work immediately on preparing urgent plans to reform the economy, education, the media, and the basic principles of foreign policy, even if complete plans would need more time.

There was no need to hurry the parliamentary or presidential elections. Elections can produce the desired results only if they meet certain basic conditions that did not exist when the revolution began and that we first had to create. We really needed a period to catch our breath after a long ordeal that had sapped our energies. The elections should have been postponed until some vital adjustments were made to the general social climate.

First, law and order needed to be restored in the streets and a good relationship established between the people and the police, because normal elections cannot be held when people are afraid of what the police might do to them or what might be done to them in the absence of the police. This requirement was self-evident and was urgently needed, whether or not elections were held.

Second, the prestige of the judiciary needed to be restored, and people needed to feel confident that they would be treated justly and addressed reasonably promptly if they were wronged, whether in elections or in some other way, and without exorbitant expenses.

Third, there should have been enough time for people to express themselves freely, to exchange ideas and form parties. Egyptians had undergone more than thirty years with severe restrictions on freedom of expression and opinion and on the freedom to form parties. They were subjected throughout to a constant cacophony of lies promoting those without merit and allowing professional deceivers and liars to monopolize the basic media and deny access to others. Amid this cacophony no real leaders were allowed to emerge, although the country had plenty of worthy people fit to lead.

The task was so much easier for the revolutionaries of July 1952 than for those of January 2011. In both cases the aims of the revolution included achieving sound democracy. But when the Free Officers carried out their revolution on July 23, there wasn't chaos in the streets of Egypt because the police had disappeared. On the contrary, the police joined up with the army, immediately and with great enthusiasm, to serve the revolution and protect the public. Decay hadn't started to burrow into the Egyptian judiciary, as it had for the past thirty years. The methods of deception and lying that were available in Mubarak's time weren't available to the monarchy, either in terms of the amount of money used or in terms of propaganda and media techniques. Under the monarchy, political party activity, despite all the corruption, was much less corrupt than it was before the January revolution. The biggest party in Egypt before July 1952, the Wafd Party, had started to weaken and was under constant attack by the palace and the royalist newspapers, but the Wafd Party did not make a truce with the king and none of its leaders, or any other party leaders in Egypt for that matter, agreed to sell their consciences cheaply to the monarchist system in the way that many leaders of so-called opposition parties had in the years leading up to January 2011.

The biggest obstacle the 1952 revolutionaries faced in trying to set up a sound democratic system in Egypt was the feudal, or quasi-feudal, system. The landowners' ability to mobilize voters and buy votes was enough to produce a parliament that did not reflect the interests of the majority of poor Egyptians, but rather the interests of landowners allied with the British. Feudalism is no longer the basic obstacle to a democratic system; instead it is the pervasive corruption in the civil service and in local councils, and the exploitation of state authority and funds to buy people and buy votes, that made possible the regime's subservience to the United States and Israel.

The Free Officers clearly understood in July 1952 that the first step toward creating a real democracy and a break with subservience to the British would be to attack feudalism, and that is what they did first. They passed the agricultural reform law in September 1952, less than two months after the revolution. It should be just as clear to us now that hopes of bringing about real democracy and escaping subservience to the United States and Israel depend on combating the corruption that is rampant in every part of the country, in political parties and economic life, in the media and culture, in the education system, and so on. Just as the July revolution tracked down the pashas and beys of the royal court and clipped their wings, the January revolution should have tracked down the pashas of the Mubarak era and eliminated the influence they derived from the nexus of money and power.

2

As mentioned before, when the revolution of July 23, 1952 took place, it wasn't called a revolution at first. It was called a movement. People and the media, and even the officers who carried it out, described it as the Army Movement, the Free Officers Movement, or the "Blessed Movement." The foreign media called it a military coup. The term 'revolution' wasn't used until a few months later; as soon as the term was used it became widely accepted, and within a few years there was no longer any doubt that what had happened really was a revolution.

In the first days it did look like just a military coup that had deposed King Farouk and replaced him with a group of officers who formed what was called a "revolutionary command council," which became the highest authority in the country. At first the term 'revolution' seemed too grand and too weighty for what the officers had done, although deposing the king was a popular demand. A revolution presupposes vast throngs coming out into the streets and forcing those in power, one way or another, to relinquish their power to those accepted and approved by the people. A revolution also implies demands for radical changes in political, economic, and social life, not just the deposition of a king or a president. Those two conditions were not met by the Officers Movement on July 23 because the movement was planned in secret and it took people by surprise as much as it surprised the king and his entourage. The officers' demands, which they summarized in the famous six principles of the revolution, even if they included the demand for some fundamental changes, looked like a brief political pamphlet mentioning very general objectives, such as creating a sound democratic system and forming a strong national army, but without anything to indicate what kind of steps the officers had decided to take.

Gradually the movement or the coup earned the right to be called a revolution. The overwhelming popular support it received made up for the fact that the masses had not played a role at the start. Then there was a succession of measures and laws that were revolutionary in the full sense of the word and that brought about deep changes in the political, social, and economic system: the agricultural reform law, which abolished feudalism almost in the blink of an eye, the dissolution of political parties, the abolition of titles, the introduction of free education, the nationalization of the Suez Canal, and the start of work on the Aswan High Dam; then the nationalization of banks and foreign insurance companies, the creation of a planning council, the drafting of an ambitious industrialization plan and then a comprehensive five-year plan for development. These were followed by widespread nationalization and an extraordinary expansion of the state's role in providing basic social services, such as education, health, and housing, and including workers in the management of the companies where they worked and in sharing the profits among them.

If all this doesn't deserve to be described as a revolution, then what does? There have been many important critiques of what the officers did in the 1952 revolution, but this is not our subject now. Our subject is that what began as a movement or an officers' coup ended up as a real revolution.

On January 25, 2011, a massive popular uprising broke out across the country, an uprising unprecedented in the history of Egypt, both in size and in the way that, from the point of view of geography, class, and religion, it was widely representative and included people of all educational levels and shades of political belief.

Yes, the slogans were vague and the demands were not clearly defined, but they included the demand for changes in multiple aspects of political, economic, and social life, and the participants behaved in a way that promised that these changes might really begin to take place, such as cooperation between Muslims and Copts, between men and women, and between members of different classes. So it wasn't strange that what happened should be widely described as a revolution, by ordinary people and in the Egyptian and foreign media, and no one seemed surprised by the use of this term.

The army protected the January revolutionaries, supported them, and helped them depose the former president, just as sixty years ago the people supported the Army Movement on July 23 and facilitated its mission. But what happened after the president stepped down on February 11, and why did progress seem to be so slow, as if it constantly needed another push by the January revolutionaries?

The basic demand of the January 25 revolutionaries was 'regime change,' and this was the slogan the revolutionaries wrote on their banners and constantly chanted. Their other top demands included the release of political detainees who had not been tried and an end to corruption. After the events of January 28 and 29, when the police withdrew from their positions, opened the prison gates, and left streets and shops prey to thugs and some policemen themselves, other demands were added, such as the arrest and trial of those responsible for withdrawing the police. Then, after the tragic events of February 2, known as the Battle of the Camel, the revolutionaries demanded the arrest and trial of those responsible for these events.

People noticed that the response to these demands was unjustifiably slow, and to some demands partial and incomplete. It was understandable that the first government formed after the revolution should be headed by a man who had long cooperated with the old regime and that it should include ministers who belonged to the same era. But when a new government was formed, even after the overthrow of the president, the prime minister was unchanged and some of the ministers affiliated to the old regime were retained. Things changed when a new government under Essam Sharaf came in, but people noted a number of things that raised questions. Why was the deputy prime minister unchanged from the previous cabinet? Why did it contain the same minister of finance who was in the first cabinet appointed after January 25, when the former president was still in power? People also noted that a number of ministers in the new government were very close, in one way or another, to the governments of the old regime, and people were surprised to discover that some senior officials in the presidency and in the state media, people who had served the old regime and cooperated with it fully, even devoted themselves to its service, were still doing their old jobs as if nothing had happened.

Yes, some senior officials accused of corruption were arrested, had their assets frozen, and were banned from leaving the country and interrogated, and some of them were charged. But it is noticeable that these measures were taken in a way that was selective and had no clear basis, as if some of the corrupt were more favored than others, and in the meantime some of the young revolutionaries were treated brutally and cruelly, in a way that could not be justified in the context of a successful revolution that had the blessing of the supreme council, which had the power to make decisions at the highest level.

All these were disturbing signs suggesting that the new authorities in Egypt were less enthusiastic about overthrowing the old regime and improving the general social climate than those who carried out the revolution in the first place.

About two years after the revolution of July 1952 there was a serious split between the leaders of the revolution. The president at the time, Muhammad Nagib, was more inclined to let political life resume its normal course as before the revolution, now that Egypt had done away with the monarchy and its corruption, and to send the army back to barracks, handing over power to an elected assembly, whereas another faction, led by Gamal Abd al-Nasser, thought it would be premature for the army to give up power and hold parliamentary elections. At the time we supported Muhammad Nagib and demanded that the army return to barracks, but Gamal Abd al-Nasser won out over Nagib, Nagib lost power forever, and the army stayed in power despite us. After that we were surprised to find the Egyptian regime starting a new phase that was historic and brilliant. Egypt joined the group of non-aligned states and became a leader in positive neutrality between the two rival blocs in the Cold War. The nationalization of the Suez Canal and the union between Egypt and Syria soon followed, then the announcement of a five-year development plan, then the nationalizations of 1961, which launched a new era of rapid economic development, industrialization, and a substantial level of social justice.

In the case of the 2011 revolution, it seemed that the opposite was happening. The army wanted to give up power quickly by holding parliamentary elections, although it had been a very short time since the end of a long period of political life that was much more corrupt than political life before the 1952 revolution. The old parties were weaker and less authentic than the pre-1952 parties, as under Mubarak there was no freedom to set up parties and the main media were monopolized in a way that prevented the emergence of any real leaders comparable to the leaders that existed at the end of the monarchy. In the 1952 revolution, the army turned out to be more revolutionary than the people, while in the case of the 2011 revolution it turned out to be quite the opposite. It began as a military coup in 1952, and then changed over time into an indisputable revolution. Is it really possible that what began as a revolution in January 2011 could change with the passage of time into a coup whose only mission was to change the head of the regime and some of the people around him, without reaching out to uproot all manifestations of corruption?

3

Some years before Hosni Mubarak stepped down from the presidency, his supporters began a campaign to pave the way for his son Gamal to succeed him. People were deeply worried that this diabolical scheme might become a reality, that after this long period of corrupt rule, which lasted more than a quarter of a century, there would come another similar reign that could last just as long or even longer, given the son's relatively young age. At the time Hosni Mubarak was asked more than once whether such a succession plan existed and he would always give exasperating answers, such as that his son had never spoken to him on the subject or that it was too early to talk about it. Such answers appeared in interviews published in newspapers or broadcast by other media. But there was another answer, more irritating and exasperating, heard by some of those close to him and passed on to others, even if it was never published in the media. I personally believe that it came from him because it's consistent with the way he spoke and thought, judging by the dozens of interviews he gave and comments he made, whether published or not.

It was said that when asked if there really was a succession plan, Mubarak answered, "And what do you think I would want to pass on to him? The country's a ruin!"

This remark is similar, for example, to a comment he made when some opposition groups planned to form an alternative parliament after the 2010 elections were completely rigged. "Let them have fun!" was all he said at the time. His comments are also consistent with his attitude when a ferry sank in the Red Sea on its way back from Saudi Arabia, killing more than a thousand Egyptians. Mubarak saw no need to go to the scene of the accident and he did not issue a statement of condolence to the families of the victims. Instead, straight after the accident, he went to watch the national soccer squad in training. It's also consistent with his attitude toward the acts of violence between Egyptians and Algerians in the wake of a soccer match, when he didn't appear to show any concern at a possible deterioration in Egypt's relations with Algeria.

He was an amazing man in more than one respect, with little ability to sense what Egyptians felt, to distinguish between a passing incident and a national disaster, or to understand that if Egypt was really "a ruin" then he was the one primarily responsible, whether or not he passed the presidency to his son. But one has to admit that if the succession plan had gone through, then when the heir inherited the country it really would have been almost a wasteland.

Since Mubarak stepped down on February 11 there have been endless revelations about very bad things, things we didn't know about or that we didn't imagine could be so bad. Only a day or two after we felt the revolution had achieved its basic objective, workers, civil servants, and professionals started demonstrating to demand better conditions. In every demonstration the protesters disclosed incidents of corruption they knew about and could easily prove and called for their bosses to be dismissed because of them. Then people working in the press and television demanded their bosses be dismissed, revealing serious abuses of power in those institutions and extraordinary and inconceivable discrepancies between what some lucky associates of the boss were earning and what the other staff earned. Then fires broke out in State Security premises in various parts of the country and the purpose was said to be to get rid of important documents that recorded instances of torture and illegal eavesdropping. Then demonstrations and sit-ins began at a university faculty to demand the immediate dismissal of the dean on the grounds that he belonged to a network of corruption in the old regime and should not be allowed to continue as dean after the regime's fall. As soon as the students and staff in other faculties heard what the students in the first faculty had done, they demonstrated in their turn for similar reasons. Then the demands escalated to include the dismissal of the university presidents for the same reasons. Some of the people who had been wronged by officials of the old regime felt that this was their chance to demand recompense. Since everyone was demonstrating and making demands, why shouldn't they speak out and strike while the iron was hot? So every day groups of men or women gathered outside the cabinet office or parliament demanding jobs or proper work contracts instead of the short-term contracts their employers had long insisted on but that gave them no right to pensions or health insurance, or demanding rights for the disabled or that a long-promised road finally be built, and so on.

In the meantime a fire broke out in a church in the village of Atfih and the Copts vehemently protested, demanding the security agencies arrest the perpetrators and rebuild the church. Then there was a succession of fights between Muslims and Copts, and people were killed, and one Copt had his ear cut off. Then there were numerous incidents of Muslims and Copts exchanging insults, and a Salafist gave a sermon likening the referendum on constitutional amendments to the first wave of Muslim invasions in the seventh century, and urging those opposed to the proposed amendments to leave Egypt and migrate to other countries if they wanted. Then new provincial governors were appointed and the people of Qena objected to their new governor because they thought he had a dishonorable record of hostility toward the objectives of the revolution. They were so angry that they blocked the railway line between Qena and Luxor, and Qena was unable to obtain necessities that came from other provinces. In the meantime one of the demonstrators came forward and said that the reason the new governor wasn't acceptable was that he was a Copt and that they wanted a Muslim governor instead.

So no new day would come without one reading in the newspapers or hearing on television about a new demonstration, a new quarrel, a new case of sectarian strife, a complaint about a new instance of previously unknown corruption, or the addition of a new name to the list of those detained or banned from leaving the country because of some allegation of corruption or wasting public money.

A dreadful scene occurred to me. There was a man who owned an amazing palace he had inherited from his wealthy ancestors, spacious, surrounded by lush gardens, and finely furnished. He lived there with his wife and children but unexpected circumstances forced him to rent the palace for some years to a tenant he hadn't met before. It then emerged that the tenant had an evil scheme that involved converting the palace into a lucrative source of ample profit for himself, even if it required turning the palace into a ruin. As soon as the tenant stepped foot in the palace he started to take measures that were sure to prevent the owner from ever coming back. For that purpose he called in a group of unscrupulous lawyers who could forge contracts and brought in a number of vicious guard dogs to pounce on anyone who tried to approach the house.

Then he began to carry out his evil scheme. While the tenant kept the upper floor for himself, the rest of the palace was divided into rooms and suites, each with its own bathroom, and he sublet each of them to separate families. Then he built some shops in the palace gardens and let them out to people who wanted to use them as shops, cafés, or restaurants. He auctioned off the palace balconies to people who wanted to take advantage of the palace's excellent location and put up boards on them advertising products such as Vodafone or Nancy Ajram's latest album.

The tenant then had another evil scheme: to split the ground floor into two wings, renting one to an Islamic association and the other to a Coptic association. He allowed both of them to set up loudspeakers facing the other wing to broadcast sermons and religious services, which aroused sectarian tensions and led to constant quarrels between them. The tenant would intervene just in time to collect protection money from both sides, on the grounds that he was defending them from an evil conspiracy the other side intended to carry out. The two sides went on submissively paying protection money, although they were not fully convinced of the man's good intentions.

The other rooms and wings had been let to people who couldn't find accommodation elsewhere because of their bad reputations. In their wings these people would entertain men and women of every kind, most of whom would sleep all day and stay up at night. The people who lived in the houses nearby would sometimes wake up in panic in the middle of the night to the sound of depraved laughter from the people living in the palace and their visitors. They would see liquor bottles being thrown from the balconies and leftovers being thrown into the gardens, and through the open windows they would glimpse scenes of debauchery.

The garden around the palace gradually turned into a rubbish dump, and the people in the nearby houses started to smell noxious odors, the cause of which they couldn't exactly determine, though there was no doubt that they all came from that house that had once been a palace but was now a collection of restaurants, cafés, shops, and brothels, even if from time to time, at various hours of days and night, the loudspeakers could be heard calling on people to worship God and perform the other rites of their religion, sometimes Islam and sometimes Christianity.

The people living nearby decided that all this had to come to an end, so they formed a delegation to go to the owner, who had come back from abroad with his family and was living nearby, but they didn't dare to approach his house because of the wild dogs. He told them he had done everything possible to regain possession of his palace but to no avail. The lawyers he consulted told him that, from the day he set foot in the house, the tenant had done everything to ensure he could stay there for the rest of his life, and that his son and then his grandson could stay on after him. The tenants' specialist lawyers had drawn up forged contracts including all this and allowing him to use the house in the manner we have described, and when the owner had challenged this in court the judge who heard the case turned out to be one of the tenants.

The only way out was to threaten to start a fire that would consume all the people living in the palace if they didn't vacate the palace immediately. The threat was made but the tenant and the others made light of it at first, saying it was the fantasy of a bunch of youngsters. But things changed completely when the wild dogs attacked and killed a group of youngsters who approached the palace in an attempt to assault it. The rest of them then marched on the house carrying torches to set fire to the palace with everyone inside.

There's no need to go into the details of what happened after that, because the story had a happy ending (or at least seemed to have one). The tenant and all the people living in the palace ran away, and the owner broke into his palace and went in with his wife and children for the first time in many years.

We can imagine how delighted the owner and his family were, and the people in the whole neighborhood, too. But the first shock came as soon as the family stepped foot in the main hall, because instead of the luxurious furniture they had left there all they found was a bare hall. They discovered that even the wooden floor, which had been designed by a famous artist, had been ripped up and all that was visible was an ugly concrete floor. All they found of the magnificent paintings that had decorated the walls was a single painting with faded colors and large black stains, and its costly frame had been replaced with one made of tin sheeting.

When the owner put his trembling hand on the doorknob to one of the rooms, dreading what he might find inside, the first thing he came across was the head of a long snake lurking behind the door and waiting for it to open. He slammed the door shut and tried another room, where he was attacked by a number of cats that had apparently been trapped inside for ages and were ravenously hungry. He stepped back and shut the door quickly, since he no longer had any doubt that the palace really was a ruin and that he and his family would have to sit on the sidewalk, think things over, and decide what to do.

It was to be expected that the sons and daughters would each have different ideas about how to restore the palace to its former glory and refurnish it, each according to his or her age and taste. Naturally all his sons and daughters were also in a hurry to go back to their rooms after such a long time away. But when their father saw that they were deeply divided and even close to fighting, he thought it necessary to tell them off and put them in their place. He told them that nothing should be done until they had exterminated the snakes and got rid of the wild cats. It's true that it wouldn't be wise to open all the doors at the same time, because it would be impossible to control all the snakes and poisonous insects that would come out, but it would be completely wrong to imagine that it was time to listen to all opinions and take votes.

4

When I saw what Dr. Nabil al-Arabi, who held the post of foreign minister, had done to reform Egyptian foreign policy in less than two months, I had many thoughts I would like to share.

Was this man a magician who visited us and touched our foreign policies with his magic wand, one after another, and suddenly they became balanced and straightforward when once they were in complete collapse from neglect or bad management?

In order to set our relationship with Iran straight, is it true that all it took was for one sensible man to come along and say just five words— "Iran is not our enemy"—instead of all that nonsense about Iran taking part in conferences that threaten our national security, accusing Iran of killing our ambassador in Iraq, or engaging in a foolish argument with Iran because it named a street after the man who assassinated President Sadat, as if we were inventing reasons for a quarrel in order to please certain parties that wish us no good?

In order to revive Palestinian confidence in us and restore respect for Egypt, is it true that all it took was for us to appoint as foreign minister a man who was able to describe accurately the blockade we had imposed on Gaza and the way its inhabitants had been deprived of some essential foodstuffs, even if it took only one word, when he said that the blockade by Egypt was "shameful"? Did it really require a magician to understand the immoral aspect of the way we had been treating the people of Gaza, when the whole world had rallied to their support and men and women had come from all over to express their rejection of Israeli policy, so much so that a young American woman had given her life standing in the way of an Israeli bulldozer?

Did it require a magician to bring the feuding Palestinian factions to meet together and reconcile in readiness to face their common enemy as a united front? Nabil al-Arabi did that, without saying anything to claim credit for himself and without filling the media with boasts and bluster. Could Egypt really have a foreign minister who wasn't as interested in his public image as in Egyptian and Arab interests and in the moral aspects of policy?

At the same time as Nabil al-Arabi was doing this or that, he traveled to central Africa in an attempt to solve the problem of Egypt's share of the Nile waters, and gave Foreign Ministry support to the unofficial Egyptian delegation that went there for the same purpose—an unusual step, as far as I know, in the history of Egyptian diplomacy. I also don't remember seeing pictures of earlier Egyptian foreign ministers sitting with the Coptic pope, as Nabil al-Arabi did, in an attempt to use the Coptic Church's influence over the Ethiopian state to solve the water problem in Egypt's favor, after coming back from visiting Rome to meet the pope at the Vatican for the same purpose.

Of course there was nothing magic about it. It was much simpler and clearer than that, to anyone with eyes, and because it was simpler and clearer Nabil al-Arabi won the esteem and affection of people in Egypt and in the rest of the Arab world almost in the blink of an eye, as was evident from daily comments by Egyptians on his doings, from the articles published in newspapers in Egypt and the Arab world, from what I heard from my Arab friends, and even from the reception official delegations gave him at meetings of the Arab League. There has been an overwhelming consensus in favor of Nabil al-Arabi, just as there was a consensus to reject what his predecessor did or didn't do. This shows yet again that right and wrong are clear and that it isn't ambiguity or incomprehension that prevents people from sticking to what is right and avoiding what is wrong, but rather something quite different that I discuss below.

The way Nabil al-Arabi behaved reminded me of another man, someone I consider to be my mentor, although he never taught me any of the courses in the faculty of law when I was a student there, and that was Dr. Hilmi Murad. He was professor of public finance and widely respected for his competence, integrity, and patriotism. He was also a political activist in the socialist party formed by Ahmad Hussein in the 1940s. I used to meet Dr. Murad from time to time at seminars and economic conferences, and we all read with great admiration his superb articles in *al-Sha'b* newspaper in the 1970s and 1980s.

Once I met him in the mid-1980s while preparations were in full swing for a big conference accompanied by an extensive publicity campaign under the slogan "Reforming Education in Egypt." The chairman of the conference was Dr. Fathi Sorour, who was minister of education at the time, before he became, or was appointed, speaker of parliament after proving himself highly competent at ruining education in Egypt. Commenting on the conference and all the hullabaloo about it, Dr. Murad said with a faint smile, "They don't need to hold a conference to reform education. If they opened any drawer in any office in the Ministry of Education they would find enough memos and proposals to fix all the flaws in Egyptian education, if only they were implemented."

So conferences weren't required because here too it was obvious what was right and what was wrong, in educational reform as in foreign policy. In fact we needed something else. So what was this other thing, the lack of which made it rare to find people who did the right thing in political life and accounted for the paucity of ministers of the caliber of Nabil al-Arabi and Hilmi Murad throughout our long history?

The answer is without doubt strongly linked to the question of democracy and dictatorship. Patriotic ministers are chosen by the people, who are necessarily concerned for the national interest. A dictator may sometimes be concerned for the national interest and appoint patriotic ministers, but he might not be concerned and he might appoint ministers who serve his own purposes or who are focused on their own personal interests. So Egypt has had very few such ministers, because it has had very little democratic rule. For the past two centuries, from the beginning of Muhammad Ali's reign to the end of the Mubarak era, the number of patriotic ministers and presidential aides has been tiny, confined to very short periods. But we should note that having patriotic ministers did not exactly correlate with enjoying democratic government, because Egypt had many patriotic ministers and advisers in the reign of Muhammad Ali and in Abd al-Nasser's time (and both of them were indisputably dictators), and it had many unpatriotic ministers and aides in much more democratic periods, such as the period between the promulgation of the 1923 constitution and the 1952 revolution. So on top of whether there is democracy or not, we must add another factor: the extent to which Egypt is truly independent or subject to the wishes of foreigners. Foreigners may sometimes be interested in reform but in most cases they have a corrupting influence, and so in most cases they choose, or encourage the choice of, people who work against the national interest and do nothing to serve that interest.

The two factors are linked but do not correlate precisely. Foreigners don't, in most cases, have any interest in Egyptians having a democratic system, usually finding dictators more useful and easier to control. If foreigners did allow us democracy, it was democracy of a particular kind, restricted by conditions, such as the requirement in the 1923 constitution that the king of Egypt obtain the approval of the British embassy in Cairo, and hence of the Foreign Office in London, for the person chosen as prime minister.

It's interesting to note, however, that from time to time Egypt goes through periods when the dictator or the foreign rulers feel they are in trouble and it's hard for them to ignore the national interest completely and not to comply, if only temporarily, with the wishes of the people. Then they resort temporarily to appointing some ministers, and perhaps also a prime minister, known to be popular for their integrity and patriotism, until the crisis passes and things calm down.

Something like that happened on February 4, 1942, in the famous incident when the British government insisted that the king appoint Mustafa al-Nahhas, the most popular leader at the time, as prime minister, despite the intense hostility between the king and al-Nahhas, because al-Nahhas insisted on opposing the king whenever the king wanted to break the law to fulfill some personal objective. The British government was forced to do that, although it also hated al-Nahhas and preferred the minority parties, because of the very serious crisis in the war with the Germans. It wanted to secure Egyptian public opinion and prevent any unrest or demonstrations that might complicate its military plans to prevent the Germans from entering Cairo. The streets of Egypt could be pacified only if Mustafa al-Nahhas took office and so the British deployed their tanks in front of Abdin Palace to force the king to accept al-Nahhas, and the king gave in. Al-Nahhas was dismissed as soon as the situation stabilized in favor of the British and the danger was over.

The king was forced to accept al-Nahhas as prime minister again in 1950 when he was going through a hard time (this time it was him rather than the British) because of the nationalistic fervor created in the wake of the Palestine war of 1948, when the king was accused of complicity in the sale of substandard weapons to the Egyptian army. Al-Nahhas came to office with some excellent ministers, including an exceptional foreign minister, Mohamed Salaheddin, and an exceptional minister of education, Taha Hussein. Overnight the government abrogated the treaty signed with the British in 1936, which people bitterly hated, and news of the unilateral abrogation won a rapturous reception. Members of parliament, stunned at the news, stood up and chanted, "Long live Egypt, long live al-Nahhas." The al-Nahhas government soon allowed Egyptian volunteers to go and fight the British lurking in the Suez Canal zone, set up training camps for them, and supplied them with weapons. The government then passed a law making education free at all levels up to university and another law protecting workers from exploitation by their bosses, known as the Individual Labor Law.

Not surprisingly, it didn't last more than a year and a half, because there was a conspiracy to contain the al-Nahhas government in the interests of the king and the British. The famous Cairo fire took place in January 1952 and the king dismissed al-Nahhas on the grounds that he had failed to maintain law and order.

Sixteen years after the Cairo fire a similar incident took place when the Abd al-Nasser regime was forced to try to placate public opinion. The regime brought in ministers who were popular and known for their integrity and patriotism until the crisis cleared. When it no longer needed their services, they were dismissed. In 1968 public anger peaked because of the military defeat of 1967, and young people came out on the streets demanding punishment for those responsible for the defeat. Gamal Abd al-Nasser felt that he had to calm things down, so he brought in a new government with two or three ministers of a new kind people hadn't been used to seeing for ages. One of them was the admirable man I mentioned earlier, Dr. Hilmi Murad, who was appointed minister of education. It wouldn't have taken Murad long to reform the educational system, but unfortunately he angered Abd al-Nasser for something not related to education but rather his strong opinions, which he stuck to. In the cabinet he spoke out in support of the independence of the judiciary and against a proposal, backed by Abd al-Nasser, that would have removed some judges from the bench. Murad was dismissed as soon as public opinion calmed down and Abd al-Nasser was confident he had the situation under control.

Anwar al-Sadat did something similar in his first years in power in the early 1970s, in the wake of the death of a strong and popular leader and unrest among young people who protested in 1972 at the government's reluctance to do what was needed to recover Sinai from Israeli occupation and before the Sadat regime fell fully into the clutches of American control. Sadat brought in a great man as prime minister, Dr. Aziz Sidqi, and some ministers known for their integrity, patriotism, and competence, such as Ismail Sabri Abdallah as planning minister, Fuad Morsi as minister of supply, and Mustafa al-Gabali as minister of agriculture. The three of them were soon actively trying to reform the sectors they were responsible for. Ismail Sabri Abdallah drew up an ambitious industrialization plan, Fuad Morsi devised a system to tackle rapacious traders, and Mustafa al-Gabali made an excellent plan that aimed to achieve self-sufficiency in wheat and other staple crops before the end of the century. But it didn't last long, as usual. Sadat got rid of these men and others like them as soon as he was well established and replaced them with people who agreed to obey the speculators, monopolists, contractors, and currency dealers, as well as the wishes of America.

Was moving Nabil al-Arabi from the foreign ministry to the secretariat of the Arab League similar to these previous cases I have mentioned? One has the right to wonder sadly, "Don't Egyptians deserve to have an excellent foreign minister for more than just three or four months?"

5

Does Egypt need economists? The question might seem surprising but I suggest you withhold judgment until you finish reading.

Let's start with the history of the Egyptian economy from the beginning of the British occupation in 1882. Throughout the period of occupation, which didn't really end until 1956, the economic policy implemented in Egypt was made in London and not in Cairo. We could exclude from that the first four years after the 1952 revolution on the grounds that British influence had been severely weakened by the revolution, but the plain fact remains that for seventy years Egypt had no free will in deciding economic policy.

Britain's economic objectives were simple. After taking the necessary measures in the first decades of the occupation to enable Egypt to pay back the money it had borrowed from foreign banks, Britain's three main aims were to obtain cheap Egyptian cotton; to maintain Egypt as a market for British exports, especially textiles, which required obstructing industrialization in Egypt; and to ensure a plentiful supply of cheap labor and prevent Egypt from adopting a protectionist policy.

This policy didn't require Egyptian economists, because British economists and politicians could do what was needed. All it required was Egyptian civil servants who could understand the instructions regarding the economy that came from London and knew how to carry them out. So it's no wonder that the number of Egyptian economists in the first half of the twentieth century was very limited and they basically worked as teachers or, if they worked in government or in banks, their job was not planning or working on development strategies but rather as I just described it: carrying out policies and instructions that came from London.

With the end of the British occupation in 1956, Egypt went through a rare period when it was free to formulate an independent economic policy (we can find a precedent for that only in the time of Muhammad Ali, more than a hundred years earlier). From then on Egypt quickly drew up an industrialization program in 1958 and then a fine development plan for the years 1960–65. Thanks to this program and this plan, Egypt achieved some stunning results, the fruits of which we are still reaping today, contrary to what is said to minimize their importance. Not only this, but successful development was coupled with a high degree of income redistribution and a narrowing of the gaps between classes.

Yes, in that short period Egypt undoubtedly needed economists; not just civil servants who understood the language of the economy but economists with vision, able and eager to devise a strategy to stimulate the economy. So no wonder it was during that period that the first faculty of economics was set up in Egypt and the first Ministry of Planning and planning institute, all of which contributed to the economic achievements of that period.

Then came the unfortunate defeat of 1967, and it looked like there would no longer be any need for Egyptian economists. It's true that after the defeat much was said about the economics of war and the need to mobilize resources for a new battle, but in fact this was more of a smokescreen to give people the impression that a real effort was being made to win back Sinai. In reality, in the years after the defeat the government was trying to keep people happy by enabling them to consume more and to pamper the middle classes in a desperate attempt to placate the anger generated by the defeat.

The eight years between 1967 and the mid-1970s were years of appalling economic recession and Egypt was dependent on aid from Arab countries. The country abandoned any real development effort and the most it could aspire to in that period was to reduce its losses to the minimum, maintain law and order, and prevent popular unrest.

When Anwar al-Sadat launched his Open Door policy in the mid-1970s, he was in fact taking Egypt back to something very like the situation during the British occupation in the sense that it lost its freedom of maneuver to devise its own economic policy. For a short time Sadat called in some economists with a comprehensive economic vision and a strongly patriotic ethos, led by men such as Aziz Sidqi, but he quickly got rid of them as soon as American influence was well established.

So the Egyptian economy, starting from the mid-1970s, was managed by people who might be described as "economic civil servants," whose only task was to interpret and implement instructions that came from abroad, that is, from the U.S. administration and the two big international financial institutions. The result was that when Sadat was killed in 1981 the Egyptian economy was in a lamentable state: a startling amount of foreign debt, rampant inflation, a big decline in the contribution of industry to GDP, very slow growth in agriculture, and heavy dependence on imported foodstuffs, while Egypt was spared high unemployment only by the opportunities for emigration to the Gulf.

Hope that the Egyptian economy might recover returned briefly with the famous economic conference convened in February 1982 at the beginning of the Mubarak era. The conference brought together the elite of Egyptian economists with incisive vision and an indubitably patriotic ethos, and they submitted important proposals for economic reform. At the time we thought that Egypt was about to begin a new phase when real economists would be in charge of the economy. But we were surprised to find the prime minister, Fuad Mohieddin, closing the conference by thanking the economists for their efforts and sending them home with a promise to form committees that would implement their recommendations, which never happened. The situation continued as it had begun in the middle of the Sadat era: mission after mission from the International Monetary Fund and the World Bank would be welcomed and their recommendations and the recommendations of the U.S. administration would be implemented, as though in the wonderful age of independence we had merely substituted decisions made in London for decisions made in Washington.

It wasn't a matter of a dispute between right and left; it was much simpler than that. The American intellectual Noam Chomsky has explained it with great clarity. Washington wasn't fighting communists in the Third World, it was fighting nationalists. Chomsky has offered ample proof of that from Latin America and Asia, but it was the same in Egypt, because the people excluded from management of the economy in Egypt from the mid-1970s were not only nationalist leftists but also nationalist rightists. I have always believed, and I still do, that Egypt can achieve a real economic renaissance under the leadership of either of these two types of economist, as long as they have integrity, are patriotic, fight corruption, and believe in the rule of law. People like Said al-Naggar were ostracized by the Abd al-Nasser regime because they believed in a free market and were hostile to excessive state intervention, and then ostracized by the Sadat regime because of their integrity, patriotism, and calls for the rule of law. The same applied to Ibrahim Shehata, a distinguished lawyer and economist. Whenever his name or that of Said al-Naggar was mentioned in the presence of senior Egyptian officials, they would nod their heads in recognition of their merit but then brush aside the possibility of calling on the services of either, for the same reasons. Said al-Naggar and Ibrahim Shehata, both of whom can be considered to hold rightist views on the economy, have written countless excellent books and articles on what needs to be done to bring about an economic revival in Egypt, but officials have paid little attention to these writings.

As for the names and writings of the patriotic economists affiliated with the left, there is plenty one could say. Most of them were in the Ministry of Planning, the planning institute, and the faculty of economics, as well as in international organizations abroad, but no officials ever summoned them for consultations or to hold a dialogue with them. They remained ensconced where they were inside Egypt, without anyone using their services other than their students. Starting in the mid-1970s the government considered the Ministry of Planning and the planning institute a burden and didn't issue a decree abolishing them and closing them down simply to avoid a scandal. Yes, there were patriotic Egyptian economists who held senior positions in international institutions, and the whole world other than Egypt benefited from their talents and their abilities. The odd thing is that the international financial institutions have no objection to employing these people in senior positions as long as they don't do any real reform to economic policy in their own country. That's because the bureaucratic system applied in these institutions enables them to extract everything these great economists have to offer and then redirect it to serving the interests of international capital and the other forces that control the world.

Things continued in this manner throughout the Mubarak era, with one minister after another taking charge of the Egyptian economy, or rather one prime minister after another, all of them of the kind I described earlier as more like civil servants who know what economic terms mean and can carry out the orders coming from Washington, rather than economists who have vision and can help devise a national strategy for economic revival. These are many and easily recognized, and it was simple for the person who appointed ministers and prime ministers to pick and choose between them, even though they are little known and enjoy little respect among their fellow economists.

This continued until the revolution of January 25, 2011, which gave us hope that relief was at hand. We looked forward to the day when the economy would be managed by economists of a different kind who had long been excluded, and I repeat that it doesn't much matter whether they are from the right or the left because an economic revival is possible under either as long as they have integrity and have the country's interests at heart. When that is the case, differences can easily be resolved and we would soon find their diverse positions converging on common ground that serves the interests of the nation. What prevents reconciliation and perpetuates the disagreement is not the divergence of opinions but the divergence of personal interests.

So what happened?

The economy was again assigned to men of the same old kind that had served as advisers and prime ministers in the overthrown regime, as if the country only has this type of civil servant. There's no harm in an economist known for his integrity taking on a small ministry provided he remains powerless, to embellish the cabinet and have his photograph in the newspapers, as long as he remains far from the process of making fundamental decisions or, more accurately, far from the process of receiving and implementing the fundamental decisions that come from abroad. Discussions continue, of course, endless meetings convene and break up, and people of various opinions are invited to say what they think, but then everyone is surprised to find the most prominent economic officials traveling to Washington, and we don't know exactly if the decision to travel is made in Cairo or in Washington. Then they and their colleagues come back triumphant with precious instructions and advice.

In short, if Egypt has highly active civil servants of this kind, why would it need economists?

The Mysteries of the Egyptian Revolution

1

The joy and pride Egyptians felt when the revolution started on January 25 were quite understandable and justified, and their feeling of joy and pride was even greater when the revolution succeeded in bringing down the head of the regime.

But surprisingly, a set of questions and riddles raised by the events of the revolution and its evolution over the subsequent months has remained without convincing answers. Yes, joy can make you forget yourself, and distract you from thinking at length about the reasons for and the details of a joyous event, especially if this joyous event has been awaited so long that you had completely lost hope that it would ever happen. But especially after things have calmed down and the outlook has started to turn gloomy, you have a duty to think about it all, and you may even have to go over the events of the revolution day by day so that you don't miss any detail that may throw light on one of the significant factors that governed all these events.

I like to imagine it as a detective story, with elements that appeared to be contradictory and that didn't fit together logically. There were so many puzzles and contradictions in the January 25 revolution in Egypt that you have to think hard to understand it, without overlooking any detail, and recall the events day by day, putting them side by side. When the picture is complete, one might be able to solve the riddles and come up with a correct interpretation of what happened.

Yes, the January 25 revolution started in Egypt in the wake of a successful revolution in Tunisia. But was the Tunisian revolution itself completely comprehensible and free of puzzles? The Tunisian people's anger was totally understandable, just like the anger of the Egyptians, but the police state in Tunisia looked stable and self-confident, just like the police state in Egypt. Both of them were strongly backed by foreign countries that showered them with aid and weapons, so how could all that suddenly be turned upside down? What was it that suddenly made it possible for so many people to assemble in this way when assembly was strictly banned? Is it just that everything comes to an end and that patience is bound to run out at some point? But why did Egyptians run out of patience at the same time as the Tunisians, the Libyans, the Yemenis, the Bahrainis, the Omanis, and the Syrians, despite the big differences in the political, social, and material circumstances of these countries and despite the big differences in how willing they were to put up with hardships?

Some might say that the domino theory makes it possible for one regime after another to collapse in this way, with the fall of each leading to the fall of another one nearby, since the people in separate Arab countries belong anyway to a single nation and all the separate peoples have common traits that might make it likely that people in one country will respond in this way to what is happening to people in another country. It's a reasonable answer but, to be honest, it doesn't completely convince me, because to have a succession of regimes falling like dominos is rare in history and it usually doesn't happen without foreign assistance. So the question is still puzzling, especially as this phenomenon of regimes falling in succession went hand in hand with other similar incidents, such as the suicide of a young man in Tunisia and some suicide attempts in Egypt in front of parliament and in Alexandria, though in Egypt the people were saved from death just in time. There were also similarities in many of the slogans used, although there are usually differences in the way the people of each Arab country express how they feel.

A demonstration had been announced, with a call to gather in Tahrir Square in Cairo, many days before the rally took place. Why, one wonders, hadn't the authorities taken the necessary steps to prevent it from happening? Over the years we had grown used to the security forces taking every precaution to prevent gatherings that were much smaller and less serious than this. The usual methods included filling the square where the gathering was to take place with security forces and trucks and armored cars and closing off the roads leading to the square so that it was impossible to assemble there. This type of thing would happen repeatedly in circumstances that were much less charged than in January 2011. In fact this would happen at election time to ensure that one candidate won and another lost, so why did the security forces decide against taking such steps this time?

Another very strange thing happened on the evening of January 28 and the next day. We saw and heard signs that the police had withdrawn completely from police stations and gone off home, and that some of them had even attacked and looted shops and carried out acts of vandalism in the street. Why did the police suddenly decide to stop maintaining order? At the same time the army command issued a statement saying that the army supported the demands of the demonstrators and would not attack them. What does this mean? The army was for the overthrow of the regime, and the police didn't like this? And at the same time the U.S. president and his secretary of state were making unambiguous statements that also supported the Egyptian demonstrations and advised the Egyptian president to step down.

A few days later, on February 2, the event known as the Battle of the Camel took place. Men mounted on camels and horses stormed into Tahrir Square carrying swords and sticks and started to attack the demonstrators, backed by snipers on the highest buildings around the square. The snipers opened fire on the demonstrators, killing or wounding several hundred and blinding about a thousand. Those who did this were called "thugs" and the prime minister at the time (appointed by the president before his overthrow) denied knowing anything about what happened. It later became apparent that what happened that day was organized by some of the leaders of the ruling party with help from some big businessmen in a desperate attempt to put an end to the unrest because they didn't know where it might lead if they didn't act. The police had withdrawn, the task of protecting people was now in the hands of hired thugs of the kind the regime had habitually used to protect itself in previous cases, and the army was not intervening either to prevent the thugs from going into the square or to attack or disperse the demonstrators.

The president and his men held out for a while, but then he was forced to step down from the presidency on February 11. So in the end what forced him to do so? It wasn't fear that the demonstrators would get into his palace, because it would have been possible to stop them by using a little brutality, especially as the demonstrators hadn't used any violence and the regime was capable, physically and psychologically, of using the necessary level of brutality. It was certainly the army commanders who finally decided in favor of the president giving up power, so why did the army commanders make this decision after cooperating closely with the regime for the previous thirty years?

It's also important to note the developments in the role played on the political scene by what is called the 'religious current'—another of the puzzles that need explanation. The religious current had no noticeable presence in the first days of the revolution, but this absence did not arouse much interest from commentators at first. Of course there were many people affiliated with the Muslim Brotherhood and other Islamist movements in the square, but they were still a minority among the masses gathered there and they didn't have any significant effect on the slogans and chants. The slogans and chants were completely neutral on their attitude toward religion, focused on overthrowing the regime, social justice, freedom, and the denunciation of corruption and corrupt people. The only obvious effect of religion was in the fine examples of complete harmony between Muslims and Copts, in agreement on the same objectives.

Soon it was announced that a committee was being set up to amend some articles of the constitution, and the man chosen to chair the committee was someone widely respected because in the last few years he had taken courageous positions hostile to the regime and to corruption. But the man was also known for his definite sympathy for the religious current, even if he wasn't a member of any religio-political group. Some people were apprehensive that his being chosen to head this committee signaled a particular attitude in favor of the religious current on the part of the people who had come to power after the president stepped down. The committee was set up nonetheless, without much complaining or grumbling, until the time came for a referendum on the constitutional amendments. Although neither the amended articles nor the substance of the amendments had anything whatsoever to do with religion, some of the people affiliated with the religious current promoted an idea that created an alarming split between the Islamists and the secularists: that anyone who voted "no" to the amendments was a secularist hostile to the application of sharia law, and that those who voted "yes" were the truly pious. Some went as far as dividing voters into two categories, Muslims and infidels! This was a very unpleasant surprise, but the media propagated the idea and the state didn't appear to be willing to intervene to bring people back to their senses.

In the meantime, and before and after, some strange events took place that were also unexpected and most unwelcome and that helped to inflame strife between Muslims and Christians. A church was set on fire in Giza, another church was attacked in Imbaba, and then the attackers walked several miles to a third church with the intention of attacking it, too, and the security forces were inexplicably and unjustifiably slow to step in to prevent the situation from deteriorating. Security had clearly been lax since the police suspiciously withdrew a few days after the revolution started, but that it should remain so lax even in the face of such serious incidents between Muslims and Copts was incomprehensible and quite unjustifiable.

A large number of those who voted "no" to the constitutional amendments objected to the timetable for holding elections for a new parliament and president and preferred to allow more time for new parties to form and associations to spring up to express new ideas about reform. Perhaps some of them were really afraid that early elections would produce a new parliament dominated either by remnants of the ruling party whose head had been overthrown or by Islamists, who had the most popularity among the people. But it was extremely reckless to portray these opponents as if they really intended to amend Article 2 of the constitution, which says that sharia law is the main source of legislation. Portraying it in this way no doubt planted the seeds of strife between advocates of the two different positions on the relationship between government and religion, and also planted the seeds of strife between Muslims and Christians.

Was this split really inevitable, or could it easily have been avoided or nipped in the bud?

In the meantime, the media were also acting suspiciously. Only a few weeks after the president stepped down, a decree was issued freeing the Gama'a al-Islamiya leader who had been imprisoned thirty years earlier for his part in the plot to assassinate President Sadat, and who hadn't been released even after he completed his sentence. When he was released we saw pictures of him in the newspapers coming out of jail surrounded by relatives and supporters congratulating him and cheering. Then, amazingly, we saw him giving an interview to the most famous television broadcaster in Egypt. The man was there with his long bushy beard and his frightening eyes, answering the interviewer's questions in full confidence, and one of the things he said, and I couldn't believe my ears when he said it, was that he was justified in taking part in the assassination of the president as long as there was no legal way to get rid of him. Should such views be broadcast to the public in this way? What message might those responsible for the television station have been hoping to convey to young Egyptians?

It was a very strange climate that prevailed after an amazing revolution in which everyone was united around a single aim, and this climate led to an ugly polarization and a schism over the relationship between religion and politics, much more severe than the split that existed before the revolution.

But that is not the last of the revolution's puzzles. There are plenty of others.

2

One of the puzzles of the January 2011 revolution was that those who seized power in its wake announced an early date for parliamentary elections. This haste in announcing new elections looked strange after a revolution that was of such importance and that ended a long reign associated with the prevalence of corruption in various areas of political and economic life. The usual and expected practice after popular uprisings of this kind is that those who take power after the revolution take some important measures, such as issuing laws to tackle widespread corruption, before they think of handing over power to newly elected people. Holding elections too early was bound to enable the return of people similar to those against whom people rose up in revolt, thanks to the influence and money they enjoy, or to let in the Islamists, who enjoyed the most popularity both before and after the revolution, or a mixture of the two groups. Did these factors enter into the calculations of the new rulers?

A few days after the president stepped down, there was also a suspicious attack on some of the police stations that held important files with information likely to incriminate people who held important positions before the revolution. The attackers burned many of the files, so what was it that they wanted to conceal? And why did those responsible for law and order take their time doing what was necessary to prevent these attacks before they started or to tackle them before they escalated? The use of the word 'thugs' started to spread to describe those who carried out criminal attacks, including attacks on the revolutionaries, on those who joined them in protests in public squares, on those who called for measures consistent with the objectives of the revolution, or those who protested at delays in taking such measures. The term 'thug' is ambiguous and absolutely useless because, like the term 'terrorist,' it does not describe people but rather what they do, without adding to our knowledge of what the perpetrators are like or what their aim is. It serves only to distract us from any attempt to find out more about them. So that's one more riddle of the revolution: Who were these thugs who took part in or led the Battle of the Camel and attacked the revolutionaries in Tahrir Square with swords and sticks while riding camels and horses? And who were the thugs who clashed with the protesters who called for quick trials for those who planned or took part in this battle, in which many were killed? And who were the thugs who threw sheets of glass and tiles from the buildings around Abbasiya Square when the Tahrir Square revolutionaries came there on their way to the Ministry of Defense? And why didn't the security officials put an end to these acts of thuggery, whatever their purpose might have been? And why didn't they choose a strong man known for his resolve as minister of interior?

But the puzzle over the choice of officials is not confined to the Interior Ministry. It has been remarkable from the start that the choice of new officials has never matched the expectations of those who made the revolution. It wasn't strange that the new cabinet formed by the president before he stepped down in the hope of placating the revolutionaries and gaining time was headed by a man who had been a minister in the previous cabinet, even if nothing was known of him that would upset people (he was even reputed to be efficient and decisive). But how was he reappointed prime minister after the president stepped down, and why wasn't someone completely new chosen who was closer to the inclinations of the revolutionaries and more willing to carry out the objectives of the revolution? Even stranger is the retention of certain important ministers, such as the finance minister and the foreign minister, for example, and some senior officials in the public prosecutor's office, despite the fact that they had been ministers under the old regime or had held important jobs in that period and shown complete cooperation with the regime. How can that be explained or understood?

This led to repeated demonstrations in Tahrir Square demanding change, and it was surprising how remarkably slow the authorities were in responding to those demands or in substituting someone who was moderately acceptable to the revolutionaries for someone else. This happened even in the choice of the prime minister. He was a man known for his integrity but from the first day he was obviously weak, indecisive, and hardly able to impose his will. On the first day he was appointed, his deputy made remarks to that effect in public, suggesting that the prime minister and his deputy were not in complete harmony, yet even so both of them continued in their posts. Similarly the foreign minister, who for ages had been responsible for the old regime's disastrous foreign policy, and other ministers known to be weak, corrupt, unsuccessful, or fully in tune with the nature of the old regime all retained their positions for no comprehensible reason. And when a new foreign minister whose views matched the aims of the revolutionaries was brought in after constant pressure from the revolutionaries, he was soon asked to give up his job to take another position where, by the nature of the job, he could not do much.

It was very possible and only to be expected that significant changes would take place in the media, but the change took much longer than necessary, it seemed to be grudging, and there was as little change of direction as possible in the newspapers and radio or television programs. The old officials, rather than being expelled, dismissed, or subjected to inquiries, were left alone and were sometimes given about as much space in the newspaper and on television as they had before. Some changes were even retracted and old faces came back to hold important positions in the media.

Another puzzle soon appeared in connection with the way senior officials in the old regime who had been removed from their positions were treated, including the president, his wife and sons, senior party officials, members of the policies committee headed by the president's son, and other ministers who had been excluded from the new cabinet. People would hear snippets of information and it was hard to uncover the logic behind them: why, for example, this person had been arrested rather than someone else, why this person had gone on trial while someone else remained free, why certain very senior officials were untouched and we never heard that they had been detained or questioned or even dismissed from their posts. There also didn't appear to be any logic in who was banned from leaving the country. Why this man but not another? Why was this man detained and questioned when there were many other people who were more dangerous and more famous for their corruption?

On the question of fortunes smuggled abroad, people found it hard to understand the measures taken. Despite what the papers kept publishing, officials in foreign countries made statements denying that they received any requests to freeze these funds. In the case of the deposed president and his wife, people were confused about reports on his health and his illness, his loss of appetite and the deterioration of his psychological condition, their ability or inability to move, the decision on whether or not to move them from where they were to some other place, and the suitability or unsuitability of this prison or that hospital to take them in, and so on. And when people had almost lost patience and started to express their suspicions and their irritation, it was announced that the trial of the president, his sons, and his interior minister was starting and would be broadcast on television. When people saw the pictures of the president coming into the cage in the courtroom on a gurney, the pictures didn't look fully convincing, especially as some people had seen pictures of his sons and his interior minister coming out of the courtroom without handcuffs on, and even laughing with each other as they came out. It was said that some of the officers along the way gave a military salute to the former interior minister, who faced charges that could carry the death penalty.

It occurred to me, and no doubt to others, that there was a very reasonable explanation for all of this, one that would work as a solution to all these puzzles and as an answer to all these questions, and that is that in any successful revolution those who carry out the revolution are usually the ones who take power as soon as it succeeds, or at least they choose the ones who take power to represent them. If that happens, it's inconceivable that the kind of absurdities I have mentioned would take place. Some unpleasant things might happen, such as unnecessary cruelty and ruthlessness, or excessive haste in changing the laws and getting rid of the procedures that have been in force, or dispensing with competent people who are needed and replacing them with less competent people who are, or pretend to be, loyal to the revolution, and so on. Some of that might happen, but after a successful revolution, after the head of the regime has been toppled, it's hard to understand why many important things should survive that the revolution set out to do away with in the first place.

So the puzzle still stands. What is it that brought the Egyptian revolution in January 2011 to this strange outcome that is unfamiliar in the history of revolutions? Does our inability to understand stem from the fact that we are dealing with a completely new age with the mentality of a former era that is over forever? Are these the revolutions of the new age, the age of modern technology that enables the governed to be treated in this way: their thoughts and emotions controlled by the media and by new methods of communication in a way that wasn't possible before, a way that mocks their hopes and aspirations and shapes their thoughts and emotions to serve hidden objectives, replacing facts with a set of moving images such that one doesn't know whether one is seeing events as they really happened or as the producers and the cameramen conceived them?

11 Muslims and Copts

1

I have a friend I met fifty years ago when he came to London to enter the same college I was studying in. We were later work colleagues and he became one of my dearest friends. Since I first met him I never noticed that the fact that his religion was different from mine had any effect on the way he behaved toward me or toward our mutual friends who were Muslims, or on the way I behaved toward him. We saw the religious difference between us in the same way as we might see a difference in height, for example, or in nose or ear size, as nothing to do with the way we judged each other.

He differed from us by being unusually gentle. That was evident by how pleased he would be to meet you and how ready he was to express his pleasure openly, and I also noticed how warmly he treated his sister when she came to London to visit him.

He spoke little but was an excellent listener, and apparently we all prefer a good listener to a good talker. His raucous laughter would cheer us up when one of us said something funny, and more than the rest of us he was willing to put up with big talkers such as me. For this and for other reasons, we didn't feel our group was complete unless he was with us.

I was surprised at his vast knowledge of Arabic poetry, his great love for the poetry of al-Mutanabbi, and his ability to recite poetry correctly and elegantly. I didn't expect that from a man who was specializing in economics, since in most of the economists I knew I hadn't seen any love or appreciation of literature of any kind. This friend of mine was an exception in this as well.

We were in London in the Abd al-Nasser years and most of us were very enthusiastic about Abd al-Nasser's economic and foreign policy, including the idea of Arab nationalism. This friend of mine was also an enthusiastic Nasserist. I don't remember that our enthusiasm for Arab nationalism and unity ever upset him. I found nothing strange about it at the time because when I was a member of the Ba'th Party in the 1950s, some of my party colleagues were Copts from Egypt and Christians from other Arab countries who believed in Arab nationalism and the advantages of unity. In fact the leader and ideologue of the Ba'th Party, whom we adored and whose honesty we trusted, was the Syrian Christian Michel Aflaq. Professor Michel, as we called him, firmly believed that there could be no Arab revival without unity, and as the motto of the party he chose the phrase "One Arab nation, with an eternal message."

Of course this was not the position of all political activists who were Copts, even during the Nasserist period. Dr. Louis Awad, for example, never disguised his rejection of Arab nationalism, because his nationalism and his love for his nation did not extend beyond the political borders of Egypt. But Louis Awad thought that the only way to national revival was through westernization and therefore was enthusiastic about following in the footsteps of Europe. People who shared this view were not as enthusiastic about Arab unity as those of us who aspired to bring about a national revival in a way that drew on our heritage rather than denying it. From the 1970s onward, events must have made our Coptic friends very disappointed and disheartened. With recurrent incidents of what was called 'sectarian strife,' it was quite natural and completely understandable that Copts would be wary of any call to "draw on heritage" and grow more fearful that Arab unity would reinforce the idea of 'minority and majority' and deepen, rather than eliminate, their sense of alienation. So when my friend became reluctant to get into any political discussion with me that had anything to do with Arab nationalism or unity, I interpreted the change in his attitude as a sign of his fear that political differences might spoil a strong friendship that went back fifty years.

That's one of the many reasons I felt shocked and disappointed when I heard that eight Copts had been killed in an attack in Nag' Hammadi in early 2010. The news was tragic in every sense, especially as it happened on Christmas Eve when they were coming out of church. I imagined how my friend would have felt when he heard the news, how it must have deepened his sense of alienation. I was sure he wouldn't bring up the subject with me, just as I too wouldn't dare to broach it. I was also sure that what had happened could not affect the way we felt about each other. But it was saddening how this incident damaged our hopes of bringing about any revival for Egypt, whether by drawing on our own heritage or through westernization.

2

There's a big difference between the rape of a Muslim girl committed by a young Coptic man in the town of Farshout in November 2009 and the killing of eight Copts (nine others were injured) by a Muslim man as they came out of church in Nag' Hammadi on their Christmas Eve, January 6, 2010. I don't mean that one incident was a rape and the other was a murder, or that there was one victim in the first case and seventeen in the second. What I mean is the difference in the role of religion in the two incidents. In the first case I see no connection between religion and what happened, while religious differences were fundamental in the second case.

The young Coptic man didn't rape the Muslim girl because he was a Copt and she was a Muslim. No, the man was a sexual deviant, mentally deficient, or weak willed. It's conceivable that this young man might have committed the same crime against a Coptic girl, just as it is conceivable that a young Muslim man who is a sexual deviant, mentally deficient, or weak willed might rape either a Coptic or a Muslim girl. In this case the religious difference is a secondary consideration that adds nothing to our understanding of the motives for the crime.

But in the second case it's inconceivable that the murder could have happened the way it did unless the murderer was taking the victims' religion into account, because the murderer wasn't targeting any one person in particular and it apparently didn't matter to him whether he killed eight people or more, whereas it is certain that the appalling timing he chose for the crime did matter to him.

So the first incident cannot be described as 'sectarian' except in a very superficial and unhelpful sense, whereas the second incident is definitely sectarian, since there is absolutely no reason to believe that there was any other motive for the crime.

Naturally I was most surprised at the statement made by the speaker of parliament and repeated by the minister for parliamentary affairs, in which they described the attack outside the church as "merely an individual crime with no religious motive" and denied it was of a sectarian nature. I interpreted these statements as inevitably driven by political motives. But it doesn't require much thought about what happened to see that the political results of these statements would be very bad in turn, because such statements cannot contribute one iota to solving the sectarian problem in Egypt and cannot alleviate the Copts' sense of bitterness and alienation in this country, but would instead exacerbate such feelings.

What disappointed me more was what I read in a statement by the public prosecutor's office on how they were proceeding with the case. The prosecution completed its investigation of the incident at an amazing speed that was quite incompatible with the gravity of the case and referred the case to the criminal court just ten days after the incident took place. In its statement referring the three defendants (Muhammad Ahmad Hassan al-Kamouni, Muhammad Ali Qurashi Aboul Hajjaj, and Muhammad Hassan Hindawi el-Sayed) to the court, the public prosecutor's office said, "The inquiry and the police investigations did not find evidence that anyone instigated the crime." It quoted the defendants as claiming that they committed the crime "under the influence of the incident in which a Muslim girl was raped in a neighboring district and after seeing pictures of Muslim girls in obscene poses." This denial that there were any instigators was repeated several times in a government newspaper, which also said, "Security sources thought that this [the rape] was probably the reason why al-Kamouni carried out his crime on Christmas Eve" (al-Ahram, January 17, 2010).

Is it conceivable that an incident such as this could take place without incitement by someone? The information available about the killer who pulled the trigger makes it close to certain that he could not have committed this act unless someone incited him. The information shows him to be a reprobate with a long record of violent crime. He was arrested in 2002 and imprisoned for three years for thuggery. In other words, he was a professional criminal who could be hired to commit any crime if he was paid the right amount, and such a person would not commit such a crime or do anything else out of enthusiasm for any cause or principle, or because he was overwhelmed by sympathy for the Muslim girl who was raped, or out of anger (as he is said to have said) that indecent photographs of Muslim girls had been published (are there any pictures that could possibly offend al-Kamouni?). Would one expect such a hardened criminal to get so upset on behalf of Islam or Muslims that he would commit such a barbaric crime? Was the public prosecutor's office really convinced of this?

Who benefited from such a crime? Was it really someone like al-Kamouni? Did Islam and Muslims benefit from it? Did Egypt and Egyptians benefit from it, or was the real beneficiary a person, a group of people, or a government that was or were interested in destroying Islam and Muslims or in dragging Egypt and Egyptians into further decline? Didn't such a question occur to the prosecutors, or did it occur to them and they knew the answer but decided to keep it a secret and not tell anyone, to serve the interests of someone, a group of people, or a government the prosecutor did not want to expose?

3

Trying to understand the reasons for the horrific incident that happened in Alexandria on New Year's Day in 2011 undoubtedly requires more effort on our part than we usually have to make to understand tragic events.

Yes, it wasn't the first time that Copts had been horrifically attacked but this was the second case of a new kind of attack on Copts, and the two incidents happened in one year, with similarities that distinguished them from previous incidents. Both involved premeditation and careful planning and were not the outcome of a sudden outburst or a quarrel between Muslims and Copts on some subject that might have inflamed passions and brought out suppressed resentment, ending in death or injury. This isn't what happened in Alexandria or in Nag' Hammadi a year earlier. The motive in both cases was not to settle old or new scores, to avenge an earlier attack, or to help a particular person or persons against a person or persons of the other religion. The attack was aimed at Copts in general and indiscriminately, not because of a mistake one of them had made, real or imagined, but simply because they were Copts. The perpetrator or perpetrators acted in cold blood without emotion, based on forethought and planning, which makes it likely that the person who planned the attack was dispassionate with a predefined aim, and therefore might not be fanatical at all and might not necessarily even be Muslim (even if the person who carried out the attack was Muslim).

The incident is ambiguous, as well as tragic, so we need to make double the effort to plumb the depths of it and find out what was behind it.

What makes it especially difficult is that we are trying to solve a puzzle on which not much information is available and much of the information that the investigators have obtained was withheld from us on grounds of security. The published information was so meager that we cannot even tell whether the attacker was killed while committing the crime or not. A few hours after it happened, some of those responsible for the investigation said it was a suicide operation, but there was no evidence that the person who blew up the car in front of the church was inside or near the car when it exploded. Some people said the attacker was a tall man with a white complexion, while others said that he was dark and short, and so on.

On top of that, the government media had a clear interest in giving a distorted impression of what happened, for example by trying to suggest right after the incident that the number of Muslim victims was not much lower than the number of Copt victims, attempting to avoid revealing the exact number of dead by lumping together the dead and the injured, and exaggerating the measures taken before the incident to prevent such a thing from happening.

Any attempt to understand is complicated further by the fact that the incident naturally gave rise to heated passions, grief, and emotion on both sides, and anger and outrage especially among Copts. Grief and anger tend to prevent a sound understanding of what has happened, because very plausible explanations are dismissed simply because they suggest that a person or persons who is or are not the object of hatred may be responsible, or because they hold responsible a foreign country or power that is hard to reach or punish or exact revenge on when what is sought is an urgent measure that gives people relief and rapidly heals their wounds.

With such meager information, with passions and anger running high, how can we think calmly in an attempt to determine who the perpetrator or perpetrators were, or even just decide that one explanation is more likely than others?

Not surprisingly in such a situation, despite the many commentaries written on the incident, it was rare to find anyone asking about the possible motives for committing the crime. The commentaries generously made do with describing the perpetrator as "a terrorist," although this term does not in the least help to define the character of the perpetrator, in that it doesn't include a description of the attacker but merely describes what he has done. The act terrorized people, so the perpetrator was bound to be "a terrorist," and more than that we were not told.

Who benefited from this criminal act? No one wanted to bring up this important question. In fact everyone, or almost everyone, merely repeated the same explanation in one form or another: "The killer was a fanatical Muslim." Then they cursed and execrated this fanatical Muslim and set about looking for whatever or whoever is responsible for making him a fanatic. Was it the absence of democracy, or the irrational media, or the terrible curriculum in schools, or failed economic policy? Of course I don't want to deny that our democracy was a fraud or that our media were full of examples of irrationality, and I completely agree that the curricula in our schools contained much that corrupted the minds of schoolchildren and needed a complete overhaul, and that our economic policy promoted the proliferation of many social maladies, including religious fanaticism, but to admit all this is one thing and to concede readily that religious fanaticism must have been responsible for the crime in Alexandria is something else altogether. To be honest, I have never approved of blaming religious fanaticism for any of the heinous crimes committed against Copts or anyone else in Egypt, unless they were directly connected with a fight between Muslims and Copts or between the perpetrators of the crime and their victims. I didn't accept (and I still don't accept) that religious fanaticism was responsible for the attack on Naguib Mahfouz in 1992, for example, or the attack on the tourists in Luxor in 1997, or the explosions on tourist buses in front of the Hilton Hotel or on Pyramids Road many years ago, or the explosions in Sharm al-Sheikh some years later, or the killing of Copts in Nag' Hammadi in 2010. I don't approve of interpreting any of these incidents, which appeared to be completely insane, as signs of religious fanaticism, and I add to those incidents what happened in Alexandria at the start of 2011.

I have strong reasons for rejecting this common explanation, including the fact that the information published about the perpetrators and the details of the crime was insufficient to make that explanation convincing, and the fact that what we know of Egyptian society is completely incompatible with such a crime and the way it was committed. Of course I am not claiming that there are no fanatics in Egypt and I admit that irrationality in religious discourse over the last thirty years has greatly increased, but I also know that Egyptians, even at their most irrational, do not behave in this manner. And anyway, what have the Copts done that would drive any Egyptian to this kind of conduct, let alone drive him to carry out a suicide operation, as some of the media claimed, in other words to sacrifice his own life in order to kill some Copts? And what did Naguib Mahfouz do or write to incite a fanatical Muslim to try to kill him? What did the tourists do to arouse the anger of fanatical Muslims to act like this?

And then, what good do such acts do Islam and Muslims, fanatics or not fanatics? The harm to Islam and Muslims is great and frightening, while not a single benefit to Islam comes to mind.

Some people believed that the Alexandria incident was probably the work of al-Qa'ida under Osama bin Laden, on the grounds that the way the car was blown up and some of the other details were similar to explosions in Iraq in recent years. I don't deny that there are indeed similarities between the explosions here and there, but on what basis have we accepted the theory that fanatical Muslims are running and making plans for what is called al-Qa'ida? In fact, what evidence was there at the time that Osama bin Laden was even alive, and that he was sending tapes to Al Jazeera claiming responsibility for various crimes attributed to Islam and Muslims? Isn't it the easiest thing in the world these days to fabricate a tape, putting together voice and pictures and attributing it to anyone at all, even someone you might have invented in the first place?

The truth is that what happened in Alexandria as part of a sequence of incidents attributed to fanatical Muslims was much too serious for us to hastily explain away in this way, and the people who benefited from this method of explanation are, in my opinion, the real beneficiaries of these crimes. So in my opinion they are the ones who planned it, even if they hired Muslims to carry it out, because there really are Muslims who are prepared to carry out such acts, as there are in every country and in every religious community, but people of this kind are not usually fanatics; they are usually hardened criminals, without beliefs of any sort, ready to sell themselves in exchange for the right amount of money.

Again we ask: Who benefits?

There were not many possible beneficiaries. Israel was one of them, because one of the things that helps it achieve its objectives is tarnishing the reputation of Islam and Muslims, and then tarnishing it further. Israel's friends in Egypt were also possible beneficiaries, as serving Israel's goals ensures that they retain their influence and such incidents, when repeated, help to portray them as the Copts' only defenders. The U.S. administration was another possible beneficiary because it works to serve Israeli objectives and the objectives of Israel's friends in Egypt.

Of course all this doesn't mean we should be lax about resisting religious fanaticism and irrational interpretations of religion, but I don't see any connection between this requirement and the criminal incident that took place in Alexandria. What we can conclude from this and similar incidents is a confirmation of the following fact: that the cause of the Copts in this country is in fact the same as the Muslim cause. The enemies of the Muslims are the same as the enemies of the Copts, at home and abroad. And so to respond to an explosion at a church by blowing up a mosque is as pointless as it is depraved. Those who benefited from the two explosions would be people who harbor no affection for either Muslims or Copts.

4

The reactions to the crime committed against Copts on New Year's Day in 2011 were extremely good and gave Egyptians hope that the country may still be in good health.

The reactions of the intellectuals were to be expected, but this time they were more heartfelt than ever before. Even better were the reactions of simple Egyptians, the least educated, least cultured, and those with the lowest incomes. A friend returning from Asyut told me it was noticeable and inspiring that Muslims there genuinely appeared to share the grief of the Copts and that many simple people in the city were eager to go to the churches in Asyut to join the Copts in their Christmas celebrations.

The response by the government and the government newspapers was, as usual, in the form of clichés in which one could not distinguish between what was real and what was fake. There were also statements on the course of the investigations and pictures published of the person alleged to have probably killed himself in order to commit the crime. It was impossible to know for sure whether what was published described what had really happened or what the government wanted people to believe had happened. But all this didn't change the general impression that the real sympathy that Egyptian Muslims felt for the Copts in this tragedy was honest and strong.

Nonetheless there can be no doubt that Egyptians as a whole also felt truly anxious about the future, including the future of relations between Muslims and Copts, because the incident was more horrendous than the attack in Nag' Hammadi one year earlier and both of them were a new type of attack on Copts, premeditated and completely unprovoked. In the same week there was a referendum in southern Sudan on whether to secede from the north of the country, and events in Iraq continued, with a widening gap between Shi'ites and Sunnis. European countries and the United States were issuing stronger-than-usual statements about the consequences if the Egyptian government was unable to protect minorities. It looked as if the devilish idea we first heard about years earlier, that there was a plan to break the Arab world into small sectarian ministates in order to weaken the Arabs, uproot the idea of Arab nationalism once and for all, and reinforce the idea of a Jewish state on the ruins of Palestine, had started to be seriously put into effect, which might have had something to do with attempts to incite strife between Egyptian Muslims and Copts. All this was bound to arise in the minds of many, myself included, weakening the effect of the encouraging responses to the latest incident and making people more inclined toward pessimism.

That was one of the reasons I was reluctant to respond when a newspaper had the idea of pulling together suggestions from a number of writers on what could be done in the future to tackle sectarian strife in Egypt. "Do we really need more suggestions?" I asked myself. Hasn't everything been said already, and every possible suggestion made? Could I really talk again about the need to reform what the media broadcast, to refrain from incitement and spreading hatred in sermons by the imams in mosques, to review the schoolbooks read by millions of children, and to stop teachers corrupting the minds of their pupils with very bad explanations in the name of religion, which spread hatred between Muslim and Coptic children? Should I talk again about the effect of economic policies, of the rise in unemployment, and of low salaries and high prices on people's feelings toward each other, and especially against minorities, when someone who is frustrated for economic reasons finds no better outlet for his indignation and frustration than venting his anger and hatred on people who do not share his religion?

All this is true, of course, and would no doubt count as a contribution to solving the problem. But there are a number of things that make one hesitant to say it again, apart from the fact that it has been said dozens of times already.

For a start there is the possibility I just mentioned: that the fundamental cause of strife between Muslims and Copts was an external conspiracy that would not be affected if television programs were improved and school curricula and even economic policies reformed. If external forces really bore prime responsibility for damaging relations between Muslims and Copts, then they would keep up their work whatever reforms we made.

In fact these same external forces may have a hand in the television, the Egyptian media, the school curricula, and the economic policies continuing as they are. Don't these foreign forces already have a hand in choosing who rules us, which of them stay in power, and which are deposed?

But let's suppose for the sake of argument that there are no foreign fingers at all involved here and it's purely up to us whether we make reforms or allow decline. Another difficulty arises here: that all the reforms we want to see in these fields (media, education, the economy) cannot bear fruit overnight; the decline that has taken place in these fields started a long time ago, and the psychological effects are deeply entrenched, so uprooting them will require a considerable period of diligent work.

But worse than this, even if the responsibility falls to us without any foreign intervention, one has to admit that the regime ruling Egypt does not appear willing to carry out these essential reforms anyway, however much it makes statements to the contrary. Those responsible for education, the media, and the economy do not want to take the steps needed to reduce the tension between Muslims and Copts, and so offering them advice is pretty much a waste of time.

"Is that credible?" some might say in response. "Isn't there anyone in the ministries and official agencies in charge of these three key sectors who is interested in the well-being of the country and in ending strife?" My response is that these ministries and bodies are in fact full of people who are interested in the well-being of the country—in fact, they are the majority in all these ministries and agencies—but they are not the ones who make the crucial and influential decisions. Even some of the people who make the crucial and influential decisions might have good intentions and might express them when they are sitting with their families and friends, but when they sit down to make these decisions they do exactly the opposite. And the reason for that is that the decisions that need to be made to put an end to sectarian conflict are inconsistent with other interests they see as more important and more deserving. Putting an end to sectarian strife means putting an end to corruption, as well as more justice, more freedom, and more independence from foreign powers.

5

Anyone who reads or hears what people in Egypt said about the case of Wafaa Constantine, and then the case of Camellia Shehata, must be greatly surprised at the way relations between Muslims and Copts in Egypt have developed in recent decades, and also at the changes in the way Egyptian Muslims see themselves and the way the Copts see themselves.

To be honest, I wasn't eager to follow the daily news about the details of what happened in the two cases because I didn't consider them at first to deserve much attention, but the constant stream of news about the two cases and the way that day by day they took up more and more space in the media, with bigger and bigger headlines, forced one to find out more about them. Nevertheless I still couldn't tell anyone with sufficient precision what exactly happened. What I know is that Wafaa and Camellia are two Christian women, or at least were Christian women, and that Wafaa Constantine converted to Islam and then reverted to Christianity and that she is now somewhere in a monastery under the eyes of the church, and that Camellia Shehata ran away from her marital home and converted to Islam, and was then said to have been arrested by police and handed over to the church, then the church denied she had ever converted to Islam, while many Muslims insisted that she did convert and was then forced to revert to Christianity. Muslim demonstrators protested that the police had interfered with the freedom of a Coptic woman who wanted to convert, and the Copts protested against the Muslim protests, and so on.

So Wafaa and Camellia became famous personalities and everyone saw their pictures published repeatedly in the newspapers, although it was no more than a case of individual preference for which we don't know the true motives, but they certainly wouldn't add to or detract from the credit of either religion. When an individual, any individual, changes his or her religion, apart from it being unusual it is also usually connected with a purely personal problem, and it's hard to imagine anyone, man or woman, making the decision to change their religion based on lengthy study and thought about what distinguishes one of the two religions from the other. That is not in the nature of things or in the nature of most of humanity, and it is especially difficult to imagine under conditions such as those that exist in Egypt today and among members of a social class such as the one Wafaa and Camellia belong to. So it is almost certain that in both cases the desire to change religion was a decision based on purely practical considerations (probably connected with the freedom to divorce and marry) and not on theological considerations. This alone was enough to make the matter unworthy of attention. So then why all this tension and hullabaloo? Why were the Muslims so agitated, and why was the church intervening to such an extent, and why were the police involved in the first place? An individual and insignificant incident that didn't deserve much thought turned into a social phenomenon that had to be explained. I came to an explanation that I will present here.

Just as individuals can have experiences that damage their self-confidence and become very sensitive about what people say about them, getting more depressed than necessary when they are criticized and more cheerful than necessary when they are praised, even if the praise is unrealistic or driven by some selfish desire or simply by flattery, it seems to me that a whole class or sect can lose its self-confidence or have it greatly weakened, and then it imagines insults where no insult is intended and rejoices when one of its qualities is praised even when there is no good reason to rejoice. Based on claims, imaginary or real, about what one group thinks of the other or about the insults that one group has aimed at the other, individual members of this class or sect clash with others of the same class (or of another sect within the same society) and exchange abuse and insults.

We know enough about the evolution of the relationship between Muslims and Copts over the last hundred years to say with certainty that none of what happened in the cases of Wafaa and Camellia could have happened (at least not in so intense a manner) at the beginning of the last century, when Islamic discourse was led by a man of the stature of Sheikh Muhammad Abduh, or in the 1930s when it was led by Hassan al-Banna, or in the 1950s in the time of Sayyid Qutb, or in the 1960s to the 1980s in the time of Sheikh Mitwalli Sha'rawi. I think it was inconceivable in any of those periods that a Christian woman converting to Islam could have created all the interest and tension that arose in 2010. The reason is that Muslims and Copts are not living under the same circumstances as they were a hundred years ago, or half a century ago, or even a quarter-century ago. Unfortunate things have happened to each community, and their very low confidence has affected the attitude of each toward the other.

To talk about self-confidence in the context of what has happened to a whole social class or a whole sect within society may be unusual, whereas it is common in describing a particular individual, but I think that the word is correct and quite appropriate to describe what has happened to the Egyptian middle class or broad swaths of it. A decline in economic conditions can undermine the self-confidence of a whole class, just as it can undermine the self-confidence of an individual. As a result of this decline unemployment spreads and those who are not unemployed work at jobs that are below their capacity, with less status than they aspired to and than their education qualifies them to expect. They worry about what the future may bring, many of them are unable to provide basic necessities for their sons and daughters, young people are forced to put off marriage, and so on. Self-confidence is also undermined when your social status declines relative to others with whom you compare yourself and whose achievements you aspire to match. This can also happen to a whole social class when there are wide disparities in income and wealth and it seems impossible to join the class above.

This sense of frustration intensifies, and self-confidence is undermined, when despair sets in after a period of rising aspirations. In the 1930s and 1940s there was a vast gap between poor Egyptians and the rich, but the poor had been accustomed for decades, possibly even for several centuries, to the idea that it was impossible to cross this gap, so to acquire self-confidence they relied on things other than increasing their incomes and their wealth. Since the 1980s, that is, for the last thirty years, this has no longer been the case because the gap between the middle class and the upper class has grown, as it has between the lower and upper layers of the middle class, after twenty years of success in reducing this gap. The shock was severe and very disappointing, greatly undermining self-confidence.

When this happens to a whole class or a large sector of society, then what happened to relations between Muslims and Copts comes to be expected, and the form and substance of religious discourse can change, along with the way people react to events and talk about them. In the light of this change, we have to look at what happened in the welter of unfortunate developments in the cases of Wafaa Constantine and Camellia Shehata.

We can easily understand that a Muslim might be pleased if he hears that a Christian, after reading the Quran and studying Islam, found that he wanted to convert from Christianity to Islam, just as we can easily understand that a Christian might be happy if he heard the opposite, that is, that a Muslim, after reading about the teachings of Christ, found that he wanted to convert from Islam to Christianity. But why would a Muslim or a Christian rejoice to hear that someone of another religion had decided to convert to his religion based only on his personal circumstances, for practical reasons that had nothing to do with ideas or belief? In this case being happy or angry must reflect emotions that in their turn have nothing to do with ideas or belief, but probably emotions that stem from feelings of frustration that in their turn are the outcome of social and economic circumstances.

It might be said that what upset the Muslims was the attitude of the police, who acted as if they were taking the side of the Coptic Church against them and mistreated a woman who should be completely free to choose whatever religion she wants, as well as the attitude of the Church, which was said to have forced one or both of the women to return to Christianity under duress. It may be said that what upset the Christians was the rumors that some Muslims were working to convert Copts to Islam and even abducting Coptic women for this purpose. But all these rumors and allegations could only arise in a depraved social climate, and could only spread from mouth to mouth in a social climate that was even more depraved. The police and the Church would act in this manner only because of the outrage and inflamed emotions they see on the two sides, either taking the side of their own sect in order to win its support or placating the other side in order to avoid more strife. This desire to win support, and this fear of further strife, are so strong only in a social climate of the kind we have in Egypt.

Amid all this, one side or the other is bound to say a loose word or make a slip of the tongue. When feelings are running high, when people are up in arms and chanting loudly, there's a strong temptation to go along with the crowd, especially when it involves the media, whose only concern is to go along with the crowd. So we hear one side talking against the other side in a way we haven't heard for decades, and we should expect more and even worse in the years to come unless we immediately set about saving what can be saved by reforming the economy and the way we live.

In the midst of these astonishing events one should recall an extraordinary story that really happened in the 1930s or 1940s and that was told by Abd al-Rahman Azzam, that exceptionally enlightened intellectual who wrote an excellent book on the tenets of Islam and was the first secretary general of the Arab League. Azzam went home one day and found his mother putting on mourning clothes, so he asked her why. She said she was going to pay her condolences to her neighbor. When he asked if anything had happened to the neighbor's son, George, his mother said that George had converted to Islam. In surprise and disbelief, he said, "You're going to pay your condolences to her because her son has converted to Islam?"

"You know what a mother's heart is like, my son," she replied.

The question is: Why was this imaginable seventy years ago but would no longer be possible today? Why, seventy years ago, were Egyptians in general more able than they are now to imagine how a mother might feel in such circumstances? And why were they more willing in the past to give their natural human emotions priority over external appearances? That is what I have just tried to explain.

6

We all know the importance of Sheikh Muhammad Abduh, but it's useful to reread him and reread about him, to understand how much we have declined since this great man dominated religious discourse in our country more than a century ago.

I read about him in my early youth, like many others, but the passion for religious discourse that has been prevalent in Egypt for some time made me want to read him and read about him again in the hope that in him I would find some solace from the present and to remind myself that we have not always been so pathetic.

I recently had the opportunity to read two small books, one by Sheikh Muhammad Abduh called *Islam between Science and Civilization* and the other by Abbas al-Aqqad on Muhammad Abduh. I also reread a long chapter written by Ahmad Amin on Muhammad Abduh in his book *Leaders of Reform in the Modern Age*.

I admit that I was awed by what I read. Yes, I knew what an amazing man he was, but to this extent? Yes, I realized we had declined since the time when such a man was among us, but had we really fallen so low? In fact, of all the problems that we face these days and that come back to trouble our peace of mind every few days, was there anything this man had not tackled and explained decisively and correctly, all more than a hundred years ago?

On those pages I read his clear-cut opinion on the correct relationship between Muslims and Copts, on the attitude sensible Muslims should take toward science and western civilization, on the correct Muslim position on the balance between piety and the enjoyment of life, and on the Muslim position on the arts, and I found in them eloquent and decisive responses to those who endlessly attack Islam and accuse Muslims of terrorism, as well as great concern to preserve the Arabic language and awareness of its role in bringing about the desired renaissance.

All this I read in those few pages. Not just this, but I found it all explained in fine language that deserves to be read for its own sake regardless of the subject matter, with the vigor and enthusiasm of someone who fully believes what he says. All this makes me wonder: Does the Ministry of Education, when it looks for good books to put into the hands of schoolchildren, need to look far when it has in front of its eyes the writings of Sheikh Muhammad Abduh, which are simple and clear and which not only teach children to hate fanaticism, love those of different religions, and value scientific inquiry and invention, but also instill in them love for the beautiful Arabic language? If that's the case and if it's so simple, does the fact that the Ministry of Education doesn't do this, and that such ideas never occur to ministry officials in the first place, mean that those in charge of education in Egypt are not interested in combating fanaticism and putting an end to sectarian conflict, or is it all just playacting?

Read what Muhammad Abduh says about Islam's attitude toward people of other religions in his book *Islam between Science and Civilization*.

Islam has allowed Muslims to marry women from *ahl al-kitab*, whether Christians or Jews, and gives such wives the right to retain their religion and perform its rites, to go to church or to the synagogue. She and her husband are part of a whole and closer to each other than their own shadows. She is his companion in good times and bad, on journeys and at home, the joy of his heart and the balm of his spirit, the mistress of his house and the mother of his children, free to handle the house and the children as she wishes. . . . Then there is the kinship between the husband's relatives and the wife's relatives, and the customary friendship between the two groups. It's splendid when that shows among the children, the maternal uncles, and the mother's relatives. Can't you see how the ties of affection between Muslims and non-Muslims are strengthened by such tolerance, which was unusual among adherents of the two previous religions? (Abduh, *al-Islam bayna al-'Ilm wa al-Madaniya* (Islam between Science and Civilization) (Damascus: Dar al-Mada li-l-Thaqafa wa-l-Nashr, pp. 84–85)

Or read what he wrote about people who think little of denouncing others as infidels, an idea that is saddening when one remembers what happened in our current age of decline to an eminent Egyptian academic, Dr. Nasr Hamid Abu Zeid. A court declared him to be an infidel and dissolved his marriage because he favored interpreting religious texts in ways consistent with reason and science. Sheikh Muhammad Abduh wrote that one feature Muslims were famous for as one of the principles behind their religious tenets was that "if someone says something that can be read as unbelief in a hundred ways and as faith in just one way, then it should be read as faith and not as unbelief. Have you seen greater tolerance than that for what philosophers and wise men say? Is a man likely to be stupid enough to say anything that doesn't suggest faith in at least one aspect out of a hundred?" (Abduh, pp. 76–77).

Sheikh Muhammad Abduh considered the use of reason to interpret religious texts to be an essential aspect of Islam.

> Members of the Islamic community, other than a negligible minority, agree that if reason and tradition are incompatible then reason should be followed, and there are then two ways of dealing with the tradition: either conceding that the tradition is sound while admitting that it is incomprehensible, and leaving the matter to God in His omniscience, or else interpreting the tradition, while preserving the rules of language, so that its meaning is consistent with the dictates of reason. . . . Could any philosopher be more far-sighted than that? (Abduh, p. 76)

Sheikh Muhammad Abduh has some very fine words to say denying the view that religion is everything in life.

> The lenient dictates of the Hanafi school, although they bring man close to his Lord and fill his heart with dread, they nevertheless do not take him from his livelihood, deprive him of the enjoyment of life, impose on him the austerity of asceticism, or force him to abandon pleasures more than is normal. The founder of this religion did not say "Sell what you possess . . . and follow me," but when he was asked how much one should give in alms, he said: "A third, and a third is plenty. It's better to leave your heirs rich than to leave them destitute to beg from others." (Abduh, p. 86)

I recently heard from one of the lecturers at the Faculty of Fine Arts in Egypt that the sculpture department was one of the least popular with students because the opinion that sculpture was *haram* had begun to spread among them. Let them read Aqqad's summary of Sheikh Muhammad Abduh's views on the fine arts in the days when he was the mufti of Egypt, written in 1903.

Painting is a form of poetry that is seen rather than heard, and poetry is a form of painting that is heard rather than seen. These paintings and statues have preserved so many aspects of real people or groups of people in various situations that they deserve to be compared to an anthology of poetry, in visual or solid form, depicting people or animals in joy and contentment, in peace of mind and resignation. The ideas behind these expressions are so similar that it is not easy to distinguish them from each other, but when you look at different paintings you can see that the difference is glaringly obvious, and to preserve these creations is in fact to preserve knowledge and an act of gratitude toward their creators. (al-Aqqad, *Muhammad Abduh* [Cairo: Egyptian Ministry of Culture, 1964], p. 264)

If anyone objects by saying, "Looking at an image raises suspicions of idolatry," in other words, that paintings and sculptures can tempt people into paganism, which Islam condemns, Sheikh Muhammad Abduh's response is: "Your tongue also raises suspicions of lying, so must it be tied up, although it can tell the truth as well as lie?" To that he adds, "In general it strikes me that Islamic sharia is most unlikely to ban one of the finest forms of learning, after establishing that it poses no danger to Islam, with respect to either belief or practice" (al-Aqqad, pp. 264–66).

One might think that such a man in the early twentieth century could only have had followers among the elite, or the elite of the elite, because how could ordinary people understand and appreciate a man of such depth, such tolerance and broadmindedness? But in fact when the man died in 1905 his funeral was a mass occasion in the full sense of the word. This is how al-Aqqad describes it:

The late mufti did not have an organized network of followers that could mobilize large numbers of people to take part in marches. In fact the official authorities [the khedive, that is] were hostile toward him and upset with those who took part in the funeral. It was a very hot summer and the number of people who were away from the cities on holiday, either abroad or in country villages, was greater than the number that had stayed, so the nationalist tone overwhelmed the official or traditional aspect when the mufti's body was taken to its final resting place, from Alexandria to Cairo. The wave of sadness that weighed on the thousands of mourners along the road came from deep in people's hearts, showing the nation how much they felt the greatness of the man who had died and how great a loss his death had brought. From early in the morning the size of the crowd was way beyond what the police had expected and had prepared for in the two cities, even before the coffin left his house. The markets came to a standstill and the shops closed their doors to take part in the funeral procession. The pavements were packed with people standing and walking. In the two cities no one of any intellect or social status did not take part in this well-attended event. (pp. 254–55)

The French-language newspaper *L'Egypte* said, "It appeared to the spectator as if all the indigenous inhabitants of Cairo had performed the last rite of reverence and veneration for this eminent sheikh, as well as a large number of Europeans."

7

From time to time I go back to thinking about the reasons for the decline in religious discourse in Egypt. Whenever I came across an example of an irrational interpretation of religion (any interpretation that is unacceptable to reason), or an example of behavior that gives the impression of piety but is intrinsically immoral, or a case where form takes precedence over substance, or a case where someone salves his conscience by carrying out the requisite religious rituals while ignoring the ethical virtues that religion demands, I go back to the question: Why, more than a hundred years ago, did we have a great religious speaker, Sheikh Muhammad Abduh, who asserted quite the opposite and gave a higher status to observing the ethical principles that religion advocates than to carrying out the rituals, and why can't our age produce such a man, or even someone close to his wisdom and his ability to transcend minutiae and to provide a rational interpretation of religion?

I reread some of his writings and came across the following passage:

Muslims have neglected their religion and paid too much attention to words. They have abandoned all the virtues and good qualities of their religion. They say, "Intent in the case of prayer means that one intends to perform this prayer rather than do something else," and this is the sense in which they interpret the saying of the Prophet, "Actions should be judged by intentions." But to aim to do something when you set about doing it is perfectly natural. If I start walking, I don't intend, by my walking, to sit down. It's absurd to imagine that the sharia would require this and give it such an important role in the discussion of what to do and how to worship. What is meant by intention in the saying of the Prophet is what one intends to achieve by the act, either to please God and to earn His approval (which is the proper intention) or for some other purpose, such as for hypocritical display. (Muhammad Imara, ed., *al-A'mal al-kamila li-l-Imam Muhammad 'Abduh* [The Complete Works of Imam Muhammad Abduh], Part 3 [Cairo: Dar El Shorouk, 1993], p. 212)

I went on reading and found in the writings of Sheikh Muhammad Abduh one example after another of how little interest he showed in formalities and how he went straight to the moral aspect. What mattered to him before anything else was purity of heart. I read, for example, an interesting conversation that took place between him and his talented disciple, Sheikh Rashid Rida, on the question of the marriage of Sheikh Ali Yusuf, a subject that preoccupied public opinion as a whole in Egypt at the beginning of the last century.

The problem was that Sheikh Ali Yusuf, who was prominent in the press and in politics and owned the newspaper *al-Muayyad*, married Sheikh al-Sadat's daughter Safiya, who had reached the age of majority, without her father's consent. Her father objected to the marriage and sued for it to be annulled on the grounds that the husband was not his daughter's equal because his daughter was a descendant of the Prophet, whereas Ali Yusuf was not.

The court ruled in favor of annulling the marriage because the husband was not her equal. Sheikh Rashid Rida went to Sheikh Muhammad Abduh and said, "Ali Yusuf is angry with you because he believes you're the reason for the ruling that he is not her equal, because you're a friend of the judge who issued it." Sheikh Muhammad Abduh's answer was, "You know I agree with what you wrote [that is, he agreed that it was wrong to dissolve the marriage on the grounds that the husband was not the equal of his wife]. But if you asked me what I thought about Sheikh Ali and al-Sadat as people, I would say they are equals—equally contemptible, not equally noble" (Imara, p. 137).

What struck me in this conversation was not just Sheikh Muhammad Abduh's boldness in expressing his beliefs but also the way he went beyond superficial matters and went straight to a moral judgment, because what matters is not one's pedigree or descent but one's morals.

The same week I happened to read an excellent article in *al-Shuruq* newspaper by Dr. Rasheed El-Enany, who is professor of Arabic literature at Exeter University and the author of two important books on the literature of Naguib Mahfouz that earned the praise and approval of Mahfouz himself. The article was about the famous writer May Ziadeh (1886–1941), whom he rightly described as a Lebanese-Egyptian writer since she was a Lebanese Christian by birth and Egyptian through the cultural environment that influenced her and that she influenced. That was in the first decades of the last century, that golden age in the cultural history of Egypt, with brilliant writers such as Sheikh Muhammad Abduh himself, Qasim Amin, Lutfi al-Sayyid, Taha Hussein, and Abbas al-Aqqad.

Dr. El-Enany wrote his article on the occasion of the publication of a book called *May Ziadeh: Forgotten Writings*, a volume of about a thousand pages with 170 articles by Miss May, as she was known in Egypt, which were first published in Egyptian publications such as *al-Ahram* and *al-Siyasa* and then compiled by a German Arabist who spent ten years studying every word May Ziadeh wrote or that was written about her.

Dr. El-Enany says that browsing through the book was painful and saddening, partly because of the contrast between the religious discourse as it was a hundred years ago in Egypt and how it is today. He quotes this beautiful passage from an article by Miss May about relations between religious sects: "Religion, ladies and gentlemen, is not something I choose or you choose. We are born in a religion, just as one is born fair or dark, tall or short. What would you say if someone who was blond fought his neighbor because he had dark skin and brown eyes? Such a conflict strikes us as ridiculous and comical, but religious conflicts appear no less ridiculous and comical to sensible people."

In an article in *al-Ahram* (June 24, 1928), she describes a visit she made to the Rifa'i and the Ibrahim Agha mosques, when she heard the muezzin giving the call to prayer and church bells ringing at the same time. "The voice of the muezzin, the sound of my childhood, you have long awoken me at dawn and moved me in the evening. You were the first token of joy and beauty impressed on my heart. In the morning and the evening you were joined by the bells that sang in their own manner the praises of the One you magnified in your manner, the two of you floating on the breeze to express a single emotion and an exemplary worship: the worship of the One, that alone is to be worshiped."

Again I wondered: What accounts for the decline in religious discourse over the past hundred years? The only explanation I was comfortable with was the amazing growth in the number of half-educated people. Sheikh Muhammad Abduh and Miss May were writing in a society that was divided into a very small minority of educated people, though they were highly educated, and a vast majority of illiterates (but illiterates who knew their own worth, without aspirations and also without any pretensions). The members of this small highly educated minority were addressing each other, speaking in an elevated and civilized manner, while the rest were silent, making no clamor nor intruding on the discussion. Now we have millions of half-educated people who truly terrorize the educated and the illiterate alike. They are the ones who now control religious discourse and put their stamp on it.

8

In a single religion there are various ways to be religious. Islam is a single whole, but Islamic ways of being religious vary from age to age and from person to person. The same applies to all religions.

Muhammad Abduh's religion was the same as that of his disciple Rashid Rida, the same as that of Hassan al-Banna and Sayyid Qutb, and so on. But the religiosity of each differed from that of the others.

The same applies to the ways people understand the same phrase. A phrase one person uses to express his belief and devotion may have different associations in his mind than it has for others. Everyone says, "God willing," for example, and using the phrase may reflect in one way or another the way the speaker is religious, but I have noticed that the meaning can vary from one person to another. The speaker might mean that the matter is out of his control and in the hands of God, but another person might use it merely to procrastinate or to avoid giving a definitive answer.

So, to be honest, I have never been comfortable with phrases such as 'renewing Islam' or 'enlightened Islam' because Islam is not something to be renewed. What is renewed is the way people interpret Islam and what they understand from it. So what is meant is the renewal of religiosity, or of the way religion is understood. 'Enlightened' and 'unenlightened' are adjectives that can be applied to a particular person or to their interpretation of religion, but not to the religion itself.

There's nothing strange about this because religion is divine, while being religious is a human activity. It's unfortunate that we often treat human decisions on religious matters as if they are divine commands, doing an injustice to religion and to our worldly concerns at the same time.

I had this train of thought when I heard about the tension in relations between Muslims and Copts after the crime in Alexandria on New Year's Day 2011. Then there was the unjustified polarization between Muslims and Copts over whether to vote yes or no in the referendum in March 2011 on amending articles of the constitution, and then, after the referendum, the burning of the church in Atfih and the appalling attack on a Coptic teacher in Qena, all of which was done in the name of religion.

These events reminded me of what devotion meant to one great man, the Indian leader Mahatma Gandhi, in the first half of the last century. This man was a victim of his own admirable concept of devotion, slain by a man who shared his religion but was "devout" in a wholly different manner.

During the 1930s and 1940s, a struggle broke out in India between the Hindu majority and the Muslim minority. The ratio between them was about three to one; in other words, the number of Muslims was about a quarter of the total number of Indians. The basic cause for India at that time was liberation from British rule, but Muslims also aspired to set up their own independent state when the British withdrew from India.

The Muslim demand for an independent state divided the Indian nationalist movement in two and weakened the efforts of those campaigning against the British. There was evidence that the British were encouraging this division between Hindus and Muslims in accordance with the well-known policy of 'divide and rule.' But Mahatma Gandhi had other reasons, more important ones in his view, for disliking the split between Muslims and Hindus and opposing the partition of India into two states.

Gandhi saw the partition of India along religious lines as a form of 'disbelief' and he regarded the campaign for partition as utterly irrational. He described the argument for partition as "untruth" and an Indian who wrote a biography of Gandhi said that in Gandhi's vocabulary there was no word stronger than the word 'untruth.' Gandhi discussed what was meant by patriotism or loyalty to one's country, saying that religious differences had nothing to do with this loyalty and that he did not think that religious differences correlated with cultural differences.

Once he wrote, "The Bengali Muslim speaks the same tongue that a Bengali Hindu does, eats the same food, has the same amusements as his Hindu neighbor. They dress alike. His [Muslim leader Muhammad Ali Jinnah's] name could be that of any Hindu. When I first met him, I did not know he was a Muslim." Gandhi's view was that even if there were religious and cultural differences, there should be no clash of interests when it came to matters such as taxation, the economy, public health, and justice. The differences could only affect religious usage and observances, with which a secular state should have no concern.

Gandhi did everything he could to prevent the nationalist movement splitting along religious lines, but when he saw that the split persisted he confined his efforts to preventing either side from using violence against the other side. Gandhi was unusually respected by both sides, which meant that merely by expressing his disapproval of Hindus and Muslims fighting he could reduce the level of tension. When the strife intensified he announced that he would start a hunger strike to the death unless the two sides ended acts of violence, and this announcement by Gandhi was enough to put an end to them. During the violence the Muslims would blame the Hindus, and the Hindus would blame the Muslims and call them "hooligans." But Gandhi said that educated people had created the "hooligans" by spreading a culture of hatred.

Conflict between Hindus and Muslims broke out again in July 1946 when the British government asked Nehru to form a government. Nehru asked Jinnah, the head of the Muslim League, to join him in government, but Jinnah refused in protest at what he called an attempt by the "Hindu fascist party," with the help of the British, to subdue Muslims and other Indian minorities. Acts of violence broke out, and in the city of Calcutta alone five thousand people were massacred in four days and more than fifteen thousand people were injured. The tragedy was repeated in other parts of India. In village after village the Muslims began to take revenge on the Hindus for what they had done to the Muslims in other villages. Gandhi announced that if the violence didn't stop immediately, not through police intervention but because both sides realized that what they were doing was pure evil, he would start fasting until death. Gandhi said that the Hindu majority should feel remorse for what it had done and should atone for its mistakes, and that the Muslim minority should forgive and show readiness to turn a new page. The amazing result was that as soon as Gandhi announced his intention to fast, the acts of violence stopped.

When the violence resumed over the following year Gandhi was greatly saddened and uncertain what to do. He had a sense that he had failed to fulfill his hope. He had worked all his life to make India an example to the world in opposing violence, so was his method of achieving this objective mistaken? Did the people who said in public that they believed in what he said really harbor quite different thoughts in their breasts?

When the British government declared India independent on August 15, 1947, and all India was expected to celebrate with jubilation, Gandhi did not hide the fact that he was far from jubilant. The day he had longed for and worked for came without bringing him any joy because India won its freedom only at the heavy price of partition. It's very much like the way we felt in Egypt when joy at the fall of the Mubarak regime gave way to apprehension and great anxiety when incidents of sectarian strife occurred.

Acts of violence and slaughter soon resumed in India as the religious majority in each area set about attacking members of the religious minority, and the panicked minorities hurried to flee from areas where they knew they would fall under the control of the other religious group.

Gandhi decided to go to one of the cities that had seen the most violence and chose to stay in the home of a Muslim worker in a neighborhood where the Muslim inhabitants were thought to be in the greatest danger. Gandhi preached to the people of the city, urging them to renounce hatred and violence, and his address had a magical effect. Young Hindus and Muslims gathered in the streets in complete harmony to celebrate independence. The London *Times* said that Gandhi's words had a greater effect than several divisions of soldiers and police could have achieved.

But these happy developments concealed a tragic ending. The first sign of this ending came when a bomb exploded on the evening of January 20, 1948, a few feet from where Gandhi was standing during communal prayers. Ten days later, on the evening of January 30, 1948, Gandhi came out of his house to address a prayer meeting, leaning on the shoulders of his sister's granddaughters. Gandhi walked through a crowd of about five hundred people who had come to the meeting. They cleared a way for him and some stood up while others bowed in respect. He apologized for being a few minutes late for the prayers. Suddenly a man came forward from the crowd and bent down as if he wanted to touch Gandhi's feet, then took a pistol out of his pocket and fired three shots, killing Gandhi on the spot. The killer was a Hindu who hated what Gandhi was doing to urge Hindus to treat Muslims well.

9

I must admit that I have never felt good about the *niqab*. I find it upsetting and depressing and when I see one, I ask myself, "What kind of thinking led this woman to wear it?" If the motive is to satisfy a religious obligation, then many distinguished scholars of Islamic law say that it is not in fact an obligation, so why have these women rejected this interpretation and adopted the opposite one? Is it motivated by the veiled woman's desire to draw closer to God and acquire merit, and by her belief that this form of dress, even if not prescribed by Islamic law, is at least commendable? And why, I wonder, should this form of dress be considered commendable? I can think of many strong arguments against the *niqab*, both in the interests of women who are thinking of wearing it and in the interests of society as a whole, so how can the attitude of religion be different from the one dictated by reason?

I, and I trust many readers, too, very much sympathize with the well-known Mu'tazilite expression 'rational right and wrong,' which refers to the theory that the intellect can know whether something is good or bad. On that basis the Mu'tazila felt free to interpret the Quran by the criteria of both reason and the sayings of the Prophet and by relying on their knowledge of language and of the style and spirit of the Quran. Given that there are few Quranic verses or sayings of the Prophet relevant to what women should wear, and even these can be interpreted in more than one way, we have no option but to judge on the basis of reason, and reason, I believe, sees many disadvantages to the *niqab*.

Islam and ethics both advocate modesty, of course, on the part of both men and women, and this is also what reason says. But I find it hard to describe wearing the *niqab* as mere modesty because it goes much further than that, almost to the extent of withdrawing from social life altogether and isolating oneself when one goes out of the house. This withdrawal is a very strange and incomprehensible attitude, strange because it goes as far as preventing people from knowing whether the person wearing the *niqab* is a man or a woman or how old the person is. If a woman in *niqab* allows an unrelated man to hear her voice or have a conversation with her, she doesn't let him know what effect his words have on her since she doesn't let him see how her facial expression changes, although he has a right to do so, I believe, as a prerequisite for natural human interaction. How can a teacher, for example, fulfill his function of teaching a group of women in *niqab* without knowing how they react to what he says? How can a woman in *niqab* who is a civil servant deal with people who come to her on official business? How can a doctor in *niqab* deal with her patients? Or should a woman in *niqab* in fact spend most of her life at home, going out only when absolutely necessary? Why treat women so cruelly?

Is all this really necessary to protect men and women from temptation? Is it true that any feeling derived from the sexual instinct is always wrong and must be suppressed? Or is it wrong only when you can't control yourself and this feeling leads to some immoral act or sin? Why such a severe approach to mankind's natural feelings, this inclination to deny human nature? Civilization doesn't mean eliminating desire but being able to control it and direct it toward making life happy and beautiful.

To insist on women wearing *niqab* is insulting to both men and women: insulting to every passing man because it implies that he cannot think about anything but sex, and insulting to women who are not in *niqab* because it implies that they do not pay due regard to modesty. Besides, wearing the *niqab* reopens the subject of sexual temptation even when one thought it irrelevant and is a constant reminder that the main preoccupation of us all should be to avoid this temptation.

But there is another aspect to this issue. Sexual desire by its nature is not aroused only by what one sees; it may also be aroused by what one hears and merely by what one imagines. So stopping the eyes from seeing is not always enough to avert attraction to the opposite sex. So what do we do then if we assume that people cannot control their feelings and are bound to sin as soon as they feel attracted to the opposite sex? Is it enough to shield women's bodies from the gazes of men, or should their voices also be prevented from reaching their ears? And even if a woman in *niqab* walks along in silence, so no eye sees her and no ear hears her voice, how can we avert the temptation that arises from pure imagination, especially as the imagination usually comes into play when the senses are inactive? Probably, if that's the case, we have only two options: to try to train ourselves in self-control or to find a way to eliminate sexual desire at the source.

10

It's normal for a society to include a majority and a minority, that one group of people which constitutes the majority of members of that society should have a different religion, language, skin color, or opinion than another smaller group. It's normal that people feel more comfortable with those with whom they share one of these traits than they do with those who are different. But it is a basic prerequisite for civilization that people who are different are treated well, that people can understand the reasons for these differences and generously accept others expressing themselves in some form, by performing religious rites, defending their personal opinions, having different customs when it comes to eating, drinking, and dress, and so on, as long as this does not prevent others from expressing themselves, offend public decorum, or disturb public order.

Civilized people must repudiate or eschew any behavior at variance with these principles, and any rational interpretation of any religion must condemn any behavior inconsistent with this attitude, regardless of how many texts can be cited that can be interpreted to mean the opposite. It is imperative that religious texts be interpreted in a way that is not inconsistent with the dictates of reason, logic, and respect for natural human rights. Interpretations that are inconsistent with the dictates of reason and civilization must be rejected because they are insulting to both reason and religion.

I remember a wonderful story I was told by Ahmad Bahaeddin, a prominent journalist and an enlightened intellectual. He told me he was visiting a sick friend in a Cairo hospital one day and as he was leaving his friend's room one of the people with him remarked that a senior member of the Muslim Brotherhood was a patient in the same hospital (it may have been the supreme guide or his deputy, I don't remember). Bahaeddin decided to drop in on him too to wish him a quick recovery. Not surprisingly, the conversation got onto the subject of applying Islamic law. Bahaeddin told me that he told the senior Islamist: "I don't have any objection at all to Islamic law being a main source or even the main source of legislation. But it's very important for me to know who is going to interpret it."

It's most unfortunate that this civilized attitude toward religion in Egypt has been severely compromised over the past forty years. That's one of the important reasons why I hated the regimes of Anwar al-Sadat and Hosni Mubarak. Those two periods helped to do the damage and added to it as the years passed, by contributing, actively and passively, to creating the circumstances that eroded that civilized attitude—actively by measures that reinforced irrational interpretations of religion, and passively by refraining from taking steps likely to undermine irrational interpretations.

Anwar al-Sadat initially encouraged religious extremists to join the political arena in the hope that they would weaken his rivals. He and Hosni Mubarak allowed the media persistently to air extremely reactionary interpretations of Islam (and even to encourage the mistreatment of the Coptic minority). Both of them tied the hands of rational politicians and intellectuals who understand Islam and interpret it in a civilized way. They even prevented many of them from crossing the threshold of the television building. They seemed to be afraid that propagating any rational interpretation of Islam would lead to their overthrow. The two of them also applied economic policies that helped increase social tensions, create a wide gap in incomes, push up the rate of inflation, and then in Mubarak's time create a startling increase in unemployment and an equally startling decline in the quality of life for a large sector of low-income people, especially in housing. All of this in turn promoted the growth of irrational interpretations of religion and diverted the anger these sectors felt toward society and economic conditions into anger and hatred toward religious minorities.

All this was one of the many reasons why we rejoiced at the revolution of January 2011. We were especially happy when, in the first days of the revolution, we saw very gratifying scenes showing that Egyptians were basically civilized human beings. We saw two young men, one a Muslim in a turban and the other a Copt carrying a cross, side by side chanting the same slogans, and we saw a Coptic woman pouring water for a Muslim man to help him wash before prayers.

Copts joined Muslims in all the demonstrations across the country, and throughout a month and a half of joint action there was not a single incident that could be classified as an incident of sectarian strife. So why, a month and half after the revolution, was there suddenly a serious incident, when Muslims set fire to a church in a village in Giza province, and then a sudden polarization between Muslims and Copts over the referendum on constitutional amendments that had nothing whatsoever to do with relations between Muslims and Copts, with one side saying to vote "yes" if you are a real Muslim and the other side saying to vote "no" if you want to protect the rights of Copts?

This sudden change was saddening and raised many questions. Did it make sense that Egyptians could change so much overnight? Was the harmony that prevailed during the weeks of the revolution just a superficial, ephemeral phenomenon that was soon superseded by the real feelings that lay beneath, feelings that give rise to much suspicion and apprehension? Were those incidents the work of someone who had an interest in undermining and obstructing the revolution as part of what was sometimes called the counterrevolution? I won't deny that such explanations did occur to me, and I have heard similar ones from some of my friends, Muslims and Copts alike. All of us are puzzled, and everyone is grieving. I also wondered whether those now in power in Egypt did everything they could to prevent those events and nip them in the bud. I wondered whether those who helped set fire to the church in Giza were stopped as quickly as necessary, and whether the media did its duty to prevent inflaming hostile emotions or whether some of the media unjustifiably helped add to the tension and fear by interviewing a man of frightening appearance affiliated with a group of religious extremists and who took part in planning and carrying out the assassination of the president in 1981. The man appeared on television in long interviews, justifying his participation in the assassination plan and describing the assassination as a legitimate act, "given that there were no legal ways of achieving the same goal." The media also published pictures of him coming out of prison surrounded by well-wishers and admirers. Couldn't those in power and those in charge of the media have found some other way to allow freedom of expression, one that did not add to the tension or revive the causes of sectarian strife?

Then there's the role of writers and intellectuals. Is it really possible to defend those who went around telling people that to vote "no" in the referendum on the constitution meant agreeing to or working to repeal Article 2 of the constitution, which says that Islam is the religion of the state, and that to vote "yes" was "true Islam"? Could any intellectual plausibly agree to this line of argument? Could any writer or intellectual even remain silent in the face of this deliberate obfuscation, whatever his or her religious or political beliefs?

The referendum result was as expected, given the political climate in Egypt and this unfortunate blending of religious belief and political opinion on a subject that had nothing to do with religion in the first place. Of the voters, 77 percent said "yes" and 23 percent said "no." Many people genuinely expressed their pleasure at the high turnout. Egyptians seemed to be showing how much they wanted something they had been deprived of for decades, that is, to express their political opinions freely. As soon as they were confident that the results would not be rigged they didn't hesitate to go to the polling stations, despite the difficulties many faced. This was a good and gratifying development. Those who favored a "yes" vote were also happy that they had won a large majority and defeated their opponents, while the opposition, which had hoped for a better result, was disappointed—and this is also normal and understandable. But many people, myself included, were sad that despite the revolution Egyptians had not been able to overcome the psychological effects of four decades of bad government—that is, the psychological effects of stupid economic policies and the deliberate use of sectarian tensions to support them by claiming that the people behind these stupid policies were the only alternative to religious extremism, as well as to overcome the psychological effects of an evil media policy that for forty years promoted extremism in various ways, with programs half of which were irrational interpretations of religion and the other half lewd dancing that led in its turn to irrational interpretations of religion.

11

The argument had been raging in Egypt for some time and it picked up after the January 25 revolution. In fact it's a bitter war between two sides, each of which is enraged at the other and never ceases to attack the other with the most violent insults, sometimes coupled with arson attacks, beatings, and killings.

We all know exactly who the two sides are in this argument but it's very difficult to agree on what to call them. If you call one side the religious trend or the pious, you face the reasonable objection that not all pious people are so fanatical and not all pious people hate those of other religions or wish them ill. If you call it the Islamist side, you face the same objection (that not all Muslims are so fanatical), as well as the objection that this extremism is not confined to any one religion, since there are Copts who exhibit extremism and hold the same hostile feelings toward the other side. If you call them advocates of a religious state, the objection is that a religious state is no part of Islam.

The same goes for the other side in the fight. We could call it the side that advocates a civil state but might face the objection that describing the state as civil might not reflect its real position, since the concept of a civil state might be confused with the concept of civil society. In fact members of the first side might go so far as saying that when the other side says it advocates a civil state, it's just a ruse to avoid describing themselves as secularists, which in their opinion is the right term for them because the term 'secularist' suggests to many a hostile attitude toward religion as a whole.

The terminology is a problem in itself, but however much we disagree over what to call them, we all know that there is a real rivalry between two sides over attitudes toward the relationship between religion and the state. One side argues that the ultimate authority when it comes to making political decisions should be Islamic law and that this should be openly declared, and another side argues that those making political decisions should not be bound by any such precondition, though the principles of Islamic law could be a source of inspiration when it comes to making decisions and drafting laws.

So what's behind this dispute and what does it mean?

Before we answer this question we have to choose a concise name for each side, despite the difficulties I have mentioned. Let's call the first side the Islamists and the other side the secularists on the understanding that each term means what I have just explained, no more and no less. What I mean by the Islamists is those who call for adherence to Islamic law but not necessarily for imposing the *hijab* and the *niqab* by force or imposing the *jizya* (poll tax) on Copts, because the position one takes on the *hijab*, the *niqab*, or the *jizya* depends on how one interprets Islamic law. What I mean by the secularists is those who argue that decision makers and legislators need not declare their adherence to Islamic law, though they do not exclude or reject it, let alone deny religion as a whole.

Let's also agree that there are large areas of policy—foreign, domestic, economic, and social—on which it is easy to imagine the two sides agreeing, just as there are large areas in these spheres of policy where it is easy to imagine sharp differences in each of the two camps. Very many examples could be provided for both possibilities. An Islamist might, for example, call for an end to subservience to any foreign power, just as a secularist might call for the same thing. They might agree on this, as they might agree that Arab unity, economic and political, is in the interests of Arabs, that the peace treaty that Anwar al-Sadat signed with Israel in 1979 was not in the interests of Egypt or the Arabs, that having a strong public sector promotes development, and that a progressive tax system is needed to achieve more social justice. But it's also highly possible to imagine an Islamist agreeing with a secularist on exactly the opposite: agreeing that the alliance with the United States is useful, that a political union between the Arab states would set back Arab progress, that making peace with Israel was beneficial to Egypt and the Arabs, or that giving the private sector priority over the public sector is better for development, and so on.

At the same time, it's also very possible that two Islamists might take different positions on any of these issues, and the same goes for two secularists.

The reason why two people from opposing sides can agree and two people from the same side can disagree is, in my opinion, that Islamic law has not taken a position on many of the questions we face in the contemporary world, or the position it has taken can be interpreted or understood in more than one way. Thus, two people might agree that Islamic law is the ultimate authority but disagree when it comes to interpretation and understanding, just as two people, one Islamist and one secularist, might agree, either because each of them ends up drawing on principles outside of but not incompatible with Islamic law or because the way the Islamist interprets Islamic law coincides with the opinion of the secularist.

I don't say all this at random or merely out of theoretical speculation, as what we actually see and hear from respected people on both sides confirms what I say. We see similar positions on foreign policy and attitudes toward Israel, and positions tending toward socialism and others tending toward capitalism, from people who belong to both of the opposing sides, just as we see sharp differences on these and other matters within each of the two sides.

If that's the case, then where does the disagreement between the two sides come from? And why does the disagreement seem to get so intense, even sometimes to the point of hatred?

The only explanation I can see for this disagreement is that it is a disagreement over 'identity.' One side never stops repeating that its identity is Islamic, while the other doesn't do that for two reasons: either because it is not Muslim or because it is worried that defining the identity of the state as Islamic in this way will lead to particular applications and interpretations of Islamic law that it does not approve of (even if it is ready to accept other interpretations), for example on the treatment of people of other religions, the treatment of women, and the penalties for certain crimes or on some economic transactions.

I repeat that the disagreement between the two sides is not in fact a disagreement over particular positions on these matters, since the Islamists themselves don't always agree on particular positions and the secularists don't know exactly what will happen if the Islamists come to power. So the disagreement is over one side's insistence on declaring a particular identity and the other side's fear of what such a declaration of identity might mean in practice.

Let's take one of many possible examples. Islam bans usury—that is beyond doubt. But what exactly is this usury that is banned? There are different opinions on that. I have heard and read contradictory opinions from various Islamists on whether it is acceptable or unacceptable to pay interest on bank loans—in other words, on whether paying such interest does or does not count as usury. If some secularists believe that abolishing interest on bank loans would do more harm than good economically, then they would not agree to define usury in such a way that the ban on usury would apply to interest payments of this kind. But this position on their part would not distinguish them from all Islamists, but only from some of them. The same can be said for female modesty. What is the necessary level of modesty that can be imposed by law? Is wearing the *hijab* and a long dress sufficiently modest? Or must women wear the *niqab*? Should the ban on alcohol apply only to Muslims or also to non-Muslims, whether foreign or not?

There's no agreement on standard interpretations on one side, and hence the other side does not have complete knowledge of the interpretations that will be applied. This uncertainty, or lack of full knowledge on the part of the secularists about what would result from an Islamist victory, is what drives most secularists to reject religious intrusions into politics, in other words to reject religious justifications for policy rather than to reject religion itself, because they think it best to choose and justify a policy based on a comparison of its probable advantages and disadvantages, each case on its own merits, and not as the application of a particular legal or political principle that is based on a religious text or a traditional axiom. On the contrary, they favor interpreting the religious text or the traditional axiom case by case by rational judgment and as dictated by utility.

When the Islamists reject this attitude on the part of the secularists, the basis for doing so cannot be anything but their attachment to declaring loyalty to a certain identity, that is, their fear that the secularist position implies contempt or insufficient reverence for Islam and Islamic law. One side constantly asserts the need to declare and adhere to a particular identity, while the other side believes that respect for identity does not necessarily require that one constantly declare it or that it be the only criterion for defining the ideal policy.

In this way, I believe, one can understand the battle that broke out and the emotions inflamed over Article 2 of the constitution, which says that sharia is the principal source of legislation. The Islamists, of course, insisted that it must stay and warned against any change, while many secularists preferred another formulation, such as describing Islamic law as "a principal source" of legislation rather than "the principal source," or that one or more phrases be added to the existing text to prevent the article from being interpreted in a way that implies insufficient regard for those of other religions. Many secularists, honestly in my view, said they preferred to leave Article 2 as it is for fear lest any change, however slight, cause unrest that we can well do without. But the disagreement between the two sides on this article is a real disagreement and cannot be denied, and it is a disagreement that in my view is part of the question of 'identity.'

If that's the case, we may well wonder whether a disagreement over 'defining identity' should be our main preoccupation now, among the mass of complex problems we face and the troubles and difficulties the country is going through.

12

When the appalling events took place at the Maspero building on October 9, 2011, I remembered what I had read about other events that took place in Alexandria on June 11, 1882, one hundred and thirty years ago, and that are known in Egyptian history as the Alexandria massacre.

Both incidents were tragic: the victims included many innocent people who had committed no offense, and neither incident was expected or could have been predicted. In the aftermath of each, the most powerful states in the world issued warnings (Britain in the first case, the United States in the second) aimed at the Egyptian government, accusing it of failing to maintain order and protect the lives of minorities (foreigners in the first case and Copts in the second). In the case of the Alexandria massacre, the warning was followed by a British occupation of Egypt that lasted seventy-four years. Could a similar disaster come about after the Maspero massacre, one wondered?

I don't want to be too speculative or too pessimistic but there seems to be real reason for worry because, despite the many differences between the state of Egypt and the world in the late nineteenth century and the conditions that prevail today in the early twenty-first century, there are also important similarities that merit attention.

The Alexandria massacre took place nine months after the start of an impressive revolution in Egypt led by Colonel Ahmad Urabi on September 9, 1881 (at the time people called it the "Urabi furor"). Urabi and a group of fellow officers went to Abdin Square to express their anger at the treatment of Egyptian officers and discrimination against them in favor of Circassian officers and to convey their demands to Khedive Tawfiq.

The following conversation took place between the khedive and Urabi, according to historian Abd al-Rahman al-Raf'i:

"Why have you brought the army here?"

"We've come, Your Highness, to submit the demands of the army and the nation. They are all just demands."

"And what are these demands?"

"The dismissal of Riyad Pasha [the prime minister], the creation of a chamber of deputies, and an increase in the size of the army to the number specified in the sultanic decrees."

"You have no right to make any of these demands. I am the khedive of the country and I act as I wish."

"And we are not slaves, and starting today we will not be passed on like chattel from one ruler to another."

The Maspero massacre took place eight and a half months after the start of a revolution that was also impressive, in which hundreds of thousands of Egyptians gathered in Tahrir Square and other squares demanding bread, freedom, and social justice, and then the downfall of the regime. In 1881 Khedive Tawfiq was forced to comply with Urabi's demands, if only temporarily. He changed the government, appointed a new government under Sherif Pasha, and Ahmad Urabi himself helped Sherif Pasha choose the new ministers. In 2011 Hosni Mubarak was forced to comply with the revolutionaries' demand by stepping down, a new government was formed under Ahmad Shafik, and it looked as if the whole regime was about to collapse. But in both cases, the old regime began gradually to recover its strength and the revolutionaries began to lose their vigor little by little.

In the meantime in both cases there were foreign forces lying in ambush, watching the progress of the revolution with great and very natural interest. Britain had ambitions that made occupying Egypt a tempting option (in brief, the desire to obtain a foothold on the route to India, including control over the Suez Canal, ensuring that Egypt paid its debts to foreign creditors, and converting Egypt into a cotton farm to serve the British textile industry). The United States had and still has ambitions in Egypt (related to subjugating the largest country in the Arab world, which possesses enormous wealth in oil and natural gas, and also to long-term Israeli ambitions, political and economic). In both cases the foreign ambitions were definitely at odds with revolutionary aims such as liberation, independence, and achieving real democracy.

It is very possible that massacres such as the Alexandria massacre in 1882 and the Maspero massacre in 2011—which spread chaos across the country, create powerful reasons for conflict and discord, and thereby stop revolutions from making any progress and provide a strong justification for foreign intervention—could be something that some foreign and domestic forces greatly desire, and so they could have taken place as part of some prearranged plan.

It's important to note another similarity in the way the massacres were carried out in the two cases or, if you wish, in the way they were directed and produced. The main protagonist in the two cases was the 'thug,' someone without a cause, with no emotions of any kind or at least no hostile feelings toward those he is attacking or killing, even if he benefits from the sense of apprehension and fear that prevails between the two sides, such as the tension between Egyptians and foreigners at the time of the Alexandria massacre or between Muslims and Copts at the time of the Maspero massacre.

The main aim, and maybe the sole aim, of the thugs when they assault and murder is merely to obtain money. They are people without conscience, with no sense of loyalty to the country or to any cause whatsoever, people who have adopted criminality as a means to make a living after opportunities to earn a living from honest work have dried up.

In the wake of the Maspero massacre, people passed around estimates of the number of thugs working on behalf of Egyptian security agencies to serve political purposes when it was inadvisable for policemen to appear in official uniform. One number was 165,000 people, and I have no reason to doubt that this number was close to the truth, given what I know of the great increase in the number of unemployed in Egypt over the last quarter-century because of economic decline and the repeated references to "thugs" in official statements to justify one attack after another on the January 2011 revolution, from the Battle of the Camel on February 2 to the repeated attacks on Copts and their churches before and after the revolution.

In the Nag' Hammadi attack, for example, when eight Copts were killed and nine injured as they came out of church on Coptic Christmas Eve on January 6, 2010, the investigation reported that Muhammad Ahmad Hassan al-Kamouni, the man accused of opening fire, was a convicted criminal who had committed crime after crime and been detained in 2002 and sentenced to three years' imprisonment for "a crime of thuggery." There was also much talk at the time, and some photographs were published, suggesting a close relationship between him and an important figure in the National Democratic Party in the Nag' Hammadi area. Now, in the Maspero massacre, it was proved that groups described as "thugs" joined the peaceful march the Copts organized in protest at the attitude of the governor of Aswan toward the building of a church. Men with swords, knives, and gasoline bombs suddenly appeared from side streets and started to attack the demonstrators and the military police at the same time. Fierce fighting broke out, and twenty-five people were killed and more than two hundred were injured.

In the Alexandria massacre in 1882, in which about fifty people were killed and about seventy injured, Abd al-Rahman al-Rafʿi wrote, "The man who provoked the strife was a British subject of Maltese origin who was the brother of the British consul's servant, and this could not have been a coincidence."

Exactly a month after the Alexandria massacre, on July 11, 1882, the British fleet began bombarding Alexandria in preparation for the British invasion. On the connection between the British occupation and the Alexandria massacre, Sheikh Muhammad Abduh wrote:

> The English government, fabricating pretexts as usual, tried to turn things on their head. It ignored the truth and followed the direction dictated by its ambitions. . . . It hastily proceeded to send its ships into

the waters off Alexandria, and some of its agents then inspired some weak-minded foreigners resident in the port to cause a riot in which the poor perished, in order to satisfy English greed, and the government of England used that as a pretext for attacking the territory of the khedive. Anyone who looked at the state of Egypt with disinterested eyes could see that the disorder in that country began with the arrival of the English fleet to the port of Alexandria, and that there can be no comparison between the security, the free flow of trade and the good governance that prevailed before that and the way it was after. (Rashid Rida, *Tarikh al-ustaz al-imam al-shaykh Muhammad Abduh*, cited in Abd al-Rahman al-Raf'i, *al-Thawra al-Orabeya wa-l-ihtilal al-inglizi* [The Orabi Revolution and the British Occupation] [Cairo: Maktabat al-Nahda al-Misriya], p. 304)

My basic aim in writing this chapter is to emphasize once again that the conflict between Muslims and Copts is a fundamentally artificial conflict that has nothing to do with either Muslims or Copts. The main purpose of stirring it up is to harm both Muslims and Copts, and to portray it in any other way would be a serious mistake that could come about only if one gave free rein to one's emotions or deliberately wanted to mislead the two sides.

13

Turkish Prime Minister Recep Tayyip Erdoğan's visit to Egypt in September 2011 was exciting and unprecedented in more than one sense. He brought joy to many Egyptians, including myself, but the visit made some anxious in Egypt and abroad.

Here was Turkey offering us an exciting experiment in combining religiosity with economic, political, and social progress in a way that Egyptians, Arabs, and Muslims had not seen for a long time. It was also a new experience for Turkey, because in its modern history Turkey has had only two types of experience: religiosity coupled with backwardness (in the last centuries of the Ottoman caliphate) or progress coupled with overt rejection of religion (in the Atatürk era). This combination of religiosity and progress, characteristic of the Turkish system for the past decade, is something new and at the same time exciting and worth thinking about.

One must nevertheless admit that this Turkish phenomenon has somewhat puzzled some Egyptian intellectuals. Mr. Erdoğan is truly religious and Turkey undoubtedly has started to flourish in various aspects of life since he came to power, but Erdoğan openly declares that his is a secular government and that the Turkish state is careful to keep an equal distance from all religions. He has said openly that although he is a pious Muslim he does not govern in the name of Islam because he knows that as a human being or as a ruler he can make mistakes, while Islam cannot make mistakes, so if he claimed that he was governing in the name of Islam he might tarnish the reputation of the religion that he reveres and believes in if he misinterpreted it.

This combination of a ruler who is personally religious and a secular state is what has puzzled some Egyptians, who hate the term 'secularism' and see it as almost a synonym for atheism. This group of Egyptians wonders how they can reconcile their admiration and respect for Erdoğan and his amazing experiment with their rejection of the secularism the man has attributed to the policies of the Turkish state.

Although I understand why these Egyptians are ambivalent, I do not see myself as one of them. I see no contradiction between being religious and being able to contribute to a national revival, or between being religious and supporting a secular state. On the other hand, I have no doubt that some forms of being religious are incompatible with national revival and progress, and that is what I will now try to explain.

For almost forty years we have been experiencing something than can be described as a religious surge. Some people call it a religious revival but I prefer the term 'religious surge' for reasons that will soon become clear.

It's been a period characterized by a religious discourse that is shrill, widespread, forceful, and even aggressive, with a clear tendency to interpret religion more strictly than in the past.

This religious surge has not been confined to any one country or even a few countries, or to one religion rather than others. The phenomenon has been Egyptian but also Arab, as well as Iranian, Pakistani, Afghan, and Turkish. It has included Muslims in Muslim-majority countries as well as Muslims in Europe, the United States, and other countries. It is a phenomenon that has included, though less strongly, peoples whose religion is Christianity and who are at various levels of economic and social development, in the west as well as in the Christian minorities in Arab countries.

The phenomenon of the religious surge has been apparent in multiple aspects of social life, in culture and social thought, in schools and the media, in the growing number of people going to mosques, churches, and other places of worship, and in the increasingly strict application of religious rituals. The effects of religiosity have been apparent in various types of social behavior, in the way people dress, especially women, in the proliferation of religious terms in conversation and in writing, in a general reduction in the level of tolerance toward people of other religions, and in increased tension between believers in different religions.

If the religious surge has gained strength and spread to this extent and if its influence has reached into various aspects of social life, why would we not expect it to spread into political activity and into political resistance movements, whether resistance against external aggression or against tyranny and despotism at home?

This is what has actually happened, and since the early 1970s a growing number of political movements have combined political and religious slogans. More and more resistance movements have taken a religious character and use religious discourse to formulate their political positions. We have seen this in the appearance and growth of Islamist movements in Egypt and other Arab countries that adopt religious slogans and put their objectives in a religious framework. The discourse of Palestinian resistance to Israeli occupation has shifted from a secularist nationalist discourse to a religious discourse. We also saw this in the resistance of the Lebanese to Israeli aggression in 1982 and then in 2006, in the Iranian revolution against the shah, in the Iraqi resistance to American and British occupation, and in the Afghan resistance to Soviet occupation and then to U.S. occupation. We might of course add to those the various movements that, rightly or wrongly, have been dubbed terrorist movements, whether they were in fact religious movements that decided to use terrorism for the sake of Islam or merely attempts to tarnish the image of Islam by associating it with terrorism.

It's difficult to separate this growing tendency for political movements to use religious discourse from the religious surge phenomenon in general. If everything is "turning religious"—daily behavior, thought, and education—why should we be surprised to find that politics and resistance movements are also turning religious? I'm inclined to see all this as part of the religious surge in general, and so we have to seek an explanation for the overall phenomenon.

I think the appearance and growth of the religious surge over the past thirty or forty years can be explained by two basic factors, one related to the changes that have taken place in the relationships between states and nations and the other to what has happened to social relationships inside one country or one nation. I think the two factors are closely related to each other and could be the effect of similar causes. I will deal with these two factors in turn.

By the changes that have affected international relations, I mean the rising new wave of globalization that has taken place over the past thirty or forty years. I call this wave of globalization "new" because globalization is an old phenomenon that rises and falls, strengthens and weakens, and the successive waves of colonization, ancient and modern, can be seen as waves of globalization that facilitated the movement of goods, people, capital, ideas, and customs. But this latest wave of globalization differs from previous waves in several respects that are strongly connected, in my opinion, with the phenomenon of the religious surge.

The colonial waves, ancient and modern, always had strong economic motives, even if they were sometimes coupled with military, political, or ideological motives. These economic motives took the form of seeking to obtain cheap raw materials or cheap labor, to open up new markets or new fields for investment, or all of these together. In phase after phase of history these economic motives drove powerful states to occupy weaker states, in other words to military aggression. But the economic motives behind the current colonial wave, even if they sometimes take the form of occupation and military aggression, drive governments and companies to be aggressive in other domains, too, and in different forms. Yes, occupation and military aggression are still tools of imperialism and a means to ensure access to cheap raw materials and cheap labor, to dispose of goods that are looking for markets, and to find new opportunities for investment, but the goods looking for markets are of a different nature than they were in the past and physical conquest is no longer the most effective means to ensure the goods are marketed and new investment opportunities open up. Instead, the most effective way now is to seduce and win over the consumer by peaceful means. Imperialism (and we should not be embarrassed to use the word now as if the phenomenon of imperialism no longer exists) now operates in the field of human psychology and attacks minds, rather than in the field of war with physical occupation. Imperialism now has ways to carry out this new kind of attack that did not exist before, or at least not to the same extent.

Threats are no longer aimed at territory so much as at identity, and when identity is under threat, religious sensibilities are aroused and religious fervor rushes to the defense. In other words, in the face of the old waves of imperialism, those threatened by imperialism rose to defend their territory and their lives by taking up real weapons to counter real weapons. In the face of the current imperialism, those threatened by globalization and alienation rise to the defense by clinging to religion, and the resistance chooses a discourse appropriate to the type of aggression, which, in many cases, is a religious discourse.

But apart from this international, or external, development, there has been another powerful factor inside each country and each nation, working in the same direction and giving more backing to the religious surge, and this is what I will deal with next.

We must have the courage to distinguish between religion on the one hand and religiosity or being religious on the other. Does it really take courage? Yes, because any form of criticism of religiosity is often seen as criticism of religion. This is a form of religious terrorism that is used against anyone who dares to criticize any form of religiosity, even if it's criticism of how high the volume is on the loudspeakers broadcasting the call to prayer.

Religion is a divine phenomenon, while being religious is a human and social phenomenon. Religiosity is subject to the same processes as any other human and social phenomenon—it evolves—whereas religion is permanent and unchangeable. Religiosity varies from country to country and from nation to nation, even if they all profess the same religion, and it is affected by the economic, political, and psychological changes that take place in society.

I can claim, for example—and everyone who, like me, has lived through the changes that Egypt has undergone since the 1940s will back me on this—that the religiosity of the 1940s and 1950s was very different from what it is today. It was less severe and less extreme, and more tolerant, whether toward people of other religions or those of the same religion. What has happened over this period, and especially since the 1970s, that is, over the last forty years, to produce this outcome?

I referred earlier to the rapid pace of globalization as a probable reason for the changes in the forms of being religious that have spread not just in Egypt but in the whole world. I want to add here another, internal factor not unconnected with the phenomenon of globalization, and that is the high rate of social mobility, or the rapid change in the relative status of the different strata of society, with some rising rapidly up the social ladder and others falling. The competition to rise and the fear of falling have intensified, reinforcing on the one hand the desire to prove and publicize the fact that one has risen, but on the other hand aggravating feelings of frustration and distress at the decline of one's social status. Rapid ascent brings to the surface traditions and customs that are invisible or concealed because of low economic status but that become dominant and prevalent when that status improves. But very rapid ascent might also have an illegal or immoral cause, since legitimate businesses that respect ethical rules do not usually lead to sudden enrichment or rapid advancement. Rapid ascent is often associated with money coming into the hands of groups that have little education or culture but have obtained their wealth by ingenuity or by being quick-witted rather than by their skills or talents. All this makes it very possible that new forms of religiosity will appear that were not known or evident before, forms that are strict instead of tolerant, that make false and dishonest claims, that are fanatical and extreme rather than rational and prudent, and that use religious expressions of morality to disguise an immoral reality or as a consolation for failure to climb the social ladder.

We also have to be willing to recognize that one feature of religious discourse is that it can be interpreted in more than one way and it can strike a chord with both cultured people and the uncultured, with both the educated and the uneducated, because of its strong links with powerful emotions that are derived from faith and have a long history of customs and traditions that lie at the heart of a nation's cultural heritage and reflect its personality. So people respond to those emotions easily regardless of whether they are cultured or not. It's easy for religious discourse to spread and gain strength in periods of rapid social mobility, when people's emotions run high and lead in more than one direction and people need to express them with a force that reflects their emotional turmoil. It's also no wonder that political activists, or a large number of them, adopt religious discourse to express their political hopes and aspirations, or that political resistance movements, whether resisting a foreign or a domestic enemy, adopt slogans drawn from religious discourse, and the political discourse changes into a religious discourse that benefits in turn from the profound influence that discourse has on a people that is religious by nature.

This domain in which the religious surge appears (or as some might say, this usage or 'mobilization' of religion), by which I mean the domain of political resistance against a foreign or domestic enemy, is one of the most worthy examples of the religious surge and the one most closely linked to the real spirit of religion and to one of religion's most honorable objectives: liberation from slavery and from subjection to anything other than God.

Just as religiosity can lead to an obsession with things that are superficial and have little effect on psychological or political liberation, and even to discrimination and the incitement of enmity, it can also lead to an affirmation of human dignity, a rejection of attacks on human freedom, and commitment to ideals. This is the reason I am inclined to call what has happened in the last forty years a religious surge rather than a religious awakening, since 'religious surge' allows for both good and bad, commendable and deplorable, types of behavior, whereas 'religious awakening' can only refer to something desirable and commendable.

In the first decades of the twentieth century, one of the slogans Egyptians chanted when they called for political democracy and resistance to despotism was "There is no king but God." It's a beautiful slogan that emphasizes human dignity by rejecting subordination to anyone. Similar slogans were used to bring an end to the despotic rule of the shah in Iran at the end of the 1970s and in the resistance to the Israeli occupation of Palestine and Lebanon. If religiosity has such power to generate emotions that lead to national revival and independence, then what a loss it would be to the nation if it ignored its religion or if its intellectuals denied that some forms of religiosity could make an effective contribution to bringing about that revival and independence.

The fundamental cause of any national revival might not be, as many believe, an economic or technological factor, or a material factor of any kind. It could be a metaphysical factor (based, that is, on belief in something that transcends the visible and tangible world). Metaphysical belief includes religiosity but also includes other forms, since nonreligious people can also come to idolize some leaders and thinkers, in which case they can be as fervent as religious people (one example is the way the Russians idolized Marxist leaders at one time). It might also include a sense of ethnic or national superiority, such as the German enthusiasm for Nazism in the 1930s.

Shakib Arslan expresses this idea well in *Why the Muslims Fell Behind and Why the Rest of the World Progressed*, a fine book that came out in the early 1930s. In it he writes:

Why is it, I wonder, that young Jews who are most advanced and modern are trying to revive the Hebrew language, the origins of which are lost in the mists of the past, and at the same time are most receptive to the principles of modern science and contemporary civilization? All these people have been educated, have advanced, have risen high in the sky, although the Christians among them have preserved their Bible and their ecclesiastical traditions, the Jews their religion and the traditional clothing of their rabbis. The Japanese are pagans, but paganism was not the reason why they were backward in the past or why they are now advanced, and the fact that the common Japanese believe in a sacred horse ridden by such-and-such a god has not been an obstacle to their making progress.

It's not tanks, planes and machine guns that make people determined and dynamic. On the contrary, it is dynamism, resolve, and courage that produce planes and tanks. (Shakib Arslan, *Limadha ta'akhkhara al-Muslimun wa-limadha taqaddama ghayruhum?* [Why the Muslims Fell Behind and Why the Rest of the World Progressed] [Beirut: Dar Maktabat al-Hayat, 1975], p. 245)

But admitting that religiosity can make a major contribution toward a national revival is not incompatible with admitting that there are forms of religiosity that lead to exactly the opposite, in other words that impede national revival and deny the nation the chance to grow strong. We must have the courage to admit that, amid the current religious surge, forms of religiosity are spreading among Egyptians and others that make them less rather than more dynamic, that make them renounce their responsibilities rather than shoulder them, that fragment the nation rather than unite it and close ranks, and the spread of these forms of religiosity stems from social and international conditions, as I have tried to explain. So what are we to do in the face of this difficult situation?

In my life I have known people who have combined deep religiosity, strong faith, sincere desire to bring about a comprehensive national revival, and a vitality that has made them political activists throughout their lives, joining this or that party in the hope of contributing to the revival they envisioned.

These unusual people interpreted religion in a completely rational manner, always understanding religious texts in a sense that is compatible with the requirements of this social and political revival. But they also realized that vast numbers of religious people in Egypt accepted less rational interpretations of religion and spent their time on minor matters that had nothing to do with the question of a national revival and that may even work against it on many occasions. This didn't weaken the resolve of these enlightened people, but I believe that because of their strong confidence in themselves and in the rightness of their position, they were able to influence the masses in a way that helped them understand religion properly and positively, and to mobilize the masses to follow them along the road to achieving the highest objectives of the nation.

One of the people I knew who was simultaneously faithful to his religion and to the question of national revival was my friend Adel Hussein. I respected him on both points but I must admit that I pitied him in his later years, when I saw him failing to achieve his purpose. Instead of convincing the broad masses of his rational interpretation of religion, I saw him gradually shifting his position toward the interpretations of the masses, which were far from rational, and I saw him spending more and more of his time on minor matters that had nothing to do with a national revival or the essence of religion in my opinion and that might have been incompatible with either.

The transformation Adel Hussein went through in his later years inevitably reminded me of a famous short story by the English writer George Orwell entitled "Shooting an Elephant," and the reason this story is famous is exactly the reason I was reminded of my old friend.

The gist of the story is that a British police officer serving in Burma (maybe Orwell himself, since he worked for a time with the British police force in Burma) is ordered to deal with an enormous elephant that has gone on a rampage in the streets of a densely populated town, threatening the lives of the people. The officer is given free rein to kill the elephant or merely hunt it down and disable it. On his way to the scene, he passes crowds of people who have heard about the elephant, and they follow the officer in the hope of seeing an exciting spectacle. They are looking forward to seeing the elephant killed and will not be satisfied if it is merely pacified and disabled. As the officer walks on, the size of the crowd walking behind him gradually increases until there are several thousand, all wanting to see the elephant killed. The officer is unable to resist the power of their communal will, if only because of their numbers, so he shoots the elephant and kills it, although the elephant has in fact calmed down by the time he finds it and there is no need for him to treat it so cruelly.

Amid the current religious surge, many educated people have a real fear, and in my opinion a justified fear, that something similar to what happened in the Orwell story will happen in Egypt, and that irrational interpretations of religion, brought to the surface by the masses, will overwhelm more rational interpretations, and the campaign to end despotism will be replaced by a new despotic system that forces people to submit and to accept new forms of injustice, imposed this time in the name of religion.

I say that this fear can be justified because being religious, as an individual and a social practice, involves a large dose of emotion, and while emotions can be subordinated to reason, they often overpower reason and drive it off course.

It's easy for irrational versions of what religion prescribes and prohibits to prevail as soon as they are the versions accepted by many of the people who have the loudest voices and the most enthusiasm. A fast-flowing river carries with it all kinds of debris, such as plants and rocks, while a slow-flowing river deposits all the debris as it goes.

It is this danger that prompts many cultured Egyptians to doubt that political movements that use religious slogans can bring about a social and political renaissance, so they prefer to see political activity and resistance movements based solely on secular ideology, in the hope that secularism will protect political activity from going astray, from despotism and irrationality. But this attitude involves a danger in its turn, because instead of preserving the strong religious enthusiasm that can reinforce the spirit of opposition and resistance and contribute to its success, and trying to get rid only of the debris, we are in fact doing without one of the basic conditions for the success of political activism and of efforts to bring about a national revival.

There's no need to explain that secularism itself is not enough to save political activity from descending into extremism and irrationality, because political activity based on purely secular principles has not always succeeded in avoiding making mistakes or going astray. In fact secularism can also go together with something that resembles idolization of its leaders, so that they are seen as tantamount to "virtuous forefathers," and it can end up being highly despotic and authoritarian, as we well know from the history of Stalinism, Nazism, and fascism.

This often leads me to tell myself that the tendency toward metaphysics (that is, belief in ideas that transcend tangible and sensible natural phenomena) might be much stronger than we think. Being religious is only one form of the metaphysical attitude, and the secularist attitude often implies a metaphysical attitude, too. It is the metaphysical attitude and not only being religious that entails a risk of letting the emotions overwhelm reason, a risk of fanaticism and extremism, and a risk of revering tradition to the extent of ignoring the historical differences that make the requirements of one age different from the requirements of another age, and hence a risk of tending toward despotism and imposing a single opinion on others.

The original source of all varieties of metaphysical thinking might be an inherent human need, maybe with a biological cause. This metaphysical attitude is often a source of strength for political activity and an important incentive for national revival and progress, but it also carries the danger that political activity will lead people astray.

So we're dealing with a complex problem that is not easy to solve: we have something very valuable, metaphysics, that generates fervor and enthusiasm, brings people together, and diffuses a strong sense of loyalty and belonging, which are very valuable things for any political activity that aims at national revival but always vulnerable to contamination by extremist emotions that work against the original purpose.

How can we rid the fast-flowing river of the debris without reducing the speed? How can we maintain the zeal, enthusiasm, and readiness for self-sacrifice that come from being deeply religious while preserving at the same time rationality and tolerance for those who have different opinions and even different beliefs but who agree with us in looking forward to seeing the country make progress? How can we remove the accretions that have stuck to the valuable core without losing the valuable core in the process?

It's a very difficult task, but our cultural history is not devoid of examples that combine both these elements. The magnificent first centuries of Arabo-Islamic civilization combined the two, and our modern history includes examples of great intellectuals who succeeded splendidly, or almost succeeded, in achieving this combination and left a commendable and lasting influence on both our cultural and political life. I am one of many who think those great intellectuals include Muhammad Abduh, as he combined the call for resistance to injustice and tyranny and for action to bring about a comprehensive national revival with a strong religious zeal that was free of any extremism, authoritarianism, or irrationality and showed exemplary tolerance for those with different opinions and beliefs.

But yet again, I claim that the relative success these great intellectuals achieved in gaining supporters and followers, while our own cultural life today is almost devoid of anyone like them, could be due to the big difference between the social climate in which they were writing and thinking at the end of the nineteenth century and in the first third of the twentieth century and the social climate we live in today.

Yes, I am in no doubt that the main tasks of Egyptian, Arab, and Muslim intellectuals now is to revive the thinking of great men such as Sheikh Muhammad Abduh, but I'm not so foolish as to imagine that it's an easy task in conditions such as we have today. I often tell myself that success in this field, that is, in combining national regeneration with being religious, will first require success in another field that is different but closely related, the field of economic progress, by raising the standard of living of the majority and bringing about a minimum of social justice.

Part 4

Prospects for the Future

12 The Economy

1

The following saying, which contains an important truth, is attributed to a major English economist: "If you ask five economists to say what they think about an economic problem, you'll get six opinions."

Unfortunately the saying is largely correct, for two reasons in my opinion. One is that analyzing an economic problem and suggesting a remedy are closely connected in most cases with the ideological positions of the people doing the analysis and prescribing the remedy, and to their allegiances, which are affected by the class to which they belong and by their political ambitions. So the analyses and the remedies economists offer are bound to reflect their inclinations and personal preferences, and it's no wonder that economists disagree over most of the issues on which they express an opinion.

The other reason why they disagree is that economic problems are not usually simple, but rather are complicated and composite in the sense that they affect, and are affected by, many other problems that are not purely economic, some of them connected with political, social, and psychological conditions. People have different ideas on how to analyze these various problems and hence on the best remedy for the problem in question. To what extent, for example, is a large increase in consumption attributable to population growth, to changes in people's tastes, to changes in economic policy, or to the degree of openness to the world? Or to what extent is a higher rate of population growth attributable to economic, social, or religious factors? Would higher population growth be the result of a rise or a fall in average incomes? The explanations and analyses vary because identifying the right answer to such questions is not at all easy, and there are rarely statistics available to make one answer more probable than any other.

It's no wonder, in the circumstances, that we find different answers from Egyptian economists to the question of the real diagnosis of Egypt's economic problem and the best ways to tackle it. When I claim that in this chapter I will try to offer a diagnosis of our economic problem and suggest a remedy, I don't at all expect to offer something that will win the support of all or most economists. How could I expect that when economists, in Egypt or elsewhere, are the way I have described them? Besides obtaining the support of some economists who share my prejudices and political and social inclinations, as well as the support of some who do not give free rein to their emotions in rejecting everything that seems inconsistent with their own prejudices, I merely want to draw attention to the importance of certain factors that have helped to create and exacerbate our current economic problems, and thus draw attention also to some of the important and necessary conditions for getting out of the crisis.

The factors and conditions to which I will try to draw attention may not be purely economic. In fact they definitely are not purely economic, but we shouldn't be surprised at that. Economics, as I mentioned earlier, is closely intertwined with politics and with prevailing social and psychological conditions, and so it's very possible that economists may not be at all qualified to guide us to the right path, especially if they are the type of economist who thinks only about economics and cannot see anything else. If it is true that war is too serious to be left to the military, then analyzing and solving our economic problems cannot be entrusted solely to economists who are too narrow-minded to grasp matters that go beyond economics.

If we want to start looking for the roots of our current economic problems, where should we go to start looking and digging?

I believe that the roots of our current economic problems lie in the military defeat of 1967. I know that as soon as I say this I will lose the sympathy of a large section of Egyptian economists who have no sympathy at all for the Nasserist period for various reasons, some of which have nothing to do with economics, so they prefer to tie the beginning of the decline to the start of the Nasserist period and perhaps to the 1952 revolution. I well understand this position, and in fact I don't absolve the Nasserist regime of responsibility for some enormous mistakes, but I believe that this regime's mistakes in the economic domain were not enormous. On the contrary, I believe that the economic achievements of that era were extraordinary and that in economics Egypt's misfortune lay not in what Abd al-Nasser did but rather in what external forces did to both the Egyptian economy and Egyptian politics.

Again, I say that the inauspicious starting point was the defeat of 1967. The Egyptian economy has been ailing ever since. It hadn't been ailing in the previous ten years, but it has been ailing since 1967, right up to now. Just as a doctor seeking the right diagnosis of a disease and the best way to treat it has to distinguish between the original causes of the disease and the symptoms, I will try to do the same thing with regard to our economic problems, distinguishing between the original causes, on the one hand, and the results and symptoms, on the other. Among the results and symptoms I include problems that many people might consider to be fundamental and that some economists might even consider to be the root scourge responsible for everything else about which we complain. Among the results, the secondary problems, or even the symptoms, I include important problems such as the slow rate of gross national product (GNP) growth (and hence the slow growth in average income and the slow improvement in living standards), the slow rate of industrialization, the growing gap in incomes, the high rate of unemployment, high inflation, the large trade deficit, the decline in the value of the Egyptian pound, the increase in external and domestic debt, the low level of productivity, the low standard of education, and so on. There must be many other things that could be included as results or symptoms, rather than as original or fundamental causes of the disease.

So what do I consider to be the fundamental cause of our economic problems, or the original site of our disease? Before answering this question, I would like to make two observations.

First, the symptoms of our economic problems (or what I call the results and not the fundamental cause of the problems), even if they began in 1967 and still exist today, have not operated at the same pace throughout this period. These symptoms were worse in some years than in others. In fact, in some years the symptoms showed noticeable improvement. The reason

I say it has continued from 1967 until now is that any improvements, when they happened, always came about for ephemeral reasons that could not be relied upon to persist, and as soon as these ephemeral causes passed, the symptoms of the disease would reappear, sometimes in a more serious form than before. It's rather like someone's body temperature falling because they have taken some aspirin or some other antipyretic while the main causes of the disease still stand and have not been eliminated.

Take, for example, what has happened to the average rate of GNP growth. It fell sharply in the eight years following the defeat of 1967, but then improved strongly in the ten years after 1975. After that, average GNP growth fell and remained low for twenty years (1985–2005), improved once again between 2005 and 2008, and then fell again and remained low.

The improvements were always the result of ephemeral causes that were not guaranteed to continue. In 1975–85 the improvement in the GNP growth rate stemmed from the high price of oil, the reopening of the Suez Canal, and the flow of remittances from workers abroad—all the result of unusual external circumstances and weakly linked to the structure of the Egyptian economy. It's no wonder that average GNP growth fell again as soon as oil prices fell in the mid-1980s and the rate of emigration slackened. The rate then saw a noticeable increase in 2005–2008 because of a jump in private foreign investment, but this too was not the result of the Egyptian economy recovering its strength but of reasons related, in my opinion, to external conditions that would not necessarily continue. Foreign investment fell sharply anyway as soon as the global crisis occurred in 2008.

We can say something similar about the problem of unemployment. The improvement in unemployment that took place in 1975–85 did not happen because the state of the Egyptian economy had improved or because economic policy was well managed, but simply because tremendous opportunities for emigration to the oil-producing countries opened up after the rise in oil prices in 1973–74 and again in 1979. When those opportunities dwindled in the mid-1980s because of low oil prices, the rate of unemployment started growing again and it has continued to grow ever since, despite all the statistics proffered to indicate an alleged improvement in some years.

I can say the same thing about everything that I consider to be a symptom or a result of the underlying problem, such as the trade deficit, the increase in external and domestic indebtedness, the high rate of inflation, and the fall in the value of the Egyptian pound, because any improvement in any one of them in some years was the result of exceptional circumstances rather than the result of an improvement in the state of the economy or in economic policy. Was the large drop in foreign debt after the Iraqi invasion of Kuwait, for example, the result of an improvement in the performance of the Egyptian economy, or of a U.S. decision to waive some of Egypt's debts to facilitate the Americans' mission in the Gulf? Was the decline in the rate of inflation in the 1990s the result of better economic performance or of a retrenchment policy imposed on us by the International Monetary Fund starting in 1991, which did reduce inflation but also damaged GNP growth and added to the unemployment rate?

Second, I do not at all deny that some of the problems I have described as secondary or as symptoms of a deeper problem are extremely important. Describing them as symptoms does not imply that they have little importance, but simply that they stem from what I consider to be the underlying problem and so can only be tackled by tackling the underlying problem. Would anyone deny, for example, that the decline in the education system in Egypt is important, given the effect it has on low productivity and even on unemployment? Similarly, would anyone deny the damage done by high rates of population growth, and how much higher the standard of living could be if the rate of population growth were lower? No, no one could deny this. In a recent article a prominent Egyptian economist said our basic problem was the persistent trade deficit, that is, the failure of exports to keep up with imports. Would anyone deny that the persistence of this deficit is a serious obstacle to raising the standard of living? No, we cannot deny that. But again I say that this trade deficit and the high rate of population growth (and the deterioration of the education system) stem from something else I consider to be the underlying malaise.

In my opinion this malaise was the severe weakening of the Egyptian state in the wake of the defeat of 1967, largely because of the defeat. The will of the state was paralyzed, corruption proliferated, money came to power, the drive to acquire more wealth controlled political decisions, and the state gradually succumbed to external forces with objectives that were quite distinct from the interests of Egyptians and incompatible with decisive solutions to the problems of the Egyptian economy.

That, in my opinion, is the correct diagnosis of Egypt's economic problems. And if that really is the correct diagnosis, then the only remedy is for the Egyptian state to recover its strength and shake itself out of the appalling torpor that it's been in for more than four decades and that lasted right through the time of Sadat and Mubarak. So I believe that the most important hope one can attach to the January 25 revolution and to the overthrow of the Mubarak regime, as far as achieving economic reform is concerned, would be that the Egyptian state might recover its strength.

It goes without saying that I do not mean the return of the police state that we did away with by overthrowing the Mubarak regime and that I hope will never return to Egypt. A police state is not in fact a strong state, but a corrupt state that tries to protect corruption by repressing the population. It's a state that has failed in everything other than enabling those in power to accumulate money and that applies only laws that allow those people to acquire more wealth. At the same time it is a state that is weak toward everyone, at home and abroad, except when it comes to crushing its opponents and abusing its citizens.

When I speak of the strong state that Egypt now needs I also don't mean a carbon copy of the state that existed in the 1950s and 1960s. The world has changed significantly in the last fifty or sixty years and much of what was appropriate fifty years ago is no longer appropriate. Yes, in my opinion Egypt's economic problems can only be solved by restoring a strong state, but with specifications that are in line with the spirit of the age and that match its requirements.

Why do I think that the absence of a strong state is the real malaise that has given rise to the various economic problems we now face in Egypt? And what exactly are the specifications of the strong state needed to tackle these problems? Now I'll try to answer those two questions, one after the other.

2

Why do I think that the emergence in Egypt of the weak state, or what I prefer to call the 'soft state,' is responsible for the economic problems we face? Look at what a strong state did in Egypt in the ten years before the military defeat of 1967, between 1957 and 1967. In those ten years Egypt had an economic planning system for the first time and drew up its first five-year development plan (1960–65), which can in fact be considered the only serious plan in Egypt's economic history. The result was an increase in investment, in the rate of industrialization, and in the rate of GNP growth. That would not have been possible under a soft state, and only under a strong state could radical measures have been taken to redistribute income, to introduce free education and health care for all and services heavily subsidized by the state, such as social housing for the masses, to amend the agricultural reform law twice in favor of small farmers, and to give industrial workers a share in profits and a say in management. Making the decision to build the Aswan High Dam also required a strong state, and building the dam, along with more industrialization and the state guarantee of jobs for graduates, led to a fall in seasonal, disguised, and overt unemployment. Decisive state intervention to limit imports for the sake of industrialization and to impose severe restrictions on capital movements led to reductions in the trade and balance of payments deficits and to a stable exchange rate, and strict monitoring of government spending led to a reduction in the budget deficit and helped maintain a high level of price stability.

These admirable achievements required a state that was strong not only in the face of feudal landowners, capitalists of dubious loyalty, and corrupt people of all classes inside Egypt, but also in the face of pressures from abroad. It was Egypt's good luck in that period, the period of the Cold War and of positive neutrality, that the international climate gave it plenty of leeway with the international financial institutions and with the great powers. Egypt made the decision to build the Aswan High Dam in defiance of the World Bank, which refused to finance it, nationalized the Suez Canal in defiance of Britain and France, and imposed a high level of protection for local industries in defiance of instructions from the International Monetary Fund. Although Egypt's dependence on American wheat did begin in that period, the level of self-sufficiency in wheat and other foodstuffs stayed within reasonable limits, with a satisfactory rate of growth in the agricultural sector.

The international climate at the time was not hostile to the presence of a strong state in many Third World countries, and Egypt, like other countries in Asia, Africa, and Latin America, was able to nationalize many private-sector enterprises, build a strong public sector, introduce an effective system of subsidies for essential goods and services, and subject foreign investment to restrictions dictated by the national interest. All of this made it possible to keep external debt within reasonable limits, so that debt servicing was not a great burden on the balance of payments.

This imposing structure began to collapse as soon as the state loosened its grip on the economy after the defeat of 1967. The state became too weak to call on people to control consumption to maintain a high rate of investment. Pampering the middle classes became an important political requirement after the defeat. With the state unable to mobilize savings and the amount of foreign aid sharply reduced as part of the pressure on Egypt, the country could not make the necessary investments and the five-year plan was a dead letter.

Considerations of security and the need to keep people quiet assumed the importance that had been attached to the economy before the defeat, and the slogan "No voice louder than the sound of battle" meant that no voice or deed would be allowed to threaten the regime's security. For the same reason that the regime grew lax about protecting domestic industry, it turned a blind eye to the smuggling of consumer goods that could not legally be imported. It also grew lax about proceeding with educational reform and let the universities enroll large numbers of students as another way to stop the middle classes from grumbling. The time was not right for making new decisions that would reduce the gaps between classes, because after the defeat the regime was no longer in a position that allowed it to make new enemies.

In spite of all this, because of all this in fact, the police state grew in strength. After 1967 the strong state became a frightened state, protecting itself not by winning people's sympathy but by monitoring them night and day, on the alert for any whisper or any trivial act that might conceal a move against the regime.

As time passed, it gradually became clear to us that one of the basic aims of Israel's military attack on Egypt in 1967 was exactly that: to do away with the strong state, because a strong Egyptian state had many implications for policy against Israel and for Arab and foreign policy. Sadat's personality proved to be totally in tune with this shift from a strong state to a soft state, and this soon showed up in the economy as it did elsewhere.

The Open Door policy Sadat launched in 1974 was not a wholly mistaken policy. There was no harm in allowing Egyptians to go work in the oil-producing countries, in paving the way for easier imports of intermediate goods, in passing a new law to encourage private foreign investment after the steep fall in foreign aid, or even in renouncing state ownership of some enterprises that had been nationalized more for political than for economic reasons. But in order to succeed, all this required other measures that Sadat's state did not take. His state became not only more open to the world but also a soft state in every sense of the word. It was an open door for consumption, not for production. The aim was to promote consumption, not production. Prudent openness would have required, for example, measures to steer transfers by Egyptians working abroad in productive directions, not just to satisfy the appetite for consumption. There should have been a distinction between allowing more imports that served the productive process and flooding the market with goods for conspicuous consumption. It would have been possible to promote private foreign investment without giving the investors complete freedom to decide which sectors they invested in and their manpower policies, and without letting them set up banks, or branches of foreign banks, whose only concern was to mobilize the savings of Egyptians, especially transfers from Egyptians working abroad, and channel them either abroad or into investments that were within Egypt but had little effect in stimulating development.

Under the Open Door policy it would have been possible to reduce gradually the subsidy burden borne by the government, so that prices slowly came to reflect the real cost of goods, provided that adequate steps were taken to achieve more justice in income distribution. But for the government to give up providing subsidies and jobs for graduates without ensuring adequate investment to provide jobs for the unemployed and raise income levels, and at the same time to be negligent about collecting taxes, was a sign not only of a state that believed in free markets but also of a soft state that carried out whatever instructions came to it from abroad and submitted to the desires of a new class inside the country, a class that had unlimited materialistic aspirations and apparently wanted to take revenge on the system of the 1960s, which had restricted its opportunities to make profits and acquire wealth.

The state grew softer and softer as the years passed in the Sadat era, and that process continued in the time of Hosni Mubarak, both toward interested foreign powers and toward the new class in Egypt, until the Egyptian economy ended up in its current state: with low GNP growth, high unemployment, a productive infrastructure distorted in favor of services and against industry and agriculture, heavy dependence on imports of some basic commodities, most importantly wheat, a high level of domestic debt, a very poor pattern of income distribution, a decrepit education system, and so on, while night and day the television cheerfully tried to amuse Egyptians and raise more consumerist aspirations in the hope of distracting them from their real problems.

If this diagnosis is correct or at least close to the truth, then there is no alternative for setting the Egyptian economy right, other than a return to the strong state. With the January 25 revolution and the overthrow of the Hosni Mubarak regime, there were high hopes the age of the strong state would return to Egypt. But I repeat that the world today is no longer as it was in 1956 or 1961. It's been more than half a century since the Egyptian state nationalized the Suez Canal and exactly half a century since Gamal Abd al-Nasser announced the comprehensive nationalization of industrial and commercial enterprises and income redistribution measures that went a long way toward bringing about social justice. So what are the changes that have taken place in Egypt and the rest of the world in the last half-century that make it impossible, and in fact undesirable, to repeat that experiment today? What can now be done within the limits set by conditions in Egypt and the rest of the world today to revive the Egyptian economy and bring about greater justice in distribution?

3

In addition to being a great man, Gamal Abd al-Nasser was lucky. Now, sixty years after the revolution of 1952, it's clear that the 1950s and 1960s were a happy period in the life of the world, not just Egypt. Of course anyone can point out unfortunate things that happened in Egypt and the rest of the world during that period, but in many important respects it's hard to find a precedent for it in modern history.

The world had just emerged from a horrendous war that left millions of people dead and caused massive destruction, but the world was buoyed by its success in defeating Nazism and fascism and in creating a new international body to secure peace, as well as international financial institutions to avert drastic economic crises and, with international cooperation, to rebuild what the war had destroyed. Europe even aspired to establish an economic union that would prevent a recurrence of the two tragic wars of the previous half-century.

The countries of the poor world were optimistic about achieving independence after the two big colonial powers emerged from the war exhausted and ceded leadership of the world to two other major powers that both raised slogans the poor world (what was later called the Third World) believed—or, at least, every state in the Third World chose to believe the slogans of one of the two superpowers, which countered the slogans of the other. The great majority of Third World countries obtained their independence from the old colonial powers (Britain, France, Belgium, the Netherlands, Spain, and Portugal), but the independent states were divided between one camp that believed the slogans of the 'Free World,' which followed those of the United States, and another camp that adopted the slogans of socialism, which the Soviet Union raised. This division was not always the result of free choice on the part of the small state, but the peoples of the Third World were in effect divided between these two sets of enticing slogans: either freedom for the market with a minimum of state intervention, or a strong state that made development plans and redistributed income among classes.

Egypt's fate in the 1950s and 1960s was to apply the strong state system and bring about greater justice in income distribution, but fortunately both the superpowers graciously accepted this partition of the Third World. As far as Egypt was concerned, the result was that for about ten years (1956–67) it enjoyed freedom of movement, and during this time it applied a form of socialism without harassment by the United States (in fact the United States continued to provide aid to Egypt throughout this period). Because of this rare freedom to act, Egypt achieved stunning results in economic development and social justice, as I explained earlier, and for the same reason Egypt was not the only state to achieve such results.

So the Cold War, or at least that phase of the Cold War, brought benefit to many Third World countries, but in Europe and Japan it was associated with a period of extraordinary economic growth unprecedented in world history that went hand in hand with the introduction of the 'welfare state,' which helped to bring about more social justice.

I won't go into the reasons that made this impressive economic development possible in both the advanced and the underdeveloped world in the 1950 and 1960s or why it became impossible, with a few exceptions here and there, in the next four decades. Earlier in this chapter I mentioned how the economic decline that took place in Egypt after the defeat of 1967 was the result of the soft state replacing the strong state, but this phenomenon was by no means confined to Egypt. The strong state began to wane in the late 1960s in country after country in both the advanced and the underdeveloped world, and it continues to wane or decline today. The simplest explanation for the waning of the state's role in economic and social life in the whole world is the rise of multinational companies.

Although it is simple, it is an explanation that can be seen as an accurate summary of the most important features in the economic history of the world in the second half of the twentieth century. It is not just an economic phenomenon, as it has repercussions that extend into various aspects of political, social, and cultural life.

It is possible to trace the effects of the rise of the phenomenon of multinational corporations on the way of life in Egypt in various domains. In politics, the state that worked in the interests of people without claiming to be a democratic state was gone, replaced by a state that pretended to be democratic but always misrepresented the will of the people and worked against their interests. In economics, unemployment rose and the disparity between incomes increased, which was all consistent with submission to the influence of giant international companies. There was also an increase in the level of control exercised over Third World countries and even over some developed countries by the international financial institutions, which in fact worked for the interests of those companies. The institutions imposed policies that matched the requirements of the new masters, who now appeared in the guise of companies rather than governments.

We are well aware of how this openness toward multinational companies has affected people's aspirations and ways of life; it has been obvious in Egypt since the mid-1970s, as elsewhere, and continues to grow worse. We know, for example, what television has done to create new aspirations, and revive old aspirations, to consume goods and services that were once unknown or seen as luxuries but are now familiar necessities. In light of these aspirations it's hard to raise the savings rate, and investment is directed toward satisfying the demands of an affluent minority at the expense of the basic needs of the majority of people. In fact governments are encouraged to adopt lenient policies toward income redistribution, to make it easier to market the goods and services that these companies produce.

Under the new system, governments in the rich countries are less able to offer aid to poor countries because financial power has gradually shifted from governments to companies, so private foreign investment, rather than official aid, becomes the basic method for financing development in Third World countries. But the development that these companies are willing to finance is very different from the development that was financed by official aid. Development thus becomes a way to enrich some at the expense of the majority, and planning loses its importance. The word 'planning' even becomes a dirty word, as has happened with the slogans of socialism and social justice. As long as this is the case, the supreme objective is to increase the ability to export, to export anything, even raw materials or tourism, because that makes it possible to import more, and increasing the capacity of Third World countries to import is an important target of international companies. In this way Third World countries end up competing with each other to attract these companies to their territory, because the companies not only are the basic source of development finance but also hold the keys to exporting because of the control they have over marketing networks in various countries. In the context of this competition to attract international companies, compliance with the directives of the International Monetary Fund becomes essential and inevitable. The fund is the institution most aware of what these companies want and it has the means to force small countries, and sometimes big countries, too, to carry out its instructions, even when they are well aware of the consequences. As a result, subsidies for the poor are sacrificed and education, health, and housing are allowed to deteriorate.

This in brief is the model of development that spread in the Third World starting in the early 1970s and that continues today. A new group of Second World countries that were previously socialist joined and succumbed in their turn to the same model after the fall of the Berlin Wall in 1989. One country after another in Central and Eastern Europe turned to this model of development under the label 'economic reform,' while in fact merely falling into the same trap that multinational companies set for everyone. Of course the citizens of these previously socialist countries did make gains in the form of rights to stand for office, to vote, to oppose the government, and to express their opinions. But many people, myself included, think that in order to obtain these rights they paid a heavy price: the monopoly of the state was replaced by the monopoly of international companies, and brainwashing by the state was replaced by brainwashing by the various advertising and marketing agencies these companies use.

Over the last four decades there have been some important exceptions whereby a few Third World countries have managed to save themselves from capitulation to giant international companies and to achieve successful development that does not sacrifice social gains or the strength of the state. But for each of these exceptions there is an explanation that does not invalidate the diagnosis I have suggested. There was the phenomenon known in the 1970s as the Asian tigers, especially the success story of South Korea, followed by that of Malaysia. In the meantime China was making extraordinary leaps, as it still is, later joined by India and Turkey. But we can scarcely find a single similar success story on the African continent, in the Middle East, or in Latin America, except for some encouraging signs in Brazil in recent years.

We could explain South Korea's success as the outcome of its particular circumstances and the threat posed by North Korea. China is a continent in itself, drawing its strength from its size and its weight. We can find special explanations for the case of India, but it's not so easy to fall back on external factors or on sheer size to explain the success stories of Malaysia and Turkey, and it might be necessary to seek inherent sources of strength in those two cases, and perhaps also in the case of Brazil.

The success stories of Malaysia and Turkey have a special significance for Egypt because both clearly show how success requires the restoration of a strong state, as in the case of Egypt, and because there are no big differences between them and Egypt in terms of size or wealth in natural resources.

Both cases, Malaysia and Turkey, have had a successful mix of a strong state highly protective of the interests of people on low incomes, encouragement of the private sector, taking the steps needed to protect the national economy, and openness to the world when it does not conflict with this protection. Both recognize the importance of and need for planning without too much centralization and without underestimating the role of incentives for individuals. Both have opened the door to private foreign investment but subjected the foreign investor to conditions and restrictions dictated by the national interest. Both have done some privatization but without destroying successful public enterprises and with provisions that prevent public money from being squandered in the interests of corrupt politicians. It's striking that in both the Malaysian and the Turkish cases all this has been coupled with a high level of democracy, freedom of expression, and respect for the nation's heritage. They have proved that economic success does not require sacrificing the character of the nation but, on the contrary, that submitting to the wishes of foreign powers leads to both material and spiritual loss.

The Malaysian and the Turkish experiences have some important similarities with the Nasserist experience in Egypt, but they are also different in significant ways. I think one must count each of the three experiments as initially successful in bringing about a modern renaissance in a Third World country. They also were helped by the fact that each enjoyed a high degree of freedom to maneuver, they refused to give in to external pressures, a strong state played an effective role in their economic and social life, there was a system for central planning, and the rule of law was well developed. Each of the three experiments relied on mobilizing internal resources while giving less scope to foreign capital, and each took significant steps to narrow class differences.

But the Nasserist regime belonged to an age when foreign aid played a large role, while the Malaysian and Turkish experiments have taken place in an age when giant international companies are dominant and private foreign investment has taken the place of official aid. The age of Abd al-Nasser was tolerant toward economic protectionism through barriers to foreign goods and services, but it was replaced by the age of openness to the world. The Malaysian and Turkish experiments have dealt with this change with success. We must also admit that the Nasserist state was more like a police state, at least in its later years after the defeat of 1967, than the states in the Malaysian or Turkish cases. But because of the circumstances of the Cold War the international climate allowed for that in the 1960s more than it would today.

Why have the two Asian states succeeded with their admirable experiments in economic, social, and cultural revival, while it did not work in Egypt, a country that is no less significant historically or culturally, that is just as populous and rich in natural resources, and that is surrounded by a vast Arab world that possesses significant wealth, is sympathetic toward Egypt and ready to help and support it, and has more than once readily conceded that Egypt is its leader?

There are of course important reasons to be optimistic that Egypt will awake from its slumber and set to work on a national revival, as happened at the start of the 1950s and in the first half of the nineteenth century. The revolution of January 25, 2011 again raised hopes that such a renaissance is possible after Egyptians spent more than four decades feeling highly frustrated.

This sense of optimism is reinforced by changes that seem to have taken place in the world and that might enable a country such as Egypt to exercise again a high degree of autonomy and to resist external pressures, as happened with Abd al-Nasser and Muhammad Ali in the past.

The United States, which leads the world, is starting to wane. It is still the strongest country in the world militarily and has the biggest economy, but its relative position in the world economy has been on the decline for several decades, and it seems inevitable that this decline will continue. In the long term the decline in the United States' economic position is bound to result in a decline in its political and military position. Even before that happens the decline in the economic position of any state is bound to lead to a decline in its bargaining power and its ability to shape the world according to its wishes.

The world is witnessing the emergence of new powers that cannot be underestimated and that are making progress at impressive speed. They belong to nonwestern civilizations and cultures and until recently were part of the Third World, and we cannot expect them to turn their backs on the rest of the Third World just because they moved close to the top of the ladder. I mean China and India, of course, but why not add Malaysia, Turkey, and Iran (when the external pressures on the latter have subsided)? I'll also add Brazil and smaller countries in Latin America, although culturally they are closer to the West than to the Asian countries. Why shouldn't this make Egyptians and other Arabs more optimistic about the possibility of a national revival?

Another source of optimism lies in the amazing changes in the new generation of the Egyptian middle class, brought to light by the January 25 revolution. They are the second generation since Egypt opened to the world and have benefited from that openness, but they are more self-confident than the previous generation and more attached to their heritage. The women among them are more liberated, intellectually and psychologically, and more self-confident, without turning their backs on the traditions of the community.

But again I have some doubts and anxieties. The Arab world is afflicted in two respects, neither of which has a parallel in any other region of the Third World or the developed world, and neither of which is easy to remedy: Israel and oil wealth. The two afflictions (I almost said disasters, though it is hard to describe oil wealth in that way) mean it is taking a long time for the prey to shake off the hunters, even though we can see that the hunters are increasingly weak. Is the national will of Egypt and the Arab world capable of achieving this? Will the new forces that have taken power or will take power in Egypt and other Arab countries where revolutions are now seething have the same vision of what a national renaissance requires and how to bring it about? Even assuming that Egypt and other Arab countries obtain a high degree of democracy and that Egyptians (and their fellow Arabs) recover their right to vote, stand for election, and express themselves, of which they have been deprived for many decades, is that form of democracy, borrowed word for word from western books, really enough for them to recover the freedom that would enable them to bring about the renaissance that is needed?

13 Democracy

1

There's a big difference between the attitude toward democracy of the officers who took power in February 2011 and the officers who created the 1952 revolution. The gap between the two revolutions is close to sixty years and Egypt has undergone many significant changes during that period, so how could we not expect big differences between the two attitudes?

As soon as the 1952 revolution succeeded in removing King Farouk from the throne, the party leaders who had been in and out of power before 1952 rushed to introduce themselves to the officers in the expectation that the officers would hand them the reins of power after magnanimously carrying out the revolution. The officers thanked the party leaders but soon issued a decree dissolving all political parties.

In 1952 the Muslim Brotherhood also thought their time had come, as some of the leaders of the revolution were their friends and Gamal Abd al-Nasser himself was on good terms with them and had attended some of their meetings before the revolution. The Brotherhood leaders rallied around Muhammad Nagib, the first president after the revolution, who showed himself willing to listen to them and who believed that the army should go back to barracks and leave politics to the politicians. But the leaders of the revolution soon sacrificed Muhammad Nagib and organized demonstrations to get rid of the president of the Council of State, Abd al-Razzaq al-Sanhouri, who also favored the army going back to barracks. The political arena was then clear for the one-man rule that lasted until the death of Abd al-Nasser eighteen years after the revolution. This was based on a sham party that had nothing to do with democracy (at first the Liberation Rally, then the National Union), despite the new constitution that was promulgated and all the elections that took place.

The situation is very different this time; in fact at times it seems to be quite the reverse. The military council that took power on February 11, 2011 immediately announced a deadline for holding elections for a new parliament. Many people called for a presidential council that would include members of the military council and some civilians, but the request was rejected. It was the ruling military council that insisted on holding elections as soon as possible, while it was much of the citizenry that was calling for elections to be postponed.

I say that this is surprising because it would make sense that people should be impatient to hold clean elections after at least three decades of election rigging and that they should be impatient for civilian rule after sixty years of government by military officers, but what we saw was the reverse. It's true that people turned out in unprecedented numbers to vote in the referendum on amending some articles of the constitution, held a few weeks after the president stepped down. These amendments were not important in reality because the few important articles among those amended were connected with what the revolution had aimed to do in the first place, so people had said what they thought of them without the need for a referendum—that is, the articles that were drafted specifically to enable the presidency to pass from father to son, an idea the revolution irrevocably eliminated. In fact people turned out to vote in the referendum because it was the first time in a very long time that the rulers appeared to respect public opinion and really want to know the people's true desires.

Nonetheless there was no apparent impatience to elect a new parliament, except from the Muslim Brotherhood and other supporters of the Islamist movement. The Muslim Brothers were a 'banned' organization before the revolution, and they naturally looked forward to elections in which they would be allowed to take part. But everyone was 'banned' in one way or another before the revolution, so what was behind the lack of enthusiasm on the part of many to hold elections quickly, compared for example with what happened in 1954, when most people and most parties called on the army to go back to barracks and some officers even resigned their positions in support of a return to democracy and in protest at the officers continuing in power?

This big difference impels me to examine the changes that had taken place in Egyptian society over the previous sixty years in search of an explanation for the change in the attitude toward democracy on the part of a broad swath of Egyptians.

First, there was the change in the amount and the nature of corruption. I don't think I would be straying far from the truth if I said that corruption before 1952 was superficial compared to the corruption that prevailed before the revolution of January 2011. It's like comparing a superficial disease that is confined to a small part of the body, has a known cause, and is easy to treat with a disease that has spread through most of the body and requires a serious surgical procedure. It's also possible to say that the corruption the 1952 revolution set out to tackle was political corruption more than social corruption, related to the connection between politics and a feudal system headed by a corrupt king. That meant that when the officers in 1952 deposed the king and removed the political parties from power (let alone issued the agricultural reform law, which eliminated feudalism at a stroke less than two months after the revolution), it was enough to eradicate the most important causes of corruption in 1952 and a promising sign that it would be possible to establish a healthy system of government that would embark on the economic and social reforms that were needed.

Compare that with the situation at the time of the 2011 revolution. Corruption had spread everywhere, through all classes, and had reached the very bottom of Egyptian society. Those in power did not originally belong to a particular social class at the top of the social ladder; it was being in power that enabled them to join that class. It was possible for anyone, whatever his class roots, to climb up and join those in power, provided they had the right personal and moral (immoral, that is, of course) qualifications for climbing. I don't mean to say that this disease is incurable, but one has to admit that it is an inveterate disease that will take much longer and much more effort to treat. It certainly won't be enough just to remove a few people from power, because unfortunately the people who now enable corruption in Egypt are far more numerous than the handful of feudalists who ruled Egypt in 1952, and they have less regard for the nation's interests than the corrupt people of old. The reasons for this are too many to go into now, and my purpose here is only to point out one of the reasons why many of those interested in reform in Egypt are not in a hurry to introduce 'democracy' but prefer to wait until social and economic reforms have put an end to corruption, or at least reduced it.

The level and nature of corruption are not the only reasons for the change in attitude toward democracy in Egypt. Over the last forty years another development has occurred that we have to recognize, and that is the spread of what can be called the "irrational interpretation of religion."

Religion is dear to almost all Egyptians and is part of our cherished heritage. It runs in our blood, whether we are Muslims or Copts. But I never tire of saying that religion is one thing and being religious is another. Religion is a constant that never changes, but being religious takes many shapes and forms. Changes in social and economic conditions do not bring about any change in religion, but changes in these conditions can bring about significant changes in the form that being religious takes, in the way religion is understood, in the way we arrange our priorities when we look at religion's injunctions and prohibitions, and in the way we view and treat those of other religions. Do strong conviction and firm faith prevent us from recognizing that there are ways of being religious that are better than others and closer to the spirit and real purposes of religion and that make a larger contribution than others to the progress of society and to peace and harmony among members of a single nation?

Strong conviction and sincere faith must not prevent us from recognizing this, and recognizing this would lead us to recognize also that many decades of foolish economic policies, of social policies that drove people apart instead of bringing them together, and of despotic government that deprived people of the right to express themselves freely have unfortunately lead to the growth of what I call "irrational interpretations of religion"—interpretations that are stricter than necessary, help to create hatred between different religions instead of tolerance and friendship, portray religion to people as though it is everything in life and not just an important part of it, and give priority to formal aspects of religion that make no contribution to social progress.

Everyone recognizes that the most powerful political movement in Egypt now is the religious movement, in the form of either the Muslim Brotherhood or various other groups known as Salafis. The January revolution has enabled the Muslim Brotherhood to engage freely in political activity and has enabled the al-Wasat Party, made up of dissident former members of the Muslim Brotherhood, to exist legally after many years without this right. Some members of Salafi organizations, some of whom took part in the assassination of President Anwar al-Sadat, have been released from prison, years after they completed their sentences, and state television has been allowed to interview one of their leaders, who made extraordinary statements justifying killing the president. In this new climate, many commentators who are sympathetic toward the Islamist movement have been active, defending more openly than ever in the past one form or another of religious government, even if some of them have used the phrase "a civil government with a religious point of reference." All this has frightened those who reject any kind of religious government. When they expressed their fears, the supporters of the Islamist movement pounced on them, accusing them of not being believers to a sufficient extent or not loving Islam enough and of hiding their true feelings toward religion behind the slogan "a civil state" while what they really meant was a state that turned its back on religion. This division began from the moment the referendum on amending the constitution was announced, with a sudden and unwarranted polarization between supporters of the Islamist movement and others, on the grounds that those who rejected the simple amendments and preferred to draft a new constitution really intended to amend Article 2 of the constitution, which relates to the application of Islamic law.

This sudden polarization was very saddening and quite unnecessary, and in my opinion can only be explained by the fact that we have long been accustomed to an economic, social, and cultural climate that encourages people to give their emotions priority over reason. The continuation of poverty and the glaring income gap, the proliferation of corruption, and the shameless behavior of people on high incomes have inflamed people's emotions and made them so discontented with life that they cling to obscurantist slogans that cannot be translated into realistic policies, and that do not distinguish between interpretations of religion that take the nation forward and unite its various elements and other interpretations that work in quite the opposite direction.

The third reason why there is a real obstacle to any transition to democracy in Egypt is that for almost sixty years Egyptians have been deprived of the right to express themselves freely, to form parties, and to have any genuine cross-pollination of ideas. Although the level of dictatorship and the extent to which freedoms have been restricted have varied from period to period since the 1952 revolution, it would not be wrong to describe the whole of the long period that ended with this latest revolution as one in which a single party, the party that held power, monopolized the right to make important decisions, without allowing other Egyptians to contribute to the decision-making process. Some periods were more oppressive than others in restricting freedoms, and in some periods more than others the rulers pretended that they wanted to hear other opinions, but the opposite was the truth. The unfortunate outcome of all this was that after the revolution of January 25, 2011, we discovered that political awareness in Egypt was lamentably atrophied, fatuous, and vacuous, as it is today. We see or hear slogans without content, outdated clichés, the veneration of leaders who emerged in completely different circumstances, and distressing ignorance about developments in the outside world, whether in reality or in political thinking.

Those who took part in the political debate after the 2011 revolution were like the Sleepers of Ephesus, just come out of a deep sleep that had lasted hundreds of years and taken by surprise by the dazzling light outside their cave and by strange bodies such as they couldn't remember seeing before. Under the circumstances they were bound to say things and state opinions that neither reflect reality nor are relevant to it. The Islamists say things that a man such as Sheikh Muhammad Abduh would not have believed could be said a hundred years after his death, such as the debate over whether Islam allowed celebration of the ancient Egyptian spring holiday of Shamm al-Nisim. Nasserists speak as though it hasn't been sixty years since Gamal Abd al-Nasser carried out his revolution, and forty years since he died. The Marxists, who said nothing when some of their leaders joined the ranks of those in power and who reorganized their party only after the January revolution, have not tried to reconsider the significance of Marxism in the age we live in. The supporters of the liberal party, the Wafd, who played a very honorable role in the period between the two world wars in support of the nationalist and liberal cause, were happy to live on the laurels of that glorious period and offered no new ideas, either on liberalism or on how to liberate the country from foreign pressures. In fact the revolution of January 25 caught the leaders of the Wafd Party red-handed as they took part in the purchase of an outspoken newspaper in order to silence it. What else was left but parties that had grand names but no new ideas of any kind?

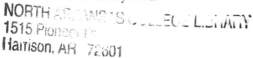

So there are three factors that impede progress toward democracy in Egypt and make it hard to feel confident about what might come out of free elections. Is there anything that can be done to save the situation?

2

After Hosni Mubarak was deposed in February 2011, Egyptians were surprised by an announcement from the military council that took power, saying that elections for a new parliament would take place in September of the same year.

Many felt that there was a real problem that couldn't be solved just by holding fair elections, but they also felt they couldn't turn their backs on democracy when the whole world now thinks that "democracy is the solution" and that the best way to solve any problem, whatever it might be, is to seek out the opinion of the majority. That's what everyone says and it's not easy to answer them. Some suggested postponing elections but the Islamists objected, saying, "Why postpone them? Don't you like what people choose?" Some suggested the military council stay in power another year or two, or that a presidential council be formed with both military and civilian members, but the democrats objected, saying, "Would you prefer a military dictatorship to democracy? So what was the revolution about then?"

I'd like to revisit an old issue much debated in political science starting more than two hundred years ago. It came up in the French revolution at the end of the eighteenth century and Marxist thought put much emphasis on it in the middle of the nineteenth century. Supporters and opponents of the Russian revolution then disagreed over it in the early twentieth century and it continued to be a fundamental part of political thinking until the socialist experiment in the Soviet Union showed severe defects. Then the question seemed to have been resolved when one socialist state after another collapsed and adopted western democracy in one form or another.

I am referring to the question of the relationship between political democracy and social democracy. The French revolution ended a long period of despotic government in which the king saw himself as, and was treated as, "God's shadow on earth." It initiated a period of political freedom based on the right to vote and to stand for election. But socialists raised a powerful objection to introducing political democracy in a society that had not yet achieved social democracy. Karl Marx and his followers poured scorn and contempt on political democracy that was not combined with fair distribution of income. They saw the democracy of the French revolution as a bourgeois curiosity and said it would benefit only those with economic power, while the only freedom the poor worker or peasant would have would be the freedom to choose between agreeing to submit to exploitation by the capitalist or the feudalist and dying of hunger.

That's how Lenin, Stalin, and their successors justified the dictatorship of the proletariat in the Soviet Union for close to seventy years: hunger perverts democracy and political freedom is meaningless unless it is coupled with the elimination, or at least the radical reduction, of class differences. In this way all the dictatorial regimes in the Third World that called themselves socialist defended themselves, from the dictatorship of Fidel Castro in Cuba to the dictatorship of Mao Zedong in China, along with many countries in Africa and Asia, including the dictatorship of Gamal Abd al-Nasser in Egypt.

When Anwar al-Sadat turned against Abd al-Nasser's system and gradually opened the door to different forms of exploitation, his defense of his new regime rested on the premise that he allowed political freedoms that were not available under Abd al-Nasser. Hosni Mubarak's regime continued to apply the same system as Sadat: a spurious political democracy with obscene social injustice. The result was the situation I described at the start: a seriously diseased polity beset by rampant corruption, poverty, and irrationality. When things are so serious, would the remedy lie merely in holding free and fair elections?

I very much doubt that the solution is so simple. I don't know of a successful revolution in history that deposed the ruler and dissolved parliament merely to hold new elections to bring in a new ruler and a new parliament, let alone if the deposed ruler was in charge of the country for thirty years, subverting everything and rigging all elections, and if more than half the population had never lived under any other ruler. The least we would expect from the revolution is that the revolutionaries or those who take power in their name, as soon as they take power, take measures or pass laws that are consistent with the objectives of the revolution and prevent the persistence of the state of affairs the revolution aimed to end. I don't necessarily mean setting detailed regulations for a new economic system, because that cannot be done in a hurry or by issuing a single law, but I do mean measures and laws that address the three factors that I have mentioned and that endanger our chances of obtaining a parliament that is able to fulfill people's hopes of a real renaissance: by eliminating corruption, the most important cause of which is the buying of influence, preventing the exploitation of religious feelings in favor of one candidate over another, and allowing more space for people to express their opinions freely while protecting freedom of opinion from the influence of money and from religious pretentiousness.

Fulfilling these three conditions by announcing some principles that reflect them before holding parliamentary elections and by taking certain measures and passing some laws to ensure they are carried out is the way to ensure that political freedom does not come about at the expense of economic freedom, which would make political freedom meaningless and dash the hopes pinned on it.

Failure to fulfill these three conditions is, in my opinion, one of the fundamental reasons why the months that have passed since the January 25 revolution have largely disappointed us. When the trials of leading members of the old regime dragged on, their supporters took comfort, including some of those responsible for the widespread corruption in Egypt. At the same time there were repeated mistakes in the choice of new officials, the authorities insisted time after time on retaining people who were implicated in corruption under the old regime, the exploitation of religious sentiment in the media was allowed, and media policy in general was obviously incoherent, with incomprehensible delays in changing senior personnel and the appointment of bland new officials who did not reflect the real objectives of the revolution and may not even have believed in them.

So there is a real cause for concern that the January revolution will not result in any noticeable progress toward economic and social democracy and hence toward real political freedom, but rather that it will bring us superficial political freedoms that look democratic but are really dictatorial.

14 Social Justice

There has been much talk of social justice in Egypt since the revolution of January 25, but unless some important things change, little can be done to bring it about.

For this reason I believe that many of those who promise to bring about social justice or even to move in that direction do not really mean what they say, because most of them realize, like me, that there are important conditions for achieving social justice that have not been met, and it looks unlikely that they can be met easily. For the same reason I believe that those who really believe in the need for social justice would do best to work first on fulfilling those conditions.

To demonstrate that this view is sound, it would be useful for us to go back a little in history.

The problem of social justice in Egypt is very old and no doubt goes back to prehistoric times. But Egypt has gone through periods that were better than others with respect to justice. In recent history one can say that the problem of social justice became prominent again about forty years ago. Gamal Abd al-Nasser tried to solve it and achieved some impressive successes. Anwar al-Sadat ignored the problem but was lucky that while he was in power there were developments to lessen the impact of the problem on the people. Hosni Mubarak ignored it too but he was unlucky, as the problem of social justice (or, properly speaking, social injustice) grew worse until it reached the state we see today.

Abd al-Nasser came to power at a time when social injustice in Egypt was appalling, alleviated only by the fact that 80 percent of the population had never seen or heard of anything better, nor had their forefathers. But Abd al-Nasser was attuned to the feelings of an enlightened middle class that knew its duty toward the deprived majority, as well as to an international situation in which the idea of social justice was alive and strong and various governments were trying to achieve it, to various extents and in various forms.

For the sake of social justice Abd al-Nasser did five things that proved to have many benefits, and the social and economic system at the end of his term in office was much fairer than it had been at the start, the disparities of income and wealth were much less than they had been, and social tensions because of injustices were much less severe than they were before 1952 and than they are now. What did Abd al-Nasser do?

First, he spearheaded the agricultural reform law, which was revolutionary from the start and became more revolutionary with amendments, each of which reduced the maximum amount of land any one person was allowed to own, redistributed the land appropriated by the state to peasants who were landless or almost landless, and set maximum rates for agricultural rents.

Second, he set into motion the wholesale nationalization of industrial and commercial properties, which was accompanied by setting a minimum wage and giving workers seats on management boards and a share in company profits.

Third, he supported a radical overhaul of the tax system to make it much more progressive and set maximum levels for incomes and for government salaries.

Fourth, he advocated that the state assume major responsibilities, including providing basic goods and services to everyone, with subsidies for essential commodities, including education, health care, and housing at very low prices or for free.

Fifth, his government reduced unemployment to a minimum. Land redistribution helped decrease unemployment in the countryside, large investment projects in agriculture and industry absorbed large numbers of the unemployed, and the government guaranteed jobs for all new graduates from universities or higher institutes.

These measures would not have been possible or even conceivable in the absence of a strong state that made laws to be enforced and not to be broken, that was able to appropriate agricultural land, using force against rebellious feudalists when necessary; to ensure that peasants had their leases renewed, against the wishes of the landowners; to defy foreign and Egyptian capitalists by nationalizing a waterway that was important to the whole world, the Suez Canal; to prepare people who would run it well; to reject threats from the most powerful states in the world, which wanted to avenge this nationalization; and to nationalize all the foreign banks and big Egyptian companies owned by men who once had control over the king himself and his entourage. Such a state was also strong enough to collect taxes, however high they might be, and to punish tax evaders and corrupt civil servants with real rather than hypothetical penalties. It was able to draw up and carry out ambitious economic plans that included building factories, schools, hospitals, and houses for the poor and to provide jobs for all those who sought them.

The Egyptian state managed to do all this in the 1950s and 1960s and it was a stunning success. Then, since the 1970s, it has shamefully neglected to do any of this, even if there has been endless talk about social justice and caring for those on low incomes. When the revolution of January 25, 2011 took place, there were renewed hopes for reform and repeated statements about determination to bring about social justice, to impose limits on salaries and incomes, to make the tax system more progressive, and to tackle the problem of unemployment by encouraging small-scale projects.

There has been much talk but not much confidence in implementation, for reasons that are fully understandable. There are no signs yet of a strong state with all the essential features I have described that would qualify it to take a serious stand in favor of social justice. The state doesn't seem able to take on those who have interests counter to those of the poor, either in the countryside or in urban areas and whether the capitalists are Egyptians or foreigners. It doesn't seem able to introduce a new tax law, or even to enforce the existing tax laws. It doesn't appear to have enough power to punish tax evaders and civil servants who take bribes, and the government hasn't said anything about any intention to draw up economic plans, ambitious or not, or to take a bold approach to the problems of education, health, and housing. It doesn't seem able to keep the streets safe, to dismiss a corrupt dean in one of the universities, or to replace a corrupt provincial governor with an honest one, so why should we trust its promise of social justice?

It might be said that the state has been going through a temporary phase during which its goal has been to hold fair elections so that the winning party can then do what is needed to bring about justice and achieve other objectives. But even in these interim conditions I have heard officials promising to go ahead with bringing about social justice starting now. I have found nothing in the political programs of the rival political parties to reassure me that the conditions I mentioned earlier will be met. The programs on offer exhibit much vagueness and generality, making do with ill-defined slogans that can be interpreted in very diverse ways when it comes to social justice and other matters. Perhaps the conflict between advocates of a civil state and of a religious state, for example, has distracted everyone from thinking about what the state, civil or religious, must do now that elections have been held.

Take, for example, the question of progressive taxation. Any policy that aims to bring about a reasonable degree of social justice must definitely have tax rates that are reasonably progressive, because one flat tax rate should not apply to both the outrageously rich and to those on modest incomes. But it's also certain that a country that is fundamentally dependent on the private sector, domestic or foreign, must be extremely cautious about raising the tax burden above a certain limit because of the effect it has on investments, which are made with the goal of achieving maximum profit. Such a state would have to be especially cautious when economic and security conditions are difficult, or when there is an international crisis that greatly reduces the incentive to invest, with or without progressive taxation. Even to talk about the need for progressive taxation might be far from prudent until Egypt gets over these difficult conditions and the international crisis eases.

But even if we assume normal conditions in Egypt and the rest of the world, to what extent is it possible to combine rapid economic development that relies on private investment, domestic or foreign, with a tax system that aims to achieve maximum social justice? Experiences with rapid economic development in the world as a whole, in the past and the present, lead us to say that it is impossible to combine the two. The history of rapid development gives us examples either of states that basically relied on the private sector and neglected considerations of justice or of states that relied largely on the public sector and gave the state a large role in the economy and at the same time achieved a high level of justice. Of course it is possible to avoid the extremes in either direction, but the trend that has prevailed in Egypt for the past forty years—low public investment, indifference toward protecting the public sector, a willingness to get rid of public ownership whether or not this is justified, and excessive pampering of foreign investors—has made the idea of applying a "fair tax system" a mere pipe dream. As a consequence, to talk today or tomorrow about making the tax system more progressive without adjusting other policies that do not allow the state a large role in the economy and that imply that the private sector and foreign investments are the basic engine of growth cannot be seen as more than a mirage.

Another example relates to setting minimum and maximum levels for salaries and incomes. Let's assume that the government now imposes a minimum wage that it asserts would guarantee a reasonable standard of living. Would it apply, I wonder, only to the civil service and the public sector or also to the private sector, Egyptian and foreign? In normal conditions the level of wages, minimum and maximum, is fixed by supply and demand, and the low minimum wage in both the private and public sectors in Egypt stems to a large extent from the availability of cheap labor and the prevalence of unemployment. How could we ensure that the private sector respects this new minimum wage when there are vast numbers of people willing to accept wages below the legal minimum? It is precisely this factor—high unemployment—that thwarted the attempt by the government of the 1952 revolution to impose a minimum wage for agricultural work, although it did succeed in implementing the other aspects of the agricultural reform law. Agricultural wages did not really start rising until the government's industrialization efforts succeeded and the High Dam was built. But assuming that the government, despite its weakness, did impose a minimum wage on the private sector, how could we avert disastrous results in the form of declining investment and growth at a time when the state has abandoned its responsibility for increasing investment, leaving the task wholly, or almost wholly, to the private sector? If the government applied the minimum wage solely to the public sector and the government, how would the government ensure that higher inflation, which is already high, would not deprive junior civil servants of any gains they might have from receiving the new minimum wage? If prices go up because of the new minimum wage, will the government keep on raising the minimum wage in line with inflation?

In the case of a maximum wage, how could you prevent the negative effect it might have if applied to the private sector, which might not be able to attract people of unusual talent, whether Egyptian or foreign? If a maximum wage were applied only to the public sector, it would make that sector less able to compete with the private sector, because public-sector workers could be enticed to leave and work in private enterprises.

Or let's take the question of low salaries and poor conditions for teachers, despite the enormous responsibilities they bear. Because the state has ignored their problem for many years, teachers have resorted to solving it by giving private lessons, even at the expense of teaching standards for the rest of their pupils. Here we have teachers trying to solve the problem of social justice by reducing the gap between their standard of living and the standard of living of other professionals through private lessons given at the cost of exacerbating the problem of social justice somewhere else—for the families of pupils who cannot afford the high cost of private lessons. How can the state tackle this problem? Would the problem be solved by raising their salaries and banning private lessons? And how could that be done when the 'institution' of private lessons has been deeply entrenched for decades and teachers have grown accustomed to setting their level of consumption and their lifestyle on the basis of what they earn from the lessons? When prices are constantly rising, how could we ensure that the phenomenon of private lessons doesn't reappear, even if we linked teachers' salaries to price levels?

I'm not saying all this as a reason for giving up hope that there can be much more social justice than there is now, but to emphasize that social justice is an issue that's too serious to be solved by a single law, by a few measures, or by budget adjustments while the state's overall policy is left as it is. It's an issue too serious to be solved by a single ministry to be called the Ministry of Social Justice (as suggested when a new minister of supply insisted that social justice be added to the name of his ministry). Social justice depends on the general philosophy of the state and its overall economic policy, and both of these depend on the state's moral stance on the question of wealth and poverty, the desired model of development, and the type of national revival required. These are matters that call for a government whose ministers and senior officials have homogeneous inclinations, since everyone will have to cooperate in implementing overall policy, so all officials have to adopt the same overall philosophy of governance. In my opinion one cannot continue to pin hopes on the ability of the January 2011 revolution to achieve social justice unless this condition is met. Short of that we must continue to treat repeated statements about the imminent achievement of social justice as mere talk, designed only to gain time and distract public opinion.

15 Dependency

What's the use of the January revolution if it doesn't enable us to do away with dependency? The Mubarak regime had many faults, too many to list, but certainly one of the worst, if not the very worst, was its extraordinary deference toward the U.S. administration and its constant submission to Washington and hence also to Israel.

Yes, this dependency began in the era of Anwar al-Sadat and continued until he was killed in 1981, but Hosni Mubarak and his men did not diverge one iota from the path of subordination Sadat pioneered, whether in economic policy, policy toward the Arab world, its position toward Israel, or the various international issues in which the United States showed any interest.

In the age of Hosni Mubarak, Egypt renounced its leadership of the Arab world and its loyalty to Arab causes because that was what the United States and Israel wanted. It renounced protecting the public sector and the national economy and opened the door without restraint to imported goods and foreign capital, regardless of the damage this might do to domestic industry and investment and of the fact that this undermined the chances of achieving the minimum self-sufficiency needed in basic commodities such as wheat. This allowed the United States to use our need for wheat as a means to put pressure on us to serve its economic and political objectives in the region.

The Mubarak regime also proved to be very amenable to directives from the International Monetary Fund, even to the extent of appointing or dismissing prime ministers and ministers in charge of the economy depending on whether the fund and the U.S. administration approved of them. Foreign organizations such as the U.S. Agency for International Development and the World Bank were allowed to interfere in Egyptian educational matters under the spurious slogan of "educational reform," including in the curricula of an ancient institution such as al-Azhar.

Egyptian foreign policy also marched in step with the wishes of the United States. Egypt made friends with the Americans' friends and was hostile to their enemies. So the Egyptian attitude toward Libya, Iraq, and Sudan shifted in line with the shifts in U.S. policy. Egypt was friends with Saddam Hussein, Ja'far Nimeiri, and Muammar Qadhafi as long as the United States approved of them, then turned against them as soon as the United States turned against them. Egypt took a position on the Iraqi invasion of Kuwait based on the dictates of the U.S. administration and even took part in the U.S. military attack on Iraq in order to give the attack some legitimacy. Egyptian–Syrian relations grew tense when America's relations with Syria grew tense, and Egypt was hostile toward the Iranian regime to exactly the same extent as the United States. It would step up attacks on Iran when the United States decided to increase the pressure on Iran, and the Egyptian attacks would die down if the United States wanted to try a policy of appeasement. Egypt would be extremely cool toward countries in Latin America that wanted to stretch out the hand of friendship toward it and that would have greatly benefited Egypt politically and economically if it made friends with them, simply because the United States did not view those countries sympathetically, as they were adopting independent and nationalistic policies.

That's how Egypt was when the revolution of January 25, 2011 took place, and the revolution was amazingly successful in generating a wonderful sense that the country had restored its dignity and could fulfill the hopes of Egyptians. Is there any hope more precious than that of regaining one's freedom against any foreign pressure, more precious, that is, than throwing off the shackles of dependency?

Whenever I have expressed this opinion, which attaches importance to the external pressure that major powers put on Egypt, I have found someone telling me that I am overlooking our own responsibility for the state we are in and that it's very easy to throw the responsibility onto someone else and wash one's hands of one's mistakes. I'm willing to concede that however great a responsibility falls on the external factors, the weaker party does bear some of the responsibility for its weakness. It has been truly said that the drunk has no right to blame his alcoholism on the owner of the bar. Similarly, the dependent country that submits to external pressures has to take some part of the responsibility, large or small. The Algerian thinker Malek Bennabi was also correct when he coined the phrase "susceptibility to colonialism" to describe the condition of such a country, meaning the internal aspects of weakness that encourage the predator to hunt its prey.

This is all true and it warns us not to be hasty in blaming others and not to make generalizations about cases of domination, exploitation, and colonialism instead of studying each case separately. But reading Egyptian history tends to make me emphasize the importance of external factors because of circumstances that make Egypt different from other countries. In fact I find it easy to explain many aspects of our internal weakness by the external aggression Egypt has faced, and I see no reason to believe that Egyptians are less intelligent than other nations that have emerged, or almost emerged, from ordeals in recent decades, nor less courageous or determined or dynamic. Egyptians have often risen up and made attempts at national revival, but they have always faced strong reactions from abroad to thwart them. When, thirty years ago, I began researching the evolution of relations between the west and Egypt and the other countries in the eastern part of the Arab world (which resulted in a book called *The Arab East and the West* [Beirut: Arab Unity Studies Center, 1980]), I found many examples of extraordinary attempts at national revival in one Arab country after another, since the late eighteenth century, all of which were nipped in the bud by interventions by one or another of the imperial states, from the Wahhabi movement in the Arabian peninsula, which in the beginning was different from what it later became, to Muhammad Ali's activities in Syria and Sudan, Emir Bashir's movement in Lebanon, the reforms by Daoud Pasha (an ally of Muhammad Ali) in Iraq, the Senoussi movement in Libya, which spread to other Arab countries, and the Mahdist movement in Sudan. All were viciously attacked by western imperialism, and the attacks continued into the twentieth century until Gamal Abd al-Nasser's experiment in Egypt and his attempt to bring Arab nationalism to life were punished by the attack in 1967.

I will allow myself to explain why I am also optimistic about this—that is, why I believe that there are changes now taking place in the world that give a country such as Egypt, and a nation such as the Arabs, an opportunity to make a new attempt at national renaissance and to be more successful in that attempt than we have ever been before.

Reading Egyptian history over the last two centuries leads to the following conclusion: the best periods for Egyptians with respect to achieving, or at least starting to achieve, a real revival in various domains have been those periods when Egypt enjoyed a measure of freedom in relation to foreign powers, even if this freedom of movement was available when international relations were in such equilibrium that no one power could single-handedly impose its will on smaller and weaker states. In my opinion the best periods in Egyptian history in this respect were the reign of Muhammad Ali, except for his last ten years, and the presidency of Gamal Abd al-Nasser, except for his last three years. The international balance of power in the time of Muhammad Ali incapacitated both Britain and France from acting in Egypt, and the balance of power in the time of Abd al-Nasser limited the freedom of the United States and the Soviet Union to act toward Egypt. Both Muhammad Ali and Abd al-Nasser set out to do what was necessary to bring about an Egyptian renaissance. We continue to benefit from their achievements despite the fact that more than half a century has passed since the end of Abd al-Nasser's experiment and more than a century and half since the end of Muhammad Ali's reign, despite all the setbacks that occurred and the dependency imposed on Egypt after they were gone.

There is strong evidence that a new era really has started in the world, with the declining fortunes of the unipolar power that dominated the world, the United States, and the rise of several other stars in various parts of the world, such as East and South Asia, Europe, Latin America, and even the Middle East. The strength of the new powers is growing and has already started to stay the hand of the United States. It's not enough for the United States to be the biggest economic and military power in the world, as it is today. What matters most is the way its relative strength in both respects has changed and is changing, and that change is moving rapidly against the interests of the United States. This greatly weakens its bargaining power, let alone its ability to impose its will unilaterally.

There is plenty of evidence, especially with the financial and economic crisis that began in 2008 and continues today, that the United States greatly needs China, India, and Europe to adopt economic policies that mitigate the crisis in the United States. Under such circumstances the United States finds itself forced to accept economic and political developments it would not have accepted before.

Under such circumstances we can understand, for example, the rapid rise in the strength of countries such as Turkey in the Middle East or Brazil in Latin America and how each of them has taken political and economic positions of which the United States does not approve. We can even understand how Iran can continue to defy the wishes of the United States, the abject failure of U.S. policy in Iraq, and the inability of the United States to get out of the mess in Afghanistan.

In such new circumstances, is it impossible for Egypt to stand on its own two feet again, brush off its dependency, and set about bringing about a national revival or even lead a revival for all Arabs? I think that international conditions herald the birth of a new age that is wholly conducive to an Egyptian renaissance, and for a similar renaissance in other Arab countries and in other countries in Africa and Asia, as happened in the 1950s and 1960s.

It might be said, "But where can we find a leader such as Turkey has found in Erdoğan, or as Brazil has found in Lula da Silva? There cannot be a renaissance and we cannot do away with dependency until the nation has a strong national leader who can inspire his people and lead them on the path to national revival." I believe that the relationship between a national revival and having an inspiring leader is the opposite of what many imagine. The leader, however inspiring and impressive he or she might be, does not create the right conditions. It is the right conditions that create leaders, or rather that create the space for them and bring them out of obscurity into the light. There are endless historical examples of this that can be cited, and the principle applies to Lula da Silva in Brazil and to Erdoğan in Turkey, just as it applies to Muhammad Ali and Gamal Abd al-Nasser in Egypt. Yes, Muhammad Ali was a strong personality with unlimited ambition and an iron will, and Abd al-Nasser was a nationalist who was also intelligent and ambitious with an iron will. But such people are not as rare as we might imagine; it is the conditions that enable such people to emerge that are rare.

16 A Secular State

A few weeks after the January 25 revolution we were taken by surprise by a deep, unexpected, and disturbing polarization between two groups of Egyptians. One group talked about politics, in one form or another, in terms of religion, while the other group insisted that politics and religion should be kept apart. This happened in particular on the occasion of the referendum on the constitutional amendments, when some people claimed that voting yes or no meant taking a certain position on religion, while others rejected this claim and condemned it as an unwarranted intrusion of religion into politics. Before this and again after, there were some unfortunate incidents of violence between Muslims and Copts and unprecedented activity by groups that called themselves Salafist, and some Salafist preachers appeared on television. This made many people anxious that a trend was starting that would end with the Salafists taking power, which might restrict the freedom of Copts and of Muslims who are not extremists.

These developments naturally reopened the discussion about the relative merits of a religious state and a secular state.

I understand the term 'religious state' to mean a state in which the rulers govern in the name of God, declaring that they apply God's law, seek to identify His intentions, and obey His injunctions and prohibitions. The term 'secular state,' on the other hand, when it is used in contrast to a 'religious state,' I understand to mean a state in which the rulers do not make such a claim but govern in the name of the people, in the name of the dictator, or in the name of political or social principles that have been professed by a renowned reformer or advocated by a revolution, or that have won general acceptance among the people.

There are many examples of religious states because they prevailed in Europe in the Middle Ages and up to the age known as the Renaissance, and during the Renaissance Savonarola imposed religious rule in the sense above on the Italian city of Florence. However, we might disagree on whether the Arabs imposed religious rule on the countries they conquered after the advent of Islam, first from Medina and then from Damascus and Baghdad. We might also disagree over the nature of government in Muslim Spain, in the Ottoman caliphate in Istanbul, and in modern times in Iran.

Examples of a secular state include the systems of government in ancient Athens and Rome, in Renaissance Europe, and in almost all the countries in the world at present.

In comparing religious states and secular states, I think it's useful to emphasize the following five facts, which tip the balance in favor of secular states rather than religious ones.

First, religious states are run by human beings, even if they are governing in the name of God and trying, with as much effort and understanding as they can muster, to apply His law and to treat His will as supreme.

So here we face an intractable problem, because in a religious state the ruler can only apply his own version of religious precepts, but he or she constantly attributes that version to divine will, confers the highest possible authority on the way the ruler applies and personally understands religion, and uses, in asserting this authority, words and phrases that people treat with the highest reverence and respect. Most people cannot easily accept that many religious texts can have more than one interpretation. In fact most people, by nature and for various reasons, have an aversion to accepting multiple interpretations of a single religious text, as if this multiplicity is an affront to their religious sensibility and to religion itself. So most people are inclined to overlook the fact that the state is run by human beings who might be wrong and might be right, and so many of them are willing to trust those who advocate a religious state without worrying about the possibility that in practice it would turn out to be different from what they expected and hoped for.

Second, religious states inevitably face changing circumstances because life does not follow the same course forever and people change as their economic and social circumstances change. Even if we assume that Islamic society stays as it is, the societies around it would always be changing and international relations would not stay unchanged for long, and this would require policy changes and a shift from an old course to a new course, even if the commitment to Islamic principles remained constant and rigorous. This need for change poses a more difficult problem for religious states than for secular states because the constants in religion are more sacred than the constants in the legal and social principles that secular states abide by. If the secular state follows the wishes of a dictator, there may not be any constants in the first place, and if it follows the wishes of the people, it's easy to deal with new circumstances by having parliament pass new laws. If the state follows the views of a renowned reformer or major social thinker, then it's easier to reinterpret those views in a way that suits the new circumstances than it is to interpret religious principles in a way that conflicts with previous practice.

Third, most states, whether religious or secular, are inhabited by minorities that follow religions other than that of the majority, and the government of a religious state, however tolerant it might be toward religious minorities, is bound to rely on the precepts of the majority religion when it comes to justifying the laws it passes and the measures it takes. In their statements and speeches, rulers will probably also use words and slogans derived from their holy books. In the educational curricula they set and the media policies they adopt, religious states aim to reinforce religious sentiment, turn to religious principles for guidance, and justify the government's actions by saying that they conform to those principles. But the principles, the texts, and the slogans used in school curricula and the media are bound to be derived from the religion of the majority, and the most that a religious government can allow if it is as tolerant and broadminded as possible is that the proportion of the various religions in the overall population should be taken into account when assigning programs, airtime, and pages in newspapers to the various religions, and that at schools people of minority religions should be given opportunities to teach their children the precepts and rituals of their religion. But the overall tone of daily life would undoubtedly be influenced by what the government does to serve its own religion, as the citizens of one state all live in the same state, go to the same schools and universities, reside in the same streets, spend their spare time in the same clubs and places of entertainment, and so on. Even if a religious government wanted to, there is no way it could take into account the feelings of other religions when they are subjected to the same television programs, the same sermons broadcast from places of worship, and the same set texts in language, literature, and history imposed by the religious government, or when they are forced to obey the same laws and the same regulations on what is right and wrong in clubs, restaurants, beaches, and other places of recreation.

This is bound to cause psychological problems, which might become social problems, of a severity that would vary depending on the tolerance and broadmindedness of the religious government. These are problems that cannot arise to the same extent in a secular state.

It might be said that this is a small or normal price that we should accept in return for a significant benefit for the majority, since the majority should not be asked to sacrifice a basic interest related to protecting its religion and underpinning its creed simply to avoid offending the feelings of the minority, who should learn how to live with whatever the interests of the majority require. This argument sounds quite reasonable as long as the minority's sacrifice does not exceed a certain level and as long as the sacrifice required of the minority is commensurate with the benefit achieved for the majority. It isn't possible to rule on this matter in general; in other words, one cannot say in general whether it is fair to demand sacrifices of the minority whenever the interests of the majority require them. Each case has to be considered individually on the basis of how large the sacrifice is compared to the benefits to the majority. We have to apply here the legal principle of "arbitrary assertion of a right." Conceding the majority's right is one thing, but disregarding the arbitrary assertion of that right is something else. I think that the government of a secular state is more likely than the government of a religious state to understand the need to make such a distinction, so the problems that can arise under a religious state because of offense to the feelings of religious minorities are bound to be greater, and it might go beyond merely offending some people's feelings and become a case of inciting strife and unrest and propagating an unhealthy social climate that damages the interests of both the minority and the majority.

Fourth, secular states are not necessarily hostile to religion. We can derive this from our earlier definition of a secular state. We defined it as a state in which the rulers do not claim to rule in the name of God or to apply His law, but in the name of the people, the dictator, or man-made political and social principles. This definition does not imply a hostile attitude toward religion and is not at all incompatible with positive attitudes toward religion and people who are religious. The basic task of a secular state is to maintain law and order, and in a state where most of the inhabitants are religious this imposes on a secular state many duties related to respect for religion, protecting religion from attack, and preventing affronts to the feelings of the religious. These duties include respect for and protection of minority religions and preventing affronts to the feelings of those who follow them, but the duties are necessarily greater and more far-reaching in the case of the majority religion.

These duties may even be extended to include the state playing a positive role in efforts to strengthen religious feelings and belief, on the grounds that such efforts might be a significant factor in bringing about a national revival, socially and morally, and in strengthening the bonds of family and social relations.

A secular state could understand its obligation toward religion in this broad sense without making it a religious state, because this understanding could be inspired by general social and political principles and could draw on acknowledgment of the requirements for a national revival that are in harmony with any religion and not drawn from any religion in particular.

This discussion of the attitude a civil state might take toward religion is not detached from reality. Most states in Western Europe still take this attitude toward religion and consider it their duty to protect it and save it from affronts as part of their function to maintain public order. In Egypt the state has been secular at least since Muhammad Ali came to power—that is, for two centuries—and the secular nature of the state became more pronounced after the British occupation in 1882 and then with Egypt's secession from the Ottoman caliphate in 1914. The state continued to be secular and allowed itself to draw on European constitutions when it regulated relations between its legislative, executive, and judicial branches, and to draw on French law when it drafted the civil, commercial, and penal codes, while applying Islamic law in civil status matters such as marriage, divorce, and inheritance. But the Egyptian state thought it had a duty to protect religion and prevent attacks on it or affronts to it as part of its function as a civil state, and it also thought it had a duty to cultivate religious knowledge among the young and to promote respect for it and observance of its rituals as part of the school curriculum. This did not apply only to the religion of the majority, for the state made the same provisions for young people of the minority religion, who in their turn had lessons at school to deepen their knowledge of their religion and instill a feeling of respect for it. The Egyptian state never made any declaration renouncing any of these duties, and if the Egyptian state seems to have grown lax about applying these principles, with judges appearing to behave as though they were legislators rather than judges and with a growing number of teachers acting as religious proselytizers even if some of their students are not of the majority religion, then the reason is not that Egypt has become a religious state but only the overall weakness of the Egyptian state.

Fifth, we now live in a world where it's difficult, if not impossible, for one country to isolate itself from the rest of the world. Modern technology has imposed mutual dependence economically, has made every nation aware of what's happening in other nations, has created new needs in each country that the country cannot satisfy by itself, and has made it easier for powerful states to intervene in weaker states, either by forcing them to open their markets to goods or to adopt lifestyles they would not have adopted of their own free will. In such a world religious states are bound to face dilemmas that secular states do not face to the same extent. If states of the two types find themselves obliged to deal with nations of different religions, cultures, and lifestyles, they constantly try to reconcile these interactions with their commitment to religious precepts and to the culture and way of life associated with religion. This constant attempt to reconcile the two, whether the state is religious or secular, is bound to be accompanied by psychological and social tensions that might reach the stage of a dangerous dualism in social and cultural life between those who advocate tradition and those who advocate modernity. But we would expect the tensions that might arise in a secular state to be less severe and less dangerous than those that might arise in a religious state, especially if the religious state is less tolerant toward those who disagree and who favor modernity.

If secular states manage to handle the world around them with tolerance toward those of different religions, cultures, and lifestyles (for example, in the way they deal with tourists and imported films) without turning their back on their religion or appearing to be negligent about protecting this religion from affronts from people of different religions, cultures, and lifestyles, then it is justifiable to say that secular states are better able than religious states to tackle the problems of globalization.

In response to all this it may be said that there's no point arguing about the relative merits of religious and secular states so long as in the end what will be decisive is the will of the people as expressed through free elections. If it happened that in elections that observe the rules of democracy and are largely free and fair the majority chooses to have a religious government, then what's the use of arguing over this or that type of government? Let the state be religious, as long as that's what people have chosen.

But even if we assume that the majority of people in Egypt would prefer to have a religious government, one shouldn't necessarily, in my opinion, conclude that a religious state is better than any other. Such a conclusion presupposes two conditions that are unlikely to be fulfilled. The first is that people know exactly what the advent of the religious state would mean, and the other is that people always know where their real interests lie.

The first condition is unlikely to be fulfilled because members of the Islamist movement, like others, do not usually reveal exactly what they intend to do if they happen to take power, and the slogan "Islam is the solution," for example, is open to a number of interpretations, some of which might not win as much support as others.

The other condition is also unlikely to be fulfilled because, contrary to popular belief, people don't in fact always know their own real needs and hence often don't know to what extent the options on offer could meet those needs. When people choose between the political options on offer, it's not very different from when they choose between goods on sale in the market. Their knowledge of the exact specifications of each commodity on sale is often imperfect, and we know what advertising does to mislead consumers about the real specifications of the goods. Consumers' knowledge of which of these goods they really need, what benefits they can expect from each of them, and whether the benefits will last long or soon pass is also imperfect knowledge. Both types of imperfect knowledge often lead us, as we are well aware, to buy a product only to find out later that it doesn't fulfill the hopes we pinned on it.

In politics, free elections are not much better than the free market system in the economy. Both are based on two assumptions—perfect or adequate knowledge of the specifications of the candidates or the goods, and perfect or adequate knowledge of our real needs—and both assumptions are unlikely to be valid.

Despite all this we might decide that free elections are the best way to decide the system of government and that the free market system is the best way to organize the economy. We might well know that the system free elections produce may not be the very best system of all and that the goods we buy in complete freedom in the market may not be the goods that best meet our real needs, but we might nevertheless decide to respect the opinion of the majority, just as a kindly father might sometimes think it best to let his children choose the product they want, even if he knows that the children will not choose what is really in their best interest. But even if the father does that, he has a duty to take any opportunity available to explain to his children the options on offer and to compare the advantages and disadvantages of each one. That's what I have tried to do in this discussion of the relative merits of religious and secular states.

An Abortive Revolution?

1

When Hosni Mubarak was president of Egypt, I never, to be honest, attached any importance to his role in governing Egypt. I was very surprised by the many references in newspapers and magazines, in local and foreign commentaries, to the fact that he did this or refused to do that or that he favored a certain course of action and that his ministers and aides put it into effect or that he disliked another idea and so these ministers and aides dropped it. Yes, perhaps he did have a role in minor matters, such as sending an Egyptian ambassador to one country rather than another (assuming the two countries were only of modest importance) or appointing a friend of his son's or a relative of his wife's to some job they wanted, but I'm confident that he had no influence over the important matters that made up Egypt's foreign and domestic policy or even in much lesser matters.

That's because I formed a certain impression of the man when he appeared on the political scene as vice president, an impression drawn from the many stories and reports about him after he assumed that position and before he took office. The stories and reports, all consistent with one another, concerned his level of intelligence, the limits of his interests and his hobbies, what did and did not attract his attention, and the surprising comments he made when he was visiting a factory or meeting an important world figure. All of them painted a coherent picture leading to the conclusion that I reached about his very limited abilities. They also, in the same way, led to a certain conception of the extent to which he understood his real stature and the limits of his abilities. A complete picture took shape, not one to inspire great admiration: limited abilities and a limited grasp of the reality of those abilities.

My thoughts were similar with respect to his younger son Gamal. There is of course the difference of age, upbringing, and education that each received and the difference between the eras in which each grew up. But I concluded that the son's abilities were bound to be limited in turn and that all the statements, comments, and ideas attributed to him did not really originate with him. There were people who had a definite interest in conveying an unrealistic image of Gamal, and he had been prompted and trained to perform particular acts and make certain statements, though it was not at all an easy task to prompt and train him.

There were certain figures who were often referred to as having real executive authority, with positions either in the secretariat of the ruling party or at the presidency, and some of their names may not have been widely known or even mentioned in the newspapers. I had no doubt that this group of people had much greater influence than the president or his son, but I tended to consider them to be carrying out policies rather than making them, and I still believe that I was right. So who were the people who were really making decisions and deciding policy?

There were of course the big businessmen, who had an interest in seeing Egyptian policy, regional and foreign as well as domestic, move in a certain direction that served their economic interests. Some of them were well known and held political positions, while others rarely appeared in public despite their importance. In my opinion, and the opinion of many others, these people were much closer to being the real rulers of Egypt. But I would attach greater importance to faces that were completely unknown to us, even if they held important positions in the various, and variously named, security agencies. These were the people able to act to tackle any crisis or unexpected problem that needed rapid attention or intervention, any significant breach of security or threat to the regime as a whole. These people must have had great influence over those mentioned earlier, from the president and his family to those who had great wealth and large companies, because of their crucial ability to protect the regime and security, including the security of these major figures.

If that was the case and if certain external powers had a clear interest in preserving the regime and maintaining Egyptian foreign and domestic policy as it was, they must have been working to ensure they had access to the circles that made the important decisions and must have had representatives inside these various security agencies—Egyptians, of course, but in constant contact with foreign powers and with the ability to understand quickly and serve the interests of these powers.

That was how I conceived the situation before the revolution of January 25. Even several months after the revolution, after the events we saw unfold and after what was sometimes called procrastination, foot-dragging, incomprehensible behavior, incompetence, or inexperience, I was inclined to believe that my conception of the state of affairs before the revolution of January 25 would serve well to describe what happened after the revolution, as it seemed better suited than any other conception to explain the mysteries we encountered day after day in the evolution of political and daily life in Egypt. So it seems to me that the people who make important and fateful decisions are still the very same people. There have of course been many changes in circumstances because of the revolution, and these people have to take into account the possibility of mass protests and the changes in the mood of the various sectors of Egyptian society, but they are still, in my opinion, governed by the same important considerations as before, foreign and domestic: foreign considerations connected with the interests of certain countries that are greatly interested in what is happening in Egypt, especially the United States and Israel, and domestic considerations that include, first, those same foreign interests and, second, the interests of big businessmen in Egypt.

This analysis is better able to explain many of the mysteries of the revolution. Why, for example, was there the sustained pretense that the former president and his family were about to undergo a just trial and would receive a just penalty for what they had done, while days and weeks passed with progress only at a snail's pace toward imposing such a penalty? And why the pretense that the money smuggled abroad would be returned to Egypt, and then the matter was completely forgotten or steps were taken when it was already too late? Why this lenience toward old-regime people (or *filoul*, as they are called) taking part in the new elections? Why is it taking so long to restore security in the streets despite its crucial importance if economic activity, including tourism, is to return to normal, as well as its importance for making people feel safe? Why has a form of censorship again been imposed on newspapers and television, with this writer banned and that broadcaster taken off the air? The examples are many and people have started talking about them constantly, and all of them suggest that the fall of Hosni Mubarak as president did not at all imply the fall of his regime. The reason is what I tried to explain: the man himself was not in the least important, nor were the other people who have been arrested and put on trial. The really important people are still in their jobs and no one has touched them, so they are still exercising their same old powers, serving the same old purposes.

<h1 style="text-align:center">2</h1>

The call for a "salvation government" first made shortly before the demonstrations and sit-ins that began on November 19, 2011, and then repeated until the end of that month (what some people called the second Egyptian revolution), was widely welcomed by Egyptians, except of course by the people from whom we wanted to save Egypt. When this second revolution began, there were loud calls for a salvation government to replace the government of Essam Sharaf, which, besides failing to run the country, had allowed innocent revolutionaries to be beaten and killed.

Nevertheless, I ask myself, "Who or what is the person or the body that we are calling on to produce a salvation government?" If the appeal was directed at the military council, which held the ultimate authority in the land, then did we really expect this council to meet this demand?

The January 25 revolution played its part in bringing the president down, and the military council then assumed power. It then turned out that the first government formed by this council after the president stepped down, the government of Ahmad Shafik, was a great disappointment and people soon demanded that the country be saved from it. When the military council formed a new government, the government of Essam Sharaf, things only grew worse. The revolutionaries then demanded a new salvation government, but what was there to make people believe that the military council would make the right choice this time?

Yes, the revolutionaries had learned that lesson and this time they demanded, in addition to a salvation government, that the military council step down, because by this time there were serious suspicions that the council was not well intentioned in its choices and was deliberately choosing weak governments for reasons that were unclear. As I sought the explanation, I inevitably remembered Karl Marx's class analysis of the state.

In fact, Marx's idea on the class analysis of the state is still useful for interpreting what is happening in the world, including what has happened and is happening in Egypt. Yes, many Marxists have habitually been over-enthusiastic about unjustifiably imposing a class-based analysis on historical events, whether major or minor. Marx himself, by virtue of the circumstances of his time, did not grasp the decisive effect that the phenomenon of colonialism and dependency would have on the course of events in countries such as ours, since Marx's analysis focused on industrially developed countries that enjoyed political independence. Marx also did not live long enough to witness the overwhelming growth of the middle class, so he saw the class struggle as confined to the struggle between the bosses and the proletariat, especially industrial workers. But all this does not exclude the possibility that Marx's class-based analysis of the state can throw useful light on modern Egyptian history, including the Mubarak period and the revolution against him.

Marx's ideas on the subject can be summarized thus: it is seriously wrong to imagine that the state, any state, can be impartial toward social classes. Those in power in any country in any age represent the class that is economically dominant, and they use the power of the state, especially the police and the army, to preserve their economic domination, and to ensure that their class continues to enjoy its privileges by oppressing the classes that are wronged and exploited and by crushing any attempt by these classes to rise up against them.

Marx and Marxists repeatedly ridiculed those who said that the state transcends class and who submitted their grievances to the state in the hope that their demands would be answered. The privileged give up their privileges only under pressure and by force. When they are forced to give up their privileges because they come under great pressure, they never cease trying to recover their positions of power, whatever brutal acts of violence this requires.

From this perspective I have looked at the reign of Hosni Mubarak, which lasted thirty years, at the revolution against him on January 25, his removal on February 11, and then at the ten months that followed his downfall, the actions of the military council during those ten months, and the nature of the governments set up to replace Mubarak's governments.

I found that this important idea of Marx's does throw a revealing light on these events.

From his predecessor, Anwar al-Sadat, Hosni Mubarak inherited a class that was amazing for its economic dominance, its ambitions, its determination to acquire more wealth and power, and the extent to which it was willing to engage in corruption to make new economic gains. This class was relatively new in Egyptian history and did not have strong links to the class that was economically dominant in the period of the monarchy. Abd al-Nasser allowed it to emerge and grow only in his last years after the devastating blow he received from abroad with the defeat of 1967. But this class flourished and gave birth to a second generation in the time of Anwar al-Sadat, who himself shared the same inclinations and aspirations. The Open Door policy Sadat launched helped this class to grow and strengthen, as did the support and encouragement this policy and this class received from external forces, especially the United States and Israel, on which Sadat was happy to become dependent. These foreign powers did not object to the corruption practiced by this new class and even encouraged the class to remain corrupt as a way to underpin its dependence.

Under Hosni Mubarak this class received yet more favors and was given every possible opportunity to engage in corruption, through permits to set up scam investment companies, massive bank loans that were then smuggled abroad, currency manipulation, the appropriation of state-owned land, legal dodges, and rigged elections.

This class mobilized all the power of the state to serve its interests, exactly as Marx predicted—the army, the police, the judiciary, ministers, and prime ministers—until, when Mubarak's last government took office under Prime Minister Ahmad Nazif, the powers of the state acted in concert with this class in a way that was unprecedented in Egypt. We saw a total and overt conjunction between those with money and those in power, to the extent that ministries were assigned to people whose private businesses and companies fell within that ministry's area of responsibility. A powerful contribution to this conjunction came from the economic, political, and security support that foreign powers, the United States and Israel, gave to this class, that is the regime—a phenomenon that was unknown in Karl Marx's time, and hence he overlooked it.

On January 25, 2011, things apparently came to a head. The resentment and sense of injustice among the oppressed classes had peaked. It's true that the thousands upon thousands who gathered in the squares did not all belong to one class. In fact, the revolution took us by surprise in the way people of different classes coalesced, unanimous in their hatred of the class that had corrupted and wrecked the country. All the classes that took part in the revolution—the middle class and the various sections of the lower class—complained of injustice and oppression, and they all came out into the squares. It was no longer a question, as it was in Marx's time, of a struggle between the proletariat and the capitalists over low wages and the appropriation of surplus value. It had become a struggle in which the exploitation of workers was combined with the exploitation of consumers, in which the oppression of workers went hand in hand with the oppression of peasants and with the hardships imposed on the families of schoolchildren by the cost of private lessons, and in which economic oppression was combined with psychological oppression.

The fact that the participants in the revolution came from a multiplicity of economic backgrounds and had suffered many different forms of oppression may have been an important reason why the revolutionaries found it so difficult to reach consensus on specific objectives. But there was another important thing that put the January 25 revolutionaries at a disadvantage, and that was the assumption that the state would not take sides among different classes and that the members of the military council, who were friends and colleagues of the rulers the revolutionaries wanted to depose, could turn their backs overnight on the class to which they belonged.

The passing of nearly two years since the January 25 revolution have been enough to realize this mistake. The brutal beatings and killings that the revolutionaries faced on November 19, 2011 and in the following days were also enough to show that the state cannot be neutral and that, if Egypt urgently needs salvation, that salvation will not come about by putting the request to the very class from whose rule the rest of the people are to be saved.

3

A whole year after the events of January 25, 2011, conditions in Egypt looked vastly different from what anyone could have expected in the early days of the revolution. On February 11, 2011, the president was successfully removed, the plan to pass the presidency to his son was completely abandoned, and so many beautiful things seemed possible. But very soon things began to deteriorate, and the revolutionaries' confidence in the military council, which had assumed the powers of the president, gradually eroded. The first prime minister, chosen by the military, quickly proved a great disappointment and was soon to betray his lack of sympathy for the revolution. When it became clear that people wanted him dismissed, he was replaced by a man who had been a member of the policies committee of the ruling party in Mubarak's era, which was chaired by Mubarak's son.

Under the new prime minister several important portfolios, such as foreign affairs and finance, were entrusted to people who occupied the same or similarly important positions before the revolution. This continued for several months, and even when members of the cabinet were replaced by others, no real change was observed in the policies they implemented.

People were amazingly inclined to find excuses for such slow change, as well as for the wrong decisions being made. People wondered, "Could it be that those making the decisions lack experience because they haven't been in power long?" But the experience of the 1952 revolution was very different. The army officers who led the earlier revolution and took power had just as little experience and were also much younger. Apparently high hopes and the fear of what the consequences might be if the revolution failed were sufficiently strong incentives, making people accept what in other circumstances they would have been reluctant to accept.

Then came the referendum of March 2011, when the people were asked to vote for or against the amendment of a small number of articles in the existing constitution. People again seemed to be genuinely happy to participate, and long queues formed in front of the polling stations, made up of men and women who had never voted in any election or referendum in their entire lives. Many were quite surprised to hear some people say that voting "no" in the referendum amounted to opposition to the famous article in the old constitution that stated that the principles of Islamic law were to be the main source of legislation. Thus secularists as well as Copts started to feel somewhat alienated—a feeling that grew stronger as increasing evidence built up to suggest that the Islamists had the sympathy of the Supreme Council of the Armed Forces (SCAF).

There also seemed to be a reluctance to take the necessary steps to restore law and order in the streets, causing a sharp decline in people's feeling of security and in the flow of tourists to the country, as well as an inevitable deterioration in economic conditions. In the early days after the fall of Hosni Mubarak, it was announced that measures were to be taken to trace the public funds that had been embezzled or smuggled out of Egypt by the Mubarak family and his entourage so that the assets could be returned to the state. As time passed, however, people heard less and less of this matter, and some European governments, which were allegedly involved in the attempt to recover the illegally processed assets, publicly denied that they had ever been approached by the Egyptian government on this matter.

The trials of the president, his sons, and senior aides were also endlessly postponed. What the people were allowed to see of these trials on television seemed more and more like theatrical performances that did not deserve to be taken seriously. Meanwhile, SCAF invited eminent people to participate in one platform or dialogue after another that never reached agreement or any obvious conclusion. One proposal after another was put forward on the principles that should guide the committee to be formed for writing the new constitution. But again, no consensus was ever reached on the principles or even on how such a committee was to be formed.

When some serious crises occurred, threatening a major decline in the credibility of SCAF, as when demonstrators were shot or arrested and sent to trial by military courts, a so-called advisory council was formed in the hope of calming people down. It took no more than a week to discover that this council was completely powerless and utterly useless.

Repeated attacks on the demonstrators who continued to gather in Tahrir Square and elsewhere, protesting against the slowness in implementing people's demands, were blamed on "thugs," whose identities were never revealed and whose purposes in their attacks were never explained. People could not, however, dissociate these new thugs from the familiar ones who had been used by Mubarak's successive governments to help security forces tackle any act of protest against the regime.

Such was the state of affairs when a whole year had passed after the uprising of January 25, 2011. An election campaign for a new parliament went ahead, and the results were not unexpected: the biggest share of seats went to members of the Muslim Brotherhood, who together with representatives of other religious groups (the Salafis) formed the majority. These Salafis have always been present in Egyptian society, but before January 25 their activities were largely confined to religious teachings and charitable work. It is interesting to note the growth of their political activity after the fall of Mubarak. Liberal, secular, and Nasserist parties (largely formed or given legal approval only after the revolution) got minority shares, but it was also interesting to know that the number of votes many of them obtained was far greater than they themselves had expected. What came as a real surprise was the quality of performance of many of the elected members of the religious groups. Members of the Muslim Brotherhood and the Salafi groups seemed to compete among themselves in showing how committed they were to Islam. On one occasion, one such member, while giving the oath required from every new member of parliament, insisted on adding a new sentence to the usual oath, saying that his observance of parliamentary duties was conditional upon these duties not contravening the law of God. On another occasion, a member suddenly stood up in the middle of a parliamentary debate and started to call for prayer. Some members of these groups proposed new laws that included further encroachments on women's rights, such as reducing the age at which divorced mothers lose custody of their children to the father. Suggestions were also made to abolish the teaching of foreign languages in schools, but fortunately these were not taken seriously.

The image of the newly won democracy was thus greatly tarnished. It was further impaired by the apparent inability of the new parliament to do anything of any importance that the military council did not approve of. It looked as if some tacit agreement had been reached between the Muslim Brotherhood and SCAF whereby the former could win the majority of seats in parliament provided that parliament did just what it was told. When after the elections SCAF chose a new prime minister, Dr. Kamal al-Ganzouri, who was not to the liking of parliament, there was nothing that the newly elected members could do to remove him, even though they kept threatening to pass a vote of no confidence. The prime minister seemed to be confident enough that he couldn't be removed unless SCAF wanted this to happen.

The new parliament thus appeared increasingly to be something of a farce, not unlike the trial of the deposed president. A new farce was then added, revolving around the choice of members of the committee responsible for drafting a new constitution. During the few weeks following the removal of the president, several prominent people suggested that rather than modifying a few articles of the old constitution and wasting time on holding a referendum on these modifications, a committee should be selected straight away to write a new constitution, which itself would be the subject of a referendum. This suggestion, for some unexplained reason, was rejected by SCAF, together with the suggestion that a "presidential council" of widely respected political figures be formed to perform the functions of a temporary president until a new one was elected. Instead, the selection of the committee to write the constitution was entrusted to the new parliament. This inevitably aroused fears among the liberal and secular opponents of the Islamists. The new parliament, dominated by Islamists, would naturally select a committee similarly dominated, leading to a constitution that could deny or restrict the rights of religious minorities and people with more liberal views, as well as those of women.

These fears were shown to be justified when the names of the members of the committee chosen by the new parliament were announced. Court cases against the formation of this committee were made and won, with the result that the time for electing a new president arrived before a new constitution was written, and even before the committee to be entrusted with writing this constitution had been formed.

The presidential election campaigns were another amazing story. When the door was declared open for nominations, the number of candidates was almost laughable. Indeed, one not particularly famous actor announced that he planned to enter the competition, only to declare a few days later that he was just trying to gain publicity for his new film. The candidates included every possible shade of political opinion. Among them one could find a member of the Muslim Brotherhood, as well as an ex-member who disagreed with the Brotherhood on some important points of principle, an independent Islamist scholar, a much less educated Salafi who attracted followers by his personal charm, a Nasserist, an ex-member of the Marxist party, and a relatively young lawyer who specialized in the protection of human rights. These were only a few in a very long list that also included the familiar names of people who were closely connected with the Mubarak regime. One of the latter, Amr Moussa, was foreign minister under Mubarak for ten years before becoming secretary general of the Arab League. Another, Ahmad Shafik, was minister of aviation until chosen as prime minister in the last few days of Mubarak's presidency. That these last two would decide to enter the race for the presidency seemed very surprising after a successful revolution, and for many Egyptians quite shocking. Could they really have dared to contemplate becoming presidential candidates without some tacit encouragement from the military council?

Some other prominent personalities suddenly withdrew from the race or suddenly joined it without convincing reasons or with no reason given at all. One of these was none other than Dr. Mohamed ElBaradei, the Nobel Prize laureate, who had been the director of the United Nations International Atomic Energy Agency before deciding to join the opposition movement in Egypt. He arrived in Cairo two days after the revolution started and was given an impressive welcome by several thousand people at the airport. He declared his decision to stand for the presidency from the very beginning, but suddenly withdrew, citing "the shady climate" in which the election campaign was being conducted. Another political figure of the old days, Mansour Hassan, who played a prominent role in politics in the last days of Sadat and then completely disappeared for the thirty years of Mubarak's rule, was suddenly given a role to play as the chairman of the ineffective advisory council and then decided to enter the presidential race. He too suddenly pulled out, giving the mysterious explanation that he had been "persuaded to withdraw by some important people." Most surprising of all was the reappearance and disappearance of Omar Suleiman, who was head of intelligence for a long time under Mubarak and was appointed vice president during Mubarak's last days in office. That a man with such a history should decide to become a presidential candidate at such a late stage in the election campaign, only to be disqualified by a court decision on the grounds of an insignificant procedural error, was indeed difficult to explain without recourse to some conspiracy theory. Finally, the Muslim Brotherhood candidate, Khairat al-Shater, was replaced by another member of the Brotherhood, Muhammad Morsi, who was much less charismatic and previously little known, also on the grounds of some unimportant formality.

A very large number of candidates still remained, and the number of people who voted was impressive, though smaller than the number of those who voted in the parliamentary elections and significantly smaller than the number who took part in the far less important referendum of March 2011. One can safely say that the results of the voting were disappointing to most Egyptians. The two candidates who got the highest number of votes were Muhammad Morsi, representing the Muslim Brotherhood, and Ahmad Shafik, who was favored by two types of people: the counterrevolutionaries and those who, after more than a year of deteriorating economic conditions and absence of law and order, came to prefer a return to the old days when at least life was less precarious.

In the second-round runoff between Morsi and Shafik, a large number of the potential voters felt that the process was hardly worth the trouble of going to the polling station. Had the whole thing really come down to this, a choice between a representative of the old regime and a representative of a religious group? Or to put it more dramatically, between going back to the dismal days of Mubarak's regime and going further back by a few centuries?

It seems a great pity that much more promising candidates were no longer on the ballot. In the first round of the election campaign there were at least four candidates who were more representative of the spirit of the January 25 revolution than the two who made it to the final round. Those four were militant opponents of the Mubarak regime and suffered imprisonment for their political views. Compared with Morsi, who was also imprisoned under Mubarak, they were much more open to liberal ideas and to more rational interpretations of Islamic teachings. The four of them—Abd al-Moneim Aboul Fotouh, Hamdeen Sabbahi, Aboul Izz al-Hariri, and Khaled Ali—managed together to secure almost 40 percent of the vote. They did represent a political orientation much more capable of putting the aims of the revolution into effect. Unfortunately they were competing separately and thus allowed the final round of the elections to be between two unpromising candidates.

But another ominous piece of news was being prepared by SCAF. A few hours before the results of the final round were to be declared, it was announced that the parliament was to be dissolved because of some fault in the parliamentary election law and that SCAF would assume the legislative power of the dissolved parliament as well as the right to object to any article in the constitution yet to be written. A new decree was also suddenly issued to replace the abolished emergency law, giving the military police wider authority than that previously vested in the Ministry of the Interior. All matters concerning the military establishment would also remain in the hands of the military. One day after Dr. Muhammad Morsi was declared winner, but before he had time to choose a prime minister, it was declared that the chairman of SCAF would have a seat in the new cabinet as the minister of defense.

By the end of June 2012 it was clear that the new president would be the prisoner of two mighty forces: the Muslim Brotherhood, of which he had been a loyal member until the day he became president, and the military establishment, which now held legislative and very wide executive powers.

The January 25 revolution declared as one of its principal aims the replacement of political despotism by a democratic system. What the people finally obtained after a period of eighteen months was a freely elected parliament that was quickly dissolved and a new president who may also have been elected freely, but only after every measure had been taken to make sure he would remain quite powerless. This is obviously a case of an abortive revolution. What started as a very promising revolution ended with something very much like a military coup d'état.

4

The deep sadness that prevailed among Egyptians ten months after the first anniversary of the January 25 revolution, coupled with their disappointment at the political developments they had seen starting within a few weeks of Hosni Mubarak stepping down, brings to mind the concept of 'alienation,' the best word I can find to describe the way Egyptians gradually felt toward their new rulers.

The sense of alienation was back after a few joyous weeks when hopes had risen sky-high and Egyptians imagined that they finally had rulers who felt as they felt and intended to work to bring about what they aspired to.

I said to myself, "Yes, that sense of alienation is back, but do you remember, throughout the past fifty or sixty years, Egyptians ever losing that feeling for more than a few months—months followed by more years of alienation?"

Let's start in 1950, when Egyptians were overjoyed at the victory of the Wafd Party in clean elections after a long period of election rigging, and their beloved leader Mustafa al-Nahhas took office as prime minister. Demonstrations across the country reflected people's happiness to see the end of a long period of alienation under one minority government after another, all of them subject to the will of the king and the British. Yes, I remember the happiness that reigned in 1950, but that feeling did not last more than a year and a half, ending with the Cairo fire in January 1952, which was taken as an excuse for dismissing al-Nahhas' government, and then things went back to how they were before 1950.

Egyptians were overjoyed again in July 1952 when the revolution took place and it looked like the new rulers and the people could work together in unison, and there was a succession of measures and laws that were very heartening: the deposition of the king, the agricultural reform law, the abolition of titles, the declaration of a republic, and so on. But did the joy last, that time too, more than a year and a half? No, it didn't last longer than that, and the sense of alienation came back suddenly in 1954 when we heard a communiqué on the radio that meant there had been a coup within the group of ruling officers and the much-loved president, Muhammad Nagib, had been pushed aside for reasons that were not at all convincing. Then began a series of unpopular measures, including what struck many people, myself included, as a contrived drama to attack the new president. Lo and behold, new songs were written and set to music in praise of this new president, and people felt only alienation toward him.

Yes, there was widespread joy at the nationalization of the Suez Canal in July 1956, and this joy lasted two whole years, maybe even two and a half years, until January 1959. In the meantime many encouraging things took place: work began on the Aswan High Dam, Egypt joined the Non-Aligned Movement, a union with Syria was proclaimed, and an ambitious industrialization program was announced, as well as an ambitious plan for economic development. But in early 1959 we were shocked to hear of a large-scale wave of detentions that included many of the most committed nationalists and Egyptians who most believed in social justice; we heard that many of them had been badly treated in prison, some of them even tortured to death. This insistence on applying socialism without any socialists was completely incomprehensible, as was all the hostility toward a new nationalist regime in Iraq. Was this based on an independent decision that stemmed from free will or was it meant to satisfy some foreign power? The sense of alienation began to come back after that, and then grew stronger as the police state became even more cruel with the passing of the years after Syria seceded from the union with Egypt in 1961 and Egypt entered the Yemen war the following year, until the sense of alienation reached its peak with the defeat of 1967.

The sense of alienation continued almost without interruption until the fall of Hosni Mubarak in February 2011. I say "almost" because we could exclude two very short periods, neither of which lasted more than a few months. The first was the period of intense rejoicing when Egyptian troops crossed the Suez Canal in October 1973, which restored Egyptians' confidence in themselves and their army. But it ended in disappointment because of the political developments that followed the military victory. Anwar al-Sadat reinforced Egyptians' sense of alienation day after day with his unjustifiable rapprochement with the Israelis, which ended in the peace treaty of 1979, his gradual repudiation of the dream of Arab unity and of the Palestinian cause, his increasing subordination to the Americans, and his adoption of an economic policy that would open the floodgates to foreign goods, which would reinforce the sense of alienation among those unable to buy them. In the end he ordered the wholesale detention of hundreds of patriots of various political leanings and suspended all the opposition newspapers.

Then, for a short period after the assassination of Sadat in 1981, it looked as if the new president would try to put things back on track by releasing political detainees, allowing banned newspapers to resume publication, rationalizing economic policy, and exercising some independence in foreign and Arab policy. After less than a year it was soon apparent that all this was a mirage. Subordination to America and deference toward Israel continued, economic policy remained subject to pressure from the International Monetary Fund and the World Bank, income disparities and unemployment worsened, and the phenomenon of Egypt's First Lady reappeared, along with restrictions on freedoms and rigged elections. The sense of alienation returned, and gradually became stronger than it had been in the days of Sadat.

As a result of all this, over a period of more than sixty years, Egyptians have not, at the very best estimate, enjoyed more than eight discontinuous years during which they felt that their government shared their hopes and was working to fulfill them: the Nahhas government (1950–51), which ended with the Cairo fire; the first months after the 1952 revolution, ending in the crisis of 1954; the two years after the nationalization of the Suez Canal in July 1956, ending with the detentions of 1959; some months after the army's victory in October 1973, ending in the disengagement agreement with Israel and the signing of a separate peace treaty; and the few months after the release of the people Sadat had detained in 1981 and the reappearance of the opposition newspapers, ending with the reimposition of newspaper censorship and election rigging.

The sense of alienation suddenly evaporated and happiness reigned on January 25, 2011, but here we are now, almost two years after that extraordinary day, again feeling the pain of alienation, which is only the more bitter when we remember how happy we were on January 25.

Young Egyptians now enjoy a major advantage of a kind that my generation of Egyptians did not enjoy. We are a generation accustomed unfortunately to repeated disappointments and a recurrent sense of alienation, time after time, but the new generation of young people has not gone through the cycles of hope and disappointment that Egypt has gone through, so they keep trying and making sacrifices. It is these people, of course, and no one else, who give Egyptians, including my much older generation, hope that Egypt will enjoy a new period when the sense of alienation disappears, and that the next period will be much longer than previous happy periods.

5

Six months after Egypt's military defeat in 1967 I was invited to attend a conference in the Cuban capital, Havana. The aim was to brief the largest possible number of Third World intellectuals who might be sympathetic toward Castro's revolution on what the revolution had achieved in its first nine years.

Egyptians were still deeply saddened by what had happened in June 1967. They had a mixture of feelings: loss of self-confidence, despair that their country could ever make any progress, and regret that they had pinned such hopes on the revolution of 1952.

On top of all that, like the rest of the Egyptians invited to the conference, I felt a certain embarrassment about having to face the intellectuals of the world when our country was in such a state and our reputation in tatters because of a crushing defeat after a conflict that had lasted only a few days (some might say only a few hours).

When we found ourselves among intellectuals who came from various parts of the world, we were surprised that, when these intellectuals thought about Egypt, the war of 1967 played a very small part and they didn't dwell long on wondering who was responsible for the Egyptian regime's failure to stand up to the Israeli attack, which had the backing of the United States. On the contrary, they attached much greater importance to how the Free Officers Movement in 1952 represented a revolution against a corrupt monarchy, and they were not surprised that such a revolution should face obstacle after obstacle, placed in its way by foreign or domestic forces. They were also clearly aware of Egypt's importance because of its long history and its special contribution to Arab culture. This was a happy surprise for us members of the Egyptian delegation and we realized it was wrong to give in to feelings that arose from a single event, however devastating, because in the end it was just a transitory event in Egypt's long history.

I remembered how my feelings evolved in those days almost half a century ago because of the sadness and disappointment Egyptians now feel after the repeated attempts to undermine the revolution of January 2011.

Let's first go back to remember how the first days of the January 25 revolution revealed that under the surface of daily life in Egypt a new and remarkable generation of Egyptians, men and women, had emerged. This extraordinary development was not a result of the revolution; the revolution was merely the reason it came to light. It suddenly became clear that the thirty or forty years that preceded the revolution of January 2011, despite all the corruption, the mistakes, and the sterility associated with this period, had failed to prevent some very positive developments that were bound to emerge and spread. Does this count as an example of "the cunning of history," in the sense that history does not run in a straight line up or down, but historical events rather generate possibilities for success or failure simultaneously and might produce good things in the middle of the most vicious and corrupt periods of history? Was not the rampant inflation caused by the mistaken economic policies adopted from the mid-1970s and the difficulties it created for many Egyptian families, who found their real income beginning to collapse because of inflation, at the same time an incentive for every member of the family, male and female, to work harder in order just to stay alive?

Similarly the development of Egyptian television in the mid-1970s was a corrupting factor in many ways and one of the reasons for the proliferation of irrational interpretations of religion. But nonetheless, didn't television, and then computers and the Internet, help people find out what was happening in the world and hone the intelligence of a whole generation of Egyptians? The benefits that some of them gained drove many to carry out the revolution of January 25.

Let's look at what has happened in the field of education. A corrupt system that was in place for about forty years led to a steep deterioration in the standard of education in Egypt at all levels. But wasn't that accompanied by a quantitative expansion in education from which vast numbers of young people were bound to benefit across the country, many of whom came out to demonstrate against this corrupt system and succeeded in bringing down the head of the regime on February 11, 2011?

Is there any similarity between the reasons that led to the setbacks to the revolution of July 1952 and the setbacks to the revolution of January 25, 2011, in spite of big differences that are the inevitable outcome of a gap of more than half a century between the two revolutions?

The revolution of 1952 was carried out by a group of young officers who were full of patriotism and who reflected the hopes of Egypt's oppressed classes—farm laborers, workers, and a small middle class—against a feudal class that enjoyed unfair privileges. Then, over fifteen years, these young officers became a new class, inheriting the privileges of the feudalists. They took a liking to the taste of power and money, grew complacent, and did not make adequate preparations to confront foreign schemes. In fact these foreign schemes had a chance to succeed only through a class that had taken a liking to power and money and had grown complacent. And so the setback of 1967 took place.

On January 25, 2011, there was another revolution in which all the oppressed classes in Egypt took part, demanding their right to take on an unjust and corrupt system. The revolution achieved brilliant success in bringing down the top of the regime, but sadly it faltered a few months later. Did the setback come about this time, too, because those who took power after the revolution belonged in turn to a class that had already developed a taste for power and money and had grown complacent? Or was it that foreign powers were horrified by the revolution and did everything they could to smother it in its cradle? Or is it true in this case, too, that foreign forces can operate only through a class with which they are allied and whose interests coincide with the interests of these foreign powers?

Whatever the interpretation, there is another important fact, and that is that the new generation of Egyptians we now have, which didn't exist in 1967, brings enormous possibilities for another attempt at a national revival. Is this what was on the mind of that extraordinary poet Ahmad Fuad Nigm when he addressed Egypt in a poem he wrote in the Qanatir prison in 1969, two years after the defeat of 1967?

O Mother Egypt, O Bahiya,
You with the headscarf and the *gallabiya*,
Time is young and so are you,
He's on his way out while you are coming,

Stepping your way over hardship,
You have passed through so many days and nights.
Your endurance is as it was
And your smile is just the same.
You smile at the morning and it smiles back,
After a night and an evening
The sun comes up and greets you,
Dashing and girlish,
O Bahiya.

Index

judiciary 75, 134, 149

Kamel, Tarek 69–70, 71–72

Lenin, Vladimir 14, 243

Mahfouz, Naguib 83, 111, 171, 172, 186
Mahmoud Khalil Museum, Cairo 25, 40
Malaysia 54, 232–34
Marx, Karl 243, 269–70, 271
masses 60–62, 114
media 26, 30, 35, 48, 60–61, 80, 89–90,
    114–17, 162; 2011 revolution 117–18;
    after 2011 revolution 159–60, 162,
    164, 244; control of/censorship
    46, 81, 97, 116, 118, 134, 268, 280;
    foreign media 75, 81, 125; govern-
    ment media 16, 27, 34, 36, 74, 88,
    108, 170, 194; radio 81, 114, 115,
    118, 279; religious extremism 170,
    174–75, 176, 194, 195, 196; television
    59, 116–17, 118–19, 160, 282; see also
    journalists; newspaper
metaphysics 210, 213–14
migration 9, 11, 20, 116, 222; illegal mi-
    gration 10–11, 15, 50, 68, 69
military 39, 98, 100, 112, 234, 277; 2011
    revolution 137, 157–58; see also
    Supreme Council of the Armed
    Forces
military coup 126, 127; 2011 revolution
    137, 139, 278; see also revolution of
    1952
ministries 26, 109, 138, 147–50, 270;
    selection of 40–41, 46, 47, 161–62,
    244; Ministry of Education 40–41,
    108, 146, 148, 149, 181; Ministry of
    Foreign Affairs 23, 145, 148, 150,
    162, 275; Ministry of Planning 149,
    151, 153
Mohieddin, Fuad 152
Mohieddin, Mahmoud 49, 50–51, 53, 57

monarchy 9, 117, 126, 134–35; see also
    Muhammad Ali
Morsi, Fuad 149
Morsi, Muhammad 2, 276–77
Moustafa, Hisham 29–31
Mubarak, Alaa 64, 65–66
Mubarak, Gamal 266; presidential suc-
    cession 1, 34, 35–36, 64–65, 72–74,
    86, 139–40
Mubarak, Hosni 1, 22–23, 140, 193–94,
    243, 251–52, 265–66, 270; corrup-
    tion 68, 121, 135; long term in office
    64, 65–66; trial of 119–20, 163, 273;
    see also regime
Mubarak, Suzanne 14, 84–86, 108
Muhammad Ali 147, 150, 233, 253, 254,
    255, 260; see also monarchy
multinational companies 71, 229–31
Murad, Hilmi 146–47, 149
Muslim Brotherhood 77, 80, 88–89,
    107, 108, 158, 193, 236, 237, 239,
    273–74
Muslim/Copt conflicts 141, 165–79,
    194–96, 200–203, 256; Alexandria
    2011 169–73, 188; beneficiaries of
    172, 174, 203–204; Maspero mas-
    sacre 200–203; media 170, 174–75,
    176, 194, 195, 196; Nag' Hammadi
    2010 166–69, 203; religious ex-
    tremism 171, 172, 173, 196; Wafaa
    and Camellia cases 175–79

al-Naggar, Said 152, 153
Nagib, Muhammad 98, 138, 236, 279
al-Nahhas, Mustafa 114, 127, 148, 278,
    280
al-Nasser, Gamal Abd 9, 67, 68, 78–79,
    138, 149, 228, 246, 254, 255
Nasserist Party 77, 78–79, 274
National Democratic Party 32–33, 35,
    47, 72, 86, 157, 203
nationalism 41, 53, 59–60, 81, 152;